Company Valuation: Measurement and Management

Company Valuation: Measurement and Management

Prof. Vinod Vasant Sople

Director,

ITM-SIA Business School

Dombivli (Mumbai)

First Edition : 2013

MUMBAI • NEW DELHI • NAGPUR • BENGALURU • HYDERABAD • CHENNAI • PUNE • LUCKNOW • AHMEDABAD • ERNAKULAM • BHUBANESWAR • INDORE • KOLKATA • GUWAHATI

First Edition : 2013

Published by : Mrs. Meena Pandey for **Himalaya Publishing House Pvt. Ltd.,**
"Ramdoot", Dr. Bhalerao Marg, Girgaon, **Mumbai - 400 004.**
Phone: 022-23860170/23863863, Fax: 022-23877178
E-mail: himpub@vsnl.com; Website: www.himpub.com

Branch Offices :

New Delhi : "Pooja Apartments", 4-B, Murari Lal Street, Ansari Road, Darya Ganj, New Delhi - 110 002. Phone: 011-23270392, 23278631; Fax: 011-23256286

Nagpur : Kundanlal Chandak Industrial Estate, Ghat Road, Nagpur - 440 018. Phone: 0712-2738731, 3296733; Telefax: 0712-2721215

Bengaluru : No. 16/1 (Old 12/1), 1st Floor, Next to Hotel Highlands, Madhava Nagar, Race Course Road, Bengaluru - 560 001. Phone: 080-32919385; Telefax: 080-22286611

Hyderabad : No. 3-4-184, Lingampally, Besides Raghavendra Swamy Matham, Kachiguda, Hyderabad - 500 027. Phone: 040-27560041, 27550139; Mobile: 09390905282

Chennai : No. 8/2, 2nd Madley Street, Ground Floor, T. Nagar, Chennai - 600 017. Mobile: 09345345055

Pune : First Floor, "Laksha" Apartment, No. 527, Mehunpura, Shaniwarpeth (Near Prabhat Theatre), Pune - 411 030. Phone: 020-24496323/24496333; Mobile: 09370579333

Lucknow : House No 731, Shekhupura Colony, Near B.D. Convent School, Aliganj, Lucknow - 226 022. Mobile: 09307501549

Ahmedabad : 114, "SHAIL", 1st Floor, Opp. Madhu Sudan House, C.G. Road, Navrang Pura, Ahmedabad - 380 009. Phone: 079-26560126; Mobile: 09377088847

Ernakulam : 39/176 (New No: 60/251) 1st Floor, Karikkamuri Road, Ernakulam, Kochi - 682011, Phone: 0484-2378012, 2378016; Mobile: 09344199799

Bhubaneswar : 5 Station Square, Bhubaneswar - 751 001 (Odisha). Phone: 0674-2532129, Mobile: 09338746007

Indore : Kesardeep Avenue Extension, 73, Narayan Bagh, Flat No. 302, IIIrd Floor, Near Humpty Dumpty School, Indore - 452 007 (M.P.). Mobile: 09301386468

Kolkata : 108/4, Beliaghata Main Road, Near ID Hospital, Opp. SBI Bank, Kolkata - 700 010, Phone: 033-32449649, Mobile: 09883055590, 07439040301

Guwahati : House No. 15, Behind Pragjyotish College, Near Sharma Printing Press, P.O. Bharalumukh, Guwahati - 781009, (Assam). Mobile: 09883055590, 09883055536

DTP by : HPH, Editorial Office, Bhandup **(Sadhana C Chandanshiv)**

Printed at : M/s. Sri Sai Art Printers, Hyderabad. On behalf of HPH.

Preface

'Business Valuation' is an interesting subject for students of finance having interest in business analysis and valuation. The business valuation analysis is done for variety of purposes. It may be required for taxation, winding up operations, spin-offs, M&A. The business valuation is done for decision making at strategic level. This book is designed for curriculum on 'Business Analysis and Valuation' taught at graduation/postgraduation level – B.Com./M.Com. - in commerce stream in Indian universities and in B-schools in finance specialisation at MBA, MMS or PGDM level. This book provides the most comprehensive analysis of a business valuation approaches and methodologies. This book covers the following:

- Introduction to the concept of business valuation;
- Understanding of business valuation process;
- Overview and importance of the existing business valuation models;
- Prevailing business valuation techniques, with their pros and cons;
- Valuation of assets (tangible and intangible) and liabilities (apparent or contingent);
- Concept application in real-life situations, with illustrations/examples;

The structure of the book is such that the book can provide vital insights into the key issues in business valuation. It also brings out the complexities involved in business valuation and the challenges thereof. The concepts in the subject are supported with the illustrations wherever necessary in its entirety. This is an introductory course on business valuation, and therefore, the student is well advised to look at this as a beginning of a long interesting journey and not an end.

This book is divided into ten chapters and each chapter is amply supported by illustrations, examples and exhaustive pedagogy of summary, review questions, video links, project assignments and bibliography. Your comments or suggestions to improve upon the quality of this book may kindly be sent to *vinodsople@yahoo.com*

Author

Content

1 CHAPTER

Business Valuation Basics

> *"Valuation provides crucial insights into how to measure, manage and maximize a company's value".*
>
> **— *Thomas E. Copeland***

Learning Objectives

To understand:

- Business valuation
- Why company needs valuation?
- Equity vs company valuations
- Approaches to company valuation
- Valuation methods and tools

Business valuation often looks like a "black box" to those not involved in the profession of valuing companies. However, company valuation is a systematic procedure for estimating the economic value of a business. It is a single value that represents the value of all the other components like brand value, insolvency, and debtor's turnover that together form a company's value. It is done under many circumstances like at the time of mergers and acquisitions, reorganization, raising public funds, and winding up of the business. Valuation process provides up to date insights and practical advice on how to create, manage, and measure the value of an organization.

INTRODUCTION

Valuation is the process of determining the current worth of an asset or company keeping in mind that the investor does not pay more for asset than it is worth. The other view of the asset value is the price the purchaser is willing to pay to the seller. But what we have to keep in mind is that the perception of value needs to be based on reality rather than the emotions of parties involved in buying and selling activity. There are many techniques covering both subjective and objective that can be used to determine value. The factors to be taken into considerations while valuating a company are company's management, the composition of its capital structure, prospect of future earnings and market value of assets. In this exercise, working out the contributions of a company's management would be more of a subjective valuation technique, while calculating intrinsic value based on future earnings would be an objective technique.

Company valuation is a systematic procedure for estimating the economic value of a business. There are two types of valuation done with regards to a company such as valuation for investments in stocks and the other one is for acquiring a company. The first one is to valuate just the equity stake in the business and second one, value the entire business, which includes, besides equity, the other claim holders in the firm. The final value represents the values of all the other components like brand value, insolvency and debtor's turnover that together form a company's value. It is done under many circumstances like at the time of mergers and acquisitions, reorganization, raising public funds and winding up of the business. Business valuations are performed for any number of reasons, such as:

- Selling business firm
- Buying a business
- Taking in a new partner
- Settling an estate that includes an owned business
- Attracting venture capital or debt capital
- Taxation

All scientific business valuations are based on a firm's recent financial statements. However, financial statements do not tell the whole story. These statements can be used for predicting future earning of a company. However, other factors need to be considered along with a company's financial statements to perform an accurate valuation. In the case of most closely held private companies, determining past earning is not as simple as looking at the firm's income statement. Business owner often take advantage of fully legal deductions. Hence, the final financial statements that don't accurately reflect real earnings. It is, in fact, an accountant's job to understand the tax code and apply it to client's business to minimize reported earnings and therefore minimize taxes due. In performing a business valuation, the appraiser's job is partly to undo the accountant's work in order to present the company's financial picture in a more real situation.

Ideally a business enterprise should have an annual business valuation policy leading to the following benefits:

- **Accountability and Performance:** An annual business valuation enables the shareholders to see the value that is being consistently created or destroyed by the management of the firm.
- **Estate Planning Purposes:** Many shareholders have on-going estate planning strategies aimed at protecting wealth for heirs.

- **Buy-sell Situations:** For those firms that do not have buy-sell agreements in place, annual business valuations are a good way of avoiding disputes that may arise when a shareholder seeks to sell his shares to other shareholders.
- **Facilitate Banking:** The ability of a firm to borrow based on the value of the goodwill or the value of the company's shares. It may expand the universe of value-creating investment options available.
- **Expands the Investment Options:** Closely held firms suffer from a lack of liquidity and the inability to use the company's shares as currency when seeking acquisitions. An annual business valuation may enable the management of the company to use it for seeking acquisition.

ENTERPRISE VALUE

The value of a business is impacted by a number of factors, many of which may change with time and which covers;

- Financial performance greatly impacts the value of a company. If a business has poor earning capacity, the value of the business may be negatively impacted.
- Growth prospects plays an important role in company valuation. Just as too high a rate of growth may lead to negative operational and financial consequences, too low a growth rate may also have a negative impact upon the business and its ability to achieve profitability. Revenue growth drives all opportunities for the business to expand.
- Competitive nature of industry impacts entry and exit decisions. If the industry in which the business is operating has become more competitive due to the entrance of new competitors, the value of a business may be impacted as a result of lost market share, lower revenue growth, shrinking margins and lower profitability.
- Management of a business influences the value of the firm. A highly experienced management team with excellent track record is highly valued by a willing buyer than an organization with only one key executive.
- The strength of the economy impacts all businesses in one way or another. If adverse economic conditions translate into long-term lower growth and profitability for a business, the value may be negatively impacted. Industry conditions are also impacted by the state of the economy but are also influenced by various other factors such as competition, technological change, trends, etc.

Company or enterprise value is a figure that represents the entire cost of a company if someone wants to acquire it. Enterprise value is a more accurate estimate of takeover cost than market capitalization because it includes a number of important factors such as preferred stock, debt, and cash reserves that are excluded from the latter one. Enterprise value is calculated by adding a corporation's market capitalization, preferred stock, and outstanding debt together and then subtracting out the cash and cash equivalents found on the balance sheet. In other words, enterprise value is what it would cost the purchaser to buy every single share of a company's common stock, preferred stock, and outstanding debt. The available cash is subtracted as in post ownership, the purchaser own the cash. The following components are included in the calculation of enterprise value:

Market Capitalization (MC): It is also called "market cap". MC is calculated by taking the number of outstanding shares of common stock multiplied by the current price-per-share. For example, Reliance Industry Ltd has 300 crore shares of stock outstanding and the current stock price was ₹ 1,000 per share, the company's MC would be ₹ 3,00,000 crore (300 crore shares × ₹ 1,000 per share = ₹ 3,00,000 crore of MC).

Preferred Stock (PS): Technically PS is an equity. However, depending upon the nature of the individual issue, PS can actually act as either equity or debt. A PS which needs to be redeemed at a certain date at a certain price is debt for all intents and purposes. PS may have the right to receive a fixed dividend plus share in a portion of the profits in "participating". PS represents a claim on the business that must be factored into enterprise value.

Debt: Along with the business, purchaser also acquires its debt in buying transaction. For example purchaser has purchased all of the outstanding shares of a business for ₹ 25 crore (MC), and the business had ₹ 10 crore in debt, the purchaser would actually have spent ₹ 35 crore. In this deal ₹ 25 crore may have come out of purchaser's own money, but he is now responsible for repaying the ₹ 35 crore which includes ₹ 10 crore in debt.

Cash and Cash Equivalents: Cash in a bank becomes property of owner who purchased the business. After acquiring complete ownership, he can simply take this cash and put it in his pocket, replacing some of the money he expended to buy the business. Cash serves to reduce his acquisition price and this is the reason, it is subtracted from the other components when calculating enterprise value.

Cash Generation: Some investors look for companies that are generating a lot of cash flow in relation to enterprise value. Such businesses require little additional reinvestment in future. Here, the owners can take the profit out of the business and put it into other investments.

FUNDAMENTAL ANALYSIS

Fundamental analysis is basically done for long and mid-term investment (stock market) which is also called as delivery-based investment or stock trading. The main important aim behind it is to study and understand the company in which investor is planning to invest money and get excellent returns. In this investor should be able to judge, how the company has done in past years, its debt status, its current valuation, its future growth prospects, its earning capacity, etc. The analysis will help him take a decision whether to invest in this company or not. The following should be looked into in a company to invest:

Company Information

Investor should find out in which industry sector the company is and what its business is? How is the current demand for the company's products and how the demand will be in future like in the long- term? The more can be obtained from company's website.

Earnings

Look into company's last 5 or 10 years earnings whether the company has posted profits or losses. The investors want to know how much money the company is making and how much it is going to make in the future. To find the earning status ratio used are EPS (Earning per share). The quarterly or yearly company's increasing earnings generally makes its stock price move up and in some cases some companies pay out a regular dividend. This indicates that the company is in growth phase. When the company declares low earnings then the market may see bearishness in the stock price and hence its share price starts deceasing and corrects further if the company doesn't provide any sufficient justification for low earnings. Every quarter, companies reports its earnings.

Current Valuation

In general, the investors invest at higher valuations of shares and when share prices start coming down then they keep worrying. Hence, before investing one should check the current valuation of the share price and invest only when the share price is at right level and not at overpriced level. To find the current valuation of the stock the ratios used are, PE ratio (price to earning ratio), Book value, PB ratio (price to book value ratio)

Future Earnings Growth

This reflects company's returns or its profits in future. Most of the investors invest in shares taking into consideration the company's future growth prospects. To find the future growth of the stock the ratios used are; PEG ratio (Price to earning growth ratio), Current and Forward EPS (Price to sales ratio)

Debt Status

For any company to perform well in the future it is very important to be debt free or less debt because if the company is having large debts like borrowings as loans then it becomes difficult for it to plan for any acquisitions, expansion plans, takeover plans, dividend payout and very important its most of the net profit goes in paying the interest and loans and other debts. If the company is having fewer debts or no debt then they are having lots of cash in hand and they are free to take any decision in coming future. To find the debt status of the company the ratio used is Debt ratio

Common Stock

The owner (shareholder) of common stock can reap two main benefits from the issuing company: Capital appreciation and dividends. Capital appreciation occurs when a stock's value increases over the amount initially paid for it. The stockholder makes a profit when he or she sells the stock at its current market value after capital appreciation. Dividends, which are taxable payments, are paid to a company's shareholders from its current earnings. Typically, dividends are paid out to stockholders on a quarterly/ annual basis. Common stock ownership has the additional benefit of enabling its holders to vote on company issues and in the elections of the organization's leadership team. Usually, one share of common stock equates to one vote.

Preferred Stock

Preferred stock doesn't offer the same potential for profit as common stock, but it's a more stable **investment option because it guarantees a regular dividend that isn't directly tied to the market like the** price of common stock. This type of stock guarantees dividends, which common stock does not. The other advantage of preferred stock is that preferred stockholders get priority when it comes to the payment of dividends. In the event of a company's liquidation, preferred stockholders get paid before those who own common stock. In addition, if a company goes bankrupt, preferred stockholders enjoy priority distribution of the company's assets, while holders of common stock don't receive corporate assets unless all preferred stockholders have been compensated (bond investors take priority over both common and preferred stockholders). Like common stock, preferred stock represents ownership in a company. However, owners of preferred stock do not get voting rights in the business.

There are many business and stock valuations methodologies depending on the reasons for performing the same. Most methods takes into consideration company's past earnings. They also work out company's future earnings based on trends observed in the company's past earnings. There are other methods to predict the future earnings too. For example, for three companies with three sets of near identical financial statements can easily have three very divergent valuations and future earning predictions because of number of reasons as shown in Exhibit 1.

Exhibit 1.1: Predictor of Future Earnings

Factor	*Reasoning*
Industry	Is the industry growing or shrinking? Are there other industry factors that need to be considered?
Customer Concentration	Do one or a few customers account for a significantly large percentage of total business on an ongoing basis
Attractiveness	This is a subjective measure. But it is a significant one. Certain industries and companies within an industry tend to be more attractive to buyers than others.
Potential	A company's demonstrated potential impacts considerably on its valuation
Stability	Companies with stable (predictable) year-over-year sales and earnings generally have higher values than companies where the earnings vary significantly from year to year.
Location	All other things being equal, a business located in a major city will have a higher value than one in the suburbs. One in the suburbs will have a higher value than one in a rural area.

The above are just a few of the factors that need to be considered along with a company's financial statements in order to perform an accurate business valuation.

EQUITY VS. BUSINESS VALUATION

The value of equity is obtained by discounting expected cash flows to equity, i.e., the residual cash flows after meeting all expenses, tax obligations and interest and principal payments, at the cost of equity, i.e., the rate of return required by equity investors in the firm.

$$\text{Value of Equity} = \Sigma\ CF^t \text{ to Equity}/(1+ Ec)^t$$

Where,

CF^t to Equity = Expected Cash flow to Equity in period t

Ec = Cost of Equity

t = Period for calculation

The dividend discount model is a specialized case of equity valuation, and the value of a stock is the present value of expected future dividends.

The value of the firm is obtained by discounting expected cash flows to the firm, i.e., the residual cash flows after meeting all operating expenses and taxes, but prior to debt payments, at the weighted average cost of capital, which is the cost of the different components of financing used by the firm, weighted by their market value proportions.

$$\text{Value of Firm} = \Sigma CF^t \text{ to Firm}/(1+WACC)^t$$

Where,

CF^t to Firm = Expected Cash flow to Firm in period t

WACC = Weighted Average Cost of Capital

To get from firm value to equity value, subtract out the value of all debt, value of all non-equity claims in the firm, that are included in the cost of capital calculation and the value of all non-equity claims in the firm. For most operating businesses, the standard of value will likely be fair market value, fair value or investment value.

Enterprise value is often referred to as the value of the invested capital of the business which includes the value of the equity and the value of the firm's liabilities. This value represents the total funding of the asset side of the balance sheet for all fixed assets, cash, receivables, inventory, and the goodwill of the business. Equity Value is the enterprise value less all liabilities of the business and represents the value that has accrued to the shareholders through retained earnings, etc. As various professionals may define these levels of value differently, it is important to understand exactly what a definition of a level of value includes or excludes under the specific circumstances.

FAIR MARKET VALUE

There are different definitions of 'value' used for different purposes. To make things more complex, different organizations may have different perspectives on what a given definition of value means.

Fair market value (FMV) is the price at which a willing buyer will buy from a willing seller. They both know the relevant facts and neither are under any compulsion to buy or sell. FMV is generally the basis for tax assessment. Fair Market Value is the price, expressed in terms of cash equivalents, at which property would change hands between a hypothetical (willing and able) buyer and a hypothetical (willing and able) seller, acting at arms length in an open and unrestricted market, when neither is under compulsion to buy or sell and when both have reasonable knowledge of the relevant fact. Fair Value is a legal standard of value that has been established by the courts for use in issues ranging from marital dissolution to dissenting shareholder suits. Investment Value is the value to a particular investor based on individual investment requirements and expectations. Investment value is typically used for transactional purposes when a buyer is assessing the value of the target company, including the potential synergies of the deal.

Basis of determining fair market value (FMV), is a dealing between independent, unrelated, and well informed parties looking out for their individual interests. Transactions involving family members, and parent companies and subsidiaries, are deemed arm-in-arm dealings. To qualify as an arm's length transaction, neither of the involved parties may have any interest in the transaction's consequences to the other party. Fair value is used in financial reporting and in certain litigation matters. It is very similar to (fair) market value.

To illustrate, consider the case of a hypothetical company 'A'. Different types of buyers seeking a control or majority interest may result in a higher price than fair market value.

- One investor may provide specific market synergies that increase revenues and/or decrease costs, resulting in a higher operating margin.
- Publicly traded company purchaser may acquire the company 'A' at any price that results in a lower valuation multiple than the price of the buyer's stock; this nature of such a transaction may increase the buyer's willingness to pay a higher price.
- Some buyer may pay a higher price than fair market value for intangible benefits, which may include the elimination of a competitor and a greater market presence.
- Some buyer may pay more than fair market value because cost of building a new facility is higher than the fair market value of the current facility.

Thus the reason for paying more or less than fair market value depends on variety of factors specific to buyer, situation around and his future plans.

COMPANY VALUATION APPROACHES AND METHODS

Some of the common approaches to company valuation are:

- **Asset valuation:** The Asset Approach adjusts a company's assets and liabilities to their fair market values and adds to the value of intangible assets and any contingent liabilities. Under this method, the value of assets of a company is determined by calculating the fair market value of the assets, the improvement cost of all the assets held under lease, and the value of inventory that includes finished goods, work-in-progress, and raw materials. This approach is appropriate for valuating manufacturing businesses. This is because their maximum investment is in assets such as machinery, equipment, power units, etc.
- **Capitalization of income valuation:** The Income Approach derives an indication of value based on the sum of the present value of expected economic benefits associated with the company. Under the Income Approach, the appraiser may select a multi-period discounted future income method or a single period capitalization method. This is suitable for valuating organizations like business consultancy firms, professional firms, etc., because they are not

asset-intensive in nature. The success of their business depends upon the quality of service and not on the level of output produced and sold. The items that can be included for the purpose of valuation are discretionary. These may cover location of a business, client portfolio, technical expertise, profit and loss trends, and portfolio of debtors and creditors.

- **Market valuation:** The market approach derives an indication of value by comparing the company to other similar companies that have been sold in the past. Under the market approach, the appraiser may utilize the guideline of publicly traded company method or the direct market data method. Under this approach, a multiplier formula for every industry is calculated depending upon the average sales figures of various companies in the industry. One can simply substitute figures in the formula to derive the value.

Valuation means how much a company is worth of. For equity investments valuation means the intrinsic worth of the company. There are various methods through which one can measure the intrinsic worth of a company. These are:

Net Asset Value (NAV)

NAV or Book value is one of the most commonly used methods of valuation. As the name suggests, it is the net value of all the assets of the company. If you divide it by the number of outstanding shares, you get the NAV per share. One way to calculate NAV is to divide the net worth of the company by the total number of outstanding shares. Say, a company's share capital is ₹ 200 crore (20 crore shares of ₹ 10 each) and its reserves and surplus is another ₹ 180 crore. Net worth of the company would be ₹ 380 crore (equity and reserves) and NAV would be ₹ 19 per share (₹ 380 crore divided by 20 crore outstanding shares). NAV can also be calculated by adding all the assets and subtracting all the outside liabilities from them. This will again boil down to net worth only. One can use any of the two methods to find out NAV. One can compare the NAV with the going market price while taking investment decisions.

Discounted Cash Flows Method (DCF)

DCF is the most widely used technique to value a company. It takes into consideration the cash flows arising to the company and also the time value of money. That's why, it is so popular. What actually happens in this is, the cash flows are calculated for a particular period of time (the time period is fixed taking into consideration various factors). These cash flows are discounted to the present at the cost of capital of the company. These discounted cash flows are then divided by the total number of outstanding shares to get the intrinsic worth per share.

In case buying and selling of company transaction, the valuation of the seller's business is an important component of the purchaser's analysis when discussing a proposed acquisition. The valuation of a business in the context of an acquisition, involves consideration of "investment" or "strategic" value beyond an analysis of fair market value. Valuation may be done by the seller prior to entertaining prospective buyers or by the buyer who identifies a specific target or by both parties during negotiations to resolve a dispute over price.

The business company valuation is not an exact science, nor will valuation issues typically decide on the pricing of the business. There are numerous acceptable valuation methods and in most of the situations, each will yield a different result. In fact, mathematical calculations in valuation plays part in the overall pricing of the deal and in determining the transactional true value to the business. Ideally, all methods should give the same result. But it is not so. This is because the factors impacting the analysis are many and not limited to only market conditions, the industry in which the target company operates and the type and nature of the business.

The above valuation methods are useful in that they provide starting points and supply a range of reasonable values backed by various valid manners of justification. In addition, the value or price of a company is dependent on the particular time of the valuation and on the true motivations and goals of the key players involved in the transaction. Fair market value is commonly defined as the amount at which property would change hands between a willing seller and a willing buyer when neither is under compulsion and both have reasonable knowledge of the relevant facts.

The small enterprises and family businesses are more difficult to evaluate, because of lack of certain information. The externally generated information is not available. No published information is available on these companies. The evaluation process with regards to these companies is more difficult because of their inability to obtain any financing or reasonably priced financing from financial institutions or public, lack of large product portfolio, lack of expansion into new markets, lack of management expertise, higher sensitivity to macro and microeconomic movements, lack of dividend history, more sensitivity to business risks, supply squeezes, and demand ups and downs, inability to control or influence regulatory and labour activity, cost disadvantage due to lack of economies of scale, lack of access to distribution channels, lack of relationships with suppliers and customers, lack of product differentiation or brand name recognition and inadequate financial backing.

To arrive at a valuation of a company analyst can study comparable companies and their transactions for using in analysis. The job can be entrusted to a professional business appraiser. An appraiser needs to look at a company and its assets, management, employees, financial, future projections objectively. In this the target company will have to cooperate with the appraiser in order for the appraiser to arrive at a reasonable range of prices. In general, managers often feel threatened by the appraiser's detailed scrutiny of every aspect of the company's operations and management. To allow analyst an access to all information about the target company is important to arrive at a fair valuation. For valuation it is essential to define clearly the terms under which a professional business appraiser will be working, in order to avoid problems in future. First, the expected time frame for completion of the appraisal must be set forth in advance and must be reasonable.

In the context of an acquisition, the first step is to normalize current operating results to establish free (net) cash flow. Next, the appraiser examines several scenarios to determine how specific line items would change under various circumstances. This process allows the appraiser to identify a range of strategic values based on the projected earnings stream of the seller's company under its proposed new ownership. The higher this earnings stream, the higher the purchase price.

For arriving at "strategic value", appraiser requires a detailed financial data and general information on many aspects of the seller's business. This covers the quality of the management and the company's reputation in the marketplace. The appraiser attempts to assess how the value of the target company will be affected by any changes to the operations or foundation of the company as a result of the proposed transaction, such as a loss of key customers or key managers. In the analysis, appraiser examines the seller's intangible assets when determining strategic value. The intangible assets covers customer lists, intellectual property, patents, license and distributorship agreements, regulatory approvals, leasehold interests and employment contracts. These may help in enhancing the valuation of selling company. The appraiser also looks at the expected effect that credit ratings have on the company's value. The company's reputation in industry is very difficult to quantify, but it will definitely affect its future value.

'Ratio' Analysis

Ratio Analysis is one of the basic tools of financial analysis. And it is a fact that financial analysis itself plays an important role in the progress of business strategic planning. In strategic analysis exercise, ratio analysis plays a vital role. It is not possible without studying the ratios to complete the analysis of a company's strengths, weaknesses, opportunities and threats, to arrive at any conclusion on its financial position.

Financial ratios are one of the most common tools of managerial decision making. A ratio is a comparison of one number to another- mathematically. It is a simple division problem. Financial ratios involve the comparison of various figures from the financial statements in order to gain information about a company's performance. It is the interpretation, rather than the calculation, that makes financial ratios a useful tool for business managers. Ratios may serve as indicators regarding worth of relationships between variables used to measure the firm's performance in terms of profitability, asset utilization, liquidity, leverage or market valuation.

Ratios are normally used to conduct a quantitative analysis of information in a company's financial statements. Ratios are calculated by comparing the current year figures to previous years, other companies, the industry, or even the economy to judge the performance of the company. This is predominately used in the fundamental analysis of a company.

Different types of ratios can be calculated from the financial statements pertaining to a company's activity, performance, liquidity and financing. When it comes to investing, ratio analysis is one of the most important element in the fundamental analysis process. Among the dozens of ratios available, the most relevant ratios are categorized into six major heads, which are:

- **Liquidity Measurement Ratios:** Liquidity ratio is calculated by comparing a company's most liquid assets. The greater the coverage of liquid assets to short-term liabilities, the better as it is a clear signal that a company can pay its debts that are coming due in the near future.
- **Profitability Indicator Ratios:** This ratio shows the different measures of corporate profitability and financial performance.
- **Debt Ratios:** These ratios give users a general idea of the company's overall debt load.
- **Operating Performance Ratios:** These ratios look at how well a company turns its assets into revenue as well as how efficiently a company converts its sales into cash.
- **Cash Flow Indicator Ratios:** These ratios can give users another look at the financial health and performance of a company.

- **Investment Valuation Ratios:** These ratios can be used by investors to estimate the attractiveness of a potential or existing investment and get an idea of its valuation.

Ratio Analysis, being the basic tool of the strategic analysis, is extremely important for an organization to carry out its business planning. Some of the key reasons why ratio analysis holds so much of importance are:

- Gives users a good understanding of how well the company utilized its resources in generating profit and shareholder value;
- Attempts to measure a company's ability to pay-off its short-term debt obligations;
- Determine the overall level of financial risk a company and its shareholders face; and
- Helps to enrich financial health and performance of a company.

The theory of buying low and selling high makes investing seem all too easy. For many, it is difficult to truly know when prices are cheap or expensive. In theory, the value of an investment is equal to the sum of its earnings or cash flows, which are discounted by some expected rate of return. From this general theory, many different shorthand methods have evolved to assist investors in making a quick determination as to a company's investment value using valuation ratios.

In many instances, a low ratio is considered a sign of an undervalued security, while a high ratio is considered an overvalued security. However, one major problem is that ratios typically do not take into account the future expected growth of the company itself. It is the prospect for the company's future growth combined with these estimated valuations that help investor/appraiser reach reasonable conclusions. While financial ratio analysis can provide important insight into a company's performance, it has some limitations too and that should be kept in mind when using financial ratios as an analytical tool in business valuation. Some of limitations of financial ratio analysis are:

- Ratio analysis is a scrutiny of the past and not a tool for future analysis;
- Ratio analysis is based on accounting not economic data;
- Ratios don't capture significant off-balance sheet items;
- Ratios can be manipulated through acceptable alterations of accounting policies (e.g., LIFO/FIFO).
- Financial statements reflect historical cost not current economic value;

Unfortunately, because of the way accounting rules work, the assets reported on the balance sheet might be held at cost or some other value that would not accurately reflect what the firm could get for them today. Additionally, the balance sheet is not always able to accurately represent the true earning power of those assets. Therefore, the ratio itself might be misleading without some form of additional analysis and modifications to balance sheet accounts. In such case analyst should go for peer comparison. However, if the market or an industry sector itself is over or undervalued, then company comparison by itself might lead to incorrect conclusions. Financial ratios definitely provide a good starting point for evaluating a company, and therefore are to be taken into evaluating a company.

GROWTH VS VALUE STOCKS

Growth stocks are those companies that generally reinvest their earnings instead of paying out dividends. Because of their current placement within the typical business cycle, their goal is to produce higher than normal rates of return on reinvested earnings into the foreseeable future. As this growth translates into higher expected future earnings, the stock prices tend to rise to reflect the market's expectations. One of the common pitfalls of buying into growth stocks is buying into a company's stock where the expectations have gone too high. When a company's stock is said to be "priced for perfection", there is no room for the company to miss estimates, and the company runs the risk of the market revaluing the shares at a much lower price.

Value stocks are typically defined as companies trading at a low multiple to earnings potential or some other form of valuation. In many cases, they might be recent growth stories that have lost favor in the marketplace, unknown companies that have been overlooked by the general investing public or companies facing financial difficulty but that may still have a reasonable probability of recovering from the burdens of debt or difficult economic times.

A typical pitfall often encountered by value investors is called a "value trap". A value trap is identified as a business that shows great promise for the future and is trading at a reasonable price relative to some measure of valuation. However, the future expected growth fails to materialize or even deteriorates further, leading to a loss of principal on the investment. Annual growth over a period of 5 years is a good way to gauge the long term health of a company. If a company has been outperforming in industry for 5 years or more, it can be said that a company is on growth trajectory.

INFORMATION SOURCES

The availability of relevant information is of great importance while attempting any valuation exercise. The information gathering exercise has to be undertaken by the valuation expert before beginning the valuation exercises. The probable sources of information are as follows:

Historical Record

The company's Annual Reports for past years is major source to get information of its working and past performance. This is available at Stock Exchanges and also at Registrar of Companies Office. In addition Directors Report, Management Discussions, Corporate Governance Reports, Auditors' Report and Notes to accounts also give insights into the company's operation and future plans. There are instances that the growth prospects and opportunities for the company mentioned in these documents are absolutely opposite to the future outlook as demonstrated in the projections. A detailed analysis of the past performance is a very important as a starting point in any valuation exercise. The valuation expert can note from the past results, various important aspects such as non-recurring income/ expenditure, non-operating income, change in Government/Tax regulations affecting business, tax benefits enjoyed, and so on.

Future Projections/Plans

This covers future expected profitability, balance sheet and cash flows along with detailed assumptions underlying the projections. Plans means the entire cycle of the business. It depends on the industry in which the company is falling. In certain industry even 3-year period will cover the cycle whereas in certain industries like heavy engineering or cement, a longer period of 5 to 7 years may be the cycle. It is impossible to predict the future due to the dynamic nature of the economy. Valuer should ensure that the assumption behind the future projections are reasonably convincing and acceptable at a point of time when they are prepared. Few common points of concerns generally observed in future plans of the businesses are; assuming production much higher than the capacities without capturing additional capital cost; showing unreasonable changes in selling price of the final products or of raw materials; showing unreasonable change in the working capital movements; capturing unreasonable tax benefits under (sunset clause) the Tax laws and unreasonable changes in manpower cost and so on.

Discussions with the Management

Lot of information can be collected through discussion in person with management executives. However, the discussions to be carried out should be fair and information given is not manipulated. Here, all critical people of the management need to be interviewed. The valuer should get the required information in writing on various inputs given by them. This helps in defending the valuation if challenged by any authority in future.

Other Secondary Data

This includes published data at various places. It maybe trade association, press release, newspaper or trade journals. The reports published by various banks, research organisation, etc., can form part of information resources. The data may be available on Internet pertaining to the industry as well as the target company.

Stock Market Data

The traded stock prices of the listed companies are available on the website of the stock exchange. Due adjustments also need to be made for illiquid or thinly traded shares, rights issue, bonus issues, stock split, open offers, buy back, etc. Stock exchange website also gives details of various announcements made by the company in the past.

Data on Comparable Companies

Data on comparable companies in same industry sector is available. Review of such data is an important feature in any valuation exercise. Sometimes this data may not be of much use as different funding pattern of two companies and investments therein also makes them non-comparable.

SUMMARY

There are a number of instances when investor may need to determine the market value of a business. Certainly, buying and selling a business is the most common reason. Estate planning, reorganization, or verification of the worth for lenders or investors are other reasons. Valuing a company is hardly a precise science and can vary depending on the type of business and the reason for coming up with a valuation. There are a wide range of factors that go into the process — from the book value to a host of tangible and intangible elements. In general, the value of the business will rely on an analysis of the company's cash flow. In other words, its ability to generate consistent profits will ultimately determine its worth in the marketplace. Valuation is challenging because it's based on the 'type' of company and the 'quality' of earnings. Growth rate, predictability and market conditions are also significant inputs to the valuation process. Some of the common methods of company valuation are; asset valuation, capitalisation of income valuation and market valuation. Ratio Analysis is one of the basic tools of financial analysis. The financial ratios are not sometimes necessarily indicative of a company's overall financial health, and the numbers mean less in some industries than in others. However, these financial ratios do provide a good starting point for evaluating a company, and therefore we take them into careful consideration when evaluating a company.

Review Questions

1. Why should a business have valuation?
2. What approaches do you consider in valuing the business?
3. What are the standards of value?
4. What is the difference between enterprise value and equity value?
5. What is the difference between an appraisal and a fairness opinion?

Video Linkages

1. *http://www.youtube.com/watch?v=7ZDf1DDtL3c*, Business Valuation-what is my company worth?, -Dave Dambro (or Mark N. Bass, or Ken Honeyman), of The Capital MatchPoint, www.capitalmatchpoint.com tells to about
2. *http://www.youtube.com/watch?v=rSNNBrt-XfE&feature=related*, Introduction to Valuation - Valuation is the process of determining what something is worth. This gives an introductory look at valuation from Discounted Cash Flow Analysis (DCF) to market multiples

ASSIGNMENT

1. Take two individual companies (listed on stock exchanges) in different industry segments. In this project, you are going to select the company you choose to value. You should get information on historical record of the company you have chosen and how it compares to the industry. In this assignment, you are going to make an estimate of the fundamental value of chosen company and use price projections

based on PE and P/Sales ratios. To begin, you will need 5 to 10 years of data for your company from various sources. Prepare the report under the following headings of I. Introduction to Company, II. Financial Analysis, III. Relative Valuation, IV. Fundamental Valuation, V. Conclusions, VI. Recommendations and VII. Half Page Summary.

BIBLIOGRAPHY

1. Ashwath Damodaran, (2009). *Damodaran on Valuation*; Wiley India P. Ltd., ND.
2. Fridson, Martin, and Fernando Alvarez (2002). *Financial Statement Analysis: A Practitioner's Guide*. New York: John Wiley,
3. Harrington, Diana R. (1993), *Corporate Financial Analysis: Decisions in a Global Environment*, 4th ed. Chicago: Richard D. Irwin, Inc.,
4. Helfert, Erich A. (1997), *Techniques of Financial Analysis: A Modern Approach*, 9th ed. Chicago: Richard D. Irwin, Inc.,
5. Koller Tim, Goedhart Marc, Wessels David (2010), *Valuation: Measuring and Managing the Value of Companies*, John Wiley and Sons, Inc. 5th edition.
6. Matschke, Manfred Jurgen; Brosel, Gerrit; and Matschke, Xenia (2010), "Fundamentals of Functional Business Valuation", *Journal of Business Valuation and Economic Loss Analysis*: Vol. 5: Iss. 1, Article 7.
7. Palepu, Healy and Bernard.(2000), *Business Analysis and Valuation Using Financial Statements*, Southwestern Publishing, 3rd edn, 2000.
8. Pereiro, (2002), *Valuation of Companies in Emerging Markets: A Practical Approach*, John Wiley and Sons, 1st edition.
9. Pratt Shannon P., Reilly Robert F. and Schweihs Robert P., (2000), *Valuing A Business*, McGraw-Hill; 4th edition.

2

CHAPTER

Discounted Cash Flow Valuation

"Customer satisfaction, Employee satisfaction and Cash flow are the three most important indicators for a business".

— Jack Welch

Learning Objectives

To understand:

- Time value of money
- Weighted average cost of capital
- DCF methodology
- DCF utility and limitations
- Company valuation using DCF
- DCF for borrowings

Discounted cash flows (DCF) have been a traditional method in business valuation. This method is most useful in judging the risk and uncertainty of an investment in a company. Many leading companies have used this approach to value their tangible and intangible assets in their balance sheet. DCF is the most fundamentally correct way of valuing an investment. The DCF methodology is not without its drawbacks. However, it makes one of the popular methods in business valuation. Valuation ratios, used in comparative valuation are simplified approximations of a DCF. Many estimates and assumptions required by a DCF, introduce a lot of uncertainty, often making it no better than simpler models. Discounted cash flow (DCF) valuation is used to evaluate the investment-worthiness of a stock. If the value derived from DCF valuation is higher than the current market price, the opportunity might be worth considering. Discounted Cash Flow valuation uses future free cash flow streams and discounts them (using a risk free rate + risk premium) to arrive at the present value.

INTRODUCTION

Discounted Cash Flow (DCF) analysis is one of the most popular valuation methodologies in use today. DCF method is a powerful tool to analyze even complex situations. However, the DCF method is subject to massive assumption bias. As a result slight changes in the underlying assumptions of an analysis can totally change the valuation results. It has received greater attention, emphasis and acceptance during last decade. DCF Analysis offers several advantages over other valuation methodologies. It has an ability to customize the financial model, which is the basis for the valuation to any given business situation. DCF Analysis is most universal and can be used to value any business, provided a reasonable financial forecast can be created. It has an ability to select an appropriate discount rate WACC (Weighted Average Cost of Capital) which addresses a unique circumstances of a given capital market. Since the applicable discount rate WACC is individually calculated for each DCF valuation analysis, a high level of flexibility exists to capture the reality of a given capital market. WACC calculation includes the following factors such as;

- Risk free rate of interest of a given capital market;
- Risk premium over risk free investments in a given capital market; and
- Sensitivity of the return on equity of a given company in relation to the market return.

Therefore, the sensitivity analysis is highly useful in negotiating and agreeing what the value of a given company is, as it allows to position the valuation as a range of values, rather than a single value. Most popular inputs which are being tested in the sensitivity analysis for company valuation include:

- Revenue growth
- EBITDA
- Net income margins
- Level of corporate synergies (M&A transactions)
- Working capital assumptions
- CAPEX levels
- New debt
- Repaying (faster) existing debt
- Obtaining funds through an IPO or an SPO
- WACC inputs (risk free rate, risk premium, Beta)
- Free cash flow growth rate after the terminal year

DCF method has an ability to perform valuation analysis which is almost totally independent from the prevailing capital market conditions. In DCF it is possible to capture the true value of a company being valued with reference only to its specific situation and without regard for the overall capital market conditions. Prevailing macroeconomic condition influences valuation of companies such as recessionary economy wherein value of the company falls in general.

The sensitivity analysis has shown that the DCF method is very vulnerable to changes in the underlying assumptions. Only marginal changes in the continuous growth rate will lead to huge variances in the terminal value. Since the terminal value accounts for a large portion of the company's value, this is of big significance for the validity of the DCF method.

In DCF analysis the inputs can be changed to get the value that is required. This is even possible by changing in the perpetual growth rate or in the WACC by a few base points. However, the DCF analysis is a great tool to analyze what assumptions and conditions have to be fulfilled in order to reach a certain company value. This is especially helpful in the case of capital budgeting and in the creation of feasibility plans.

The company valuation using discounted cash flows is a valid method to assess the company's value if some care is put on the validity of the underlying assumptions. As with all other financial models, the validity of the DCF method almost completely depends on the quality and validity of the data that is used as input. If used properly with right inputs, DCF valuation is a powerful tool to evaluate the values of a variety of assets and to analyze the effects on value under different economic scenarios.

WEIGHTED AVERAGE COST OF CAPTIAL

Before understanding the DCF, it is a must to understand the concept of WACC. For example to start with first understand WACC on your own investment portfolio. You may own ₹ 200 in a money market fund that has an expected yearly return of 8%. You also may own ₹ 200 of a preferred stock with an expected return of 9% and you also may own ₹ 600 of a common stock with an expected return of 10%. The expected weighted average return of ₹ 1,000 (in total) investment portfolio equals:

Expected Return = (₹ 200 × .08) + (₹ 200 × .09) + (₹ 600 × .10) = ₹ 78 (7.8%)

For a company's WACC is similar as described above. It's the weighted average expected cost for the company's various types of liabilities debt, preferred stock, and common stock issued by the corporation to finance its operations and investments.

The company's WACC is a very important number for stock valuation purposes and to the company's management for capital budgeting purposes. In an analysis of a potential investment by the company, the investment in the projects should have an expected return always greater than the company's WACC. This will generate additional cash flow and will create positive net present value for stock owners. These investments should result in an increase in stock prices. Investments that earn less than the firm's WACC will result in a decrease in stockholder value and should be avoided by the company.

One of the most important aspects of financial theory in valuation is the weighted average cost of capital (WACC) which is the discount rate. In other words it is a time value of money, to convert expected future cash flow into present value. In practical terms, WACC represents what it would cost, on average, to raise money for the company.

The common choice for the risk free rate for valuation of long-term investments is the yield on long-term Indian treasury bonds. The Beta of a stock indicates the degree to which the stock's return moves with that of the overall market. If Beta = 1.0, the stock is as risky as the overall market and therefore will provide expected returns equal to those of the market. Stocks with Beta of 1.5 will, on an average rise 150% of overall market during rising prices and fall 150% of overall market during falling prices. Beta incorporates only the systematic risk that affects every stock. Always, taking systematic risk is awarded with a risk premium. In case of publicly traded companies, published estimates of historical beta are available. For unlisted companies, Betas of listed companies with similar risk profile are used as proxy after adjusting for the degree of leverage. The long-term expected return on market (Rm) index is estimated using historical data on the average returns on the stock market. A common practice is to use a long data series to reduce volatility. The cost of debt can be defined by the minimum after tax rate of return that a company must earn on the debt-financed portion of its investments in order to leave unchanged the market price of its stock.

ILLUSTRATION[1]

Balance Sheet Data

- Assets = 100
- Liabilities = 100 (Equity, E = 55 + Long-term debt, D = 25 + Current Liabilities, CL = 20)

Calculating Cost of Debt as follows

- Pre-tax yields to maturity of outstanding debt = 11.0%
- Prevailing Tax Rate = 30%
- Kd = Debt (1-tax rate) = 10% (1-.030) = 7.7 %

Calculating Cost of Equity

- Risk free rate of return (10 year Govt. Bond), Rf = 5.5%
- Market Risk Premium = 6.75%
- Beta = 1.2
- Ke = Rf + (Beta) × (Market Risk Premium)
- Ke = 5.5 + (1.2) × (6.75) = 13.6

Calculating WACC

WACC = Cost of Equity* + Cost of Debt* (after tax)

(*Weighted by the proportion of debt and equity in the capital structure)

- WACC = { E/(D+E) } Ke + {D/(D+E)}Kd (1-t)
- WACC = [{55/(25+55)} × 13.6] + [{25/(25+55)} × 7.5]
- WACC = 11.69

1. Financial Modeling Guide (www.financialmodelingguide.com)

TIME VALUE OF MONEY

Time Value of Money (TVM) is an important concept in financial management. It can be used to compare investment alternatives and to solve problems involving loans, mortgages, leases, savings and annuities.

TVM is based on the concept that a rupee today is worth more than the one that will be received in the future. Money today is worth more because it can be invested and earn interest. For that one should receive some compensation for foregoing spending. For instance, a rupee can be invested for one year at a 8% annual interest rate and accumulate ₹ 1.08 at the end of the year. Hence, the future (after a year) value of the rupee is ₹ 1.08 based on bank interest rate of 8% pa. It follows that the present value of the ₹ 1.08 to receive in one year is only ₹ 1. Thus a key concept of TVM is that a single sum of money or a series of equal, evenly-spaced payments or receipts promised in the future can be converted to an equivalent value today. Thus, an investor can determine the value to which a single sum or a series of future payments will grow to at some future date.

Illustration

If ₹ 100 are invested today at a rate of 7% pa, for a period of 12 years, the future value of today's ₹ 100 becomes ₹ 225.22 at the end of 12th year. This means that if an investor had a choice between taking an amount higher than the ₹ 100 today and taking the ₹ 225.22 at the end of 12th year time periods, he should take the money today. By doing so, he would be able to invest the higher amount at 7% for 12 equal time periods, which would end up giving him more than ₹ 225.22.

The value of a stock is equal to the present value of its future cash flows. No more and no less. Companies create economic value by investing capital and generating a return. Some of that return pays operating expenses, some get re-invested in the business and the rest is free cash flow. In all above free cash flow (money) that could be taken out of the business each year without harming its operations. A firm could use free cash flow to benefit shareholders in a number of ways. It can pay a dividend, which essentially converts a portion of each investor's interest in the firm to cash. It can buyback stock, which reduces the number of shares outstanding and thus increases the percentage ownership of each shareholder. Alternatively, the firm can retain the free cash flow and re-invest it in the business. The free cash flows are what gives the firm its investment value. A present value calculation adjusts those future cash flows to show money being received in future is worth less than money we receive today.

In general, future cash flows are worth less than the current ones. This is because the money that is being received today can be invested to generate return, whereas future cash flows cannot be invested until it is received. This is the time value of money. And it needs to be compensated for that risk with the risk premium. The time value of money is essentially the opportunity cost of receiving money in the future versus receiving it today, and is often represented by the interest rates being paid (by government/bank which is certain). In market many cash flows are as certain as those from the government, so we need to take an additional premium to compensate us for the risk that we may never receive the money we have been promised. Add the government interest rate to the risk premium and arrive at a discount rate.

This is the reason why stocks with stable, predictable earnings often have such high valuations. The future cash flow of such stocks are discounted at a lower rate, because they believe lower risk happening in future cash flows. On the other side, a business with an extremely uncertain future has a lower valuation. The reason is a substantial risk about the happening of potential future cash flows. That is why a rational investor is willing to pay more for a company that's profitable now relative to one that promises profitability in the future. Not only does the latter carry a higher risk (and thus, a higher discount rate), but the promised cash flows won't arrive until some years in the future. This will further reduce their value. Changing discount rates and the timing of cash flows can have a great effect on present value of a company.

DCF MATHEMATICS

DCF method is widely accepted and popularly used in investment valuation process. The scope of its usage is:

- Company valuations for the merger and acquisition transactions;
- Compliance valuations;
- Investment analysis for the venture capital and private equity investors;
- Restructuring valuation analysis;
- Specialized reports on intangible asset valuations, purchase price allocations and goodwill impairment analysis;
- Reports supporting litigation and dispute resolution (e.g., income loss reports); and
- Analysis prepared for the legal opinions and expert testimony used in the court trials.

The basic principle behind a discounted cash flow model is that the value is determined by the amount, timing, riskiness of a firm's future cash flows, and these are the three items one should always be thinking about when deciding how much to pay for an asset/stock. The value of an asset is the value of the future benefits it brings. The value of an investment is what cash flows will generate for the investor: interest payments, dividends, repayments, returns of capital, etc. These cash flows need to be adjusted for two things:

- Time value of money
- Risk anticipated in expected value of money

In a DCF valuation, a discount rate is chosen which reflects the risk. Here, higher discount rate is selected for higher degree of risk. The selected discount rate is used to discount all forecasted future cash flows to calculate a present value:

DPV = [CF1 / (1+r) 1] + [CF 2 / (1+r)2]+ ... + [CFn / (1+r) n]

Where,

- DPV - discounted present value of the stream of future cash flows.
- CF1 - cash flow the investor receives in the first year.

- CF2 - cash flow the investor receives in the second year.
- CFn - cash flow the investor receives in the nth year.
- r - discount rate.

The formula above can be adjusted for periods other than a year in the same way as the NPV (net projected value) formula. The formula differ because this excludes the time zero cash flow: e.g., the cost of buying a security. The discounted cash flow formula is derived from the future value formula for calculating the time value of. Thus the discounted present value (for one cash flow in one future period) is expressed as:

FV = DPV × (1+i) n

DPV = {FV}/{(1+i) n} = {FV} × {(1-d) n}

where,

- DPV is the discounted present value of the future cash flow (FV), or FV adjusted for the delay in receipt;
- FV is the nominal value of a cash flow amount in a future period;
- i is the interest rate, which reflects the cost of tying up capital and may also allow for the risk that the payment may not be received in full;
- d is the discount rate, which is i/(1+i), i.e., the interest rate expressed as a deduction at the beginning of the year instead of an addition at the end of the year;
- n is the time in years before the future cash flow occurs.

Where multiple cash flows in multiple time periods are discounted, it is necessary to sum them as follows:

$$DPV = \sum_{t=o}^{t=n} \{FVt\} / \{(1+i)t\}$$

for each future cash flow (FV) at any time period (t) in years from the present time, summed over all time periods. The sum can then be used as a net present value figure. If the amount to be paid at time 0 (now) for all the future cash flows is known, then that amount can be substituted for DPV and the equation can be solved for i, that is the internal rate of return.

All the above assumes that the interest rate remains constant throughout the whole period.

For continuous cash flows, the summation in the above formula is replaced by an integration:

$$DPV = \sum_{o}^{t} \left\{FV(t)\, e^{\lambda} t\right\} dt$$

where,

FV(t) = rate of cash flow, and

$\lambda = \log(1+i)$.

To show how discounted cash flow analysis is performed, consider the following simplified example.

Illustration

➢ Reliable Industries Ltd (RIL) buys a building for ₹ 5,00,000/- Three years later, he expects to be able to sell this bldg for ₹ 7,50,000

➢ Simple subtraction suggests that the value of his profit on such a transaction would be ₹ 7,50,000- ₹ 500,000 = ₹ 2,50,000, or 50%. If that ₹ 2,50,000 is amortized over the three years, his implied annual return (known as the internal rate of return) would be about 14.5%. Looking at those figures, RIL might be justified in thinking that the purchase looked like a good idea.

➢ However, since three years have passed between the purchase and the sale, any cash flow from the sale must be discounted accordingly. At the time RIL buys the house, the 3-year Treasury Bond rate is 5% per annum. Treasury Bonds are generally considered to be inherently less risky than real estate, since the value of the Bond is guaranteed by the Indian Government and there is a liquid market for the purchase and sale of Bonds. If he hadn't put his money into buying the house, he could have invested it in the relatively safe Bonds instead. This 5% per annum can therefore be regarded as the risk-free interest rate for the relevant period (3 years).

➢ Using the DPV formula above (FV= ₹ 7.50,000, i = 0.05, n = 3), that means that the value of ₹ 5,00,000 received in three years actually has a present value of ₹ 6,47,880. In other words we would need to invest ₹ 6,47,880/- in a Bond now to get ₹ 7,50,000 in 3 years almost risk free. This is a quantitative way of showing that money in the future is not as valuable as money in the present (₹ 7,50,000 in 3 years is worth the same as ₹ 7,50,000 now; it is worth ₹ 6,47,880/- now).

➢ Subtracting the purchase price of the house (₹ 500,000) from the present value results in the net present value of the whole transaction, which would be ₹ 2,50,000/- or a little more than 29.57% of the purchase price.

➢ Another way of looking at the deal as the excess return achieved (over the risk-free rate) is (14.5%-5.0%)/(100%+5%) or approximately 9.0% (still very respectable).

➢ It is assumed that the ₹ 7,50,000 is RIL's best estimate of the sale price that he will be able to achieve in 3 years time (after deducting all expenses, of course). There is of course a lot of uncertainty about house prices, and the outcome may end up higher or lower than this estimate.

➢ The house RIL is buying is in a "good neighborhood," but market values have been rising quite a lot lately and the real estate market analysts in the media are talking about a slow-down and higher interest rates. There is a probability that one might not be able to get the full ₹ 7,50,000 RIL is expecting in three years due to a slowing of price appreciation, or that loss of liquidity in the real estate market might make it very hard for him to sell at all.

➢ Under normal circumstances, people entering into such transactions are risk-averse, that is to say that they are prepared to accept a lower expected return for the sake of avoiding risk. For the sake of the example (and this is a gross simplification), let's assume that he values this particular risk at 5% per annum (we could perform a more precise probabilistic analysis of the risk, but that is beyond the scope of this article). Therefore, allowing for this risk, RIL's expected return is now 9.0% per annum.

- And the excess return over the risk-free rate is now (9.0%-5.0%)/(100% + 5%) which comes to approximately 3.8% per annum.

- That return rate may seem low, but it is still positive after all of our discounting, suggesting that the investment decision is probably a good one: it produces enough profit to compensate for tying up capital and incurring risk with a little extra left over. When investors and managers perform DCF analysis, the important thing is that the net present value of the decision after discounting all future cash flows at least be positive (more than zero). If it is negative, that means that the investment decision would actually lose money even if it appears to generate a nominal profit.

- If the house was located in an undesirable neighborhood and the Reserve Bank was about to raise interest rates by five percentage points, then the risk factor would be a lot higher than 5%: it might not be possible for him to predict a profit in discounted terms even if he thinks he could sell the house for 10,00,000 in three years.

In this example, only one future cash flow was considered. For a decision which generates multiple cash flows in multiple time periods, all the cash flows must be discounted and then summed into a single net present value. In the case of bonds, the cash flows would be interest payments and repayments. Shares are more complex and give a choice of methods. Hybrid securities may be bond like (and therefore can be valued using a DCF), or contain embedded options that need more complex valuation. A four step DCF valuation technique is explained below

1. **Forecast Expected Cash Flow:** Forecast the expected cash flow for the company based on assumptions regarding the company's revenue growth rate, net operating profit margin, income tax rate, fixed investment requirement and incremental working capital requirement.

2. **Estimate the Discount Rate:** Estimate the company's weighted average cost of capital, which is the discount rate that's used in the valuation process.

3. **Calculate the Cash Flow:** Using WACC discount the expected cash flows during the excess return period to get the company's cash flow from its operations. WACC may also be used to calculate the company's residual value and add the value of Short-Term Assets on hand to get the corporate value.

4. **Calculate Intrinsic Stock Value:** Subtract the values of the company's liabilities-debt, preferred stock, and other short-term liabilities to get value to common equity, divide that amount by the amount of stock outstanding to get the per share intrinsic stock value.

Exhibit 2.1: Discounted Cash Flow Company Valuation Process

Step 1	Forecast 10 years cash flow	Use the estimated growth rate based on past FCF in last 10 years	Generate FCF in next 10 years based on estimated possible consistent FCF growth for next 10 years
Step 2	Discount this FCF to present value	Using a discounted growth rate value	After having all the FCF that is estimated the company will be able to generate for the following 10 years, and need to discount it to present value by assuming on a 10% growth rate. (i.e., 10% bank interest rate).
Step 3	Calculate the Discounted Perpetuity Value	Use a perpetuity growth rate	A stock can't grow at a high value infinitely. The company's growth will start to drop and come to a time to get saturated. Then get steady and in line with the economic growth of it's individual industry.
Step 4	Calculate Total Equity Value	Can also be assumed as the Enterprise Value	After 10 years, need to know what total free cash the company is able to generate. Therefore, add all the FCF generated by the company throughout the next 10 years and also the Perpetuity Value. This is all for calculating the Total Equity Value which is discounted to it's present value,
Step 5	Calculate Per Share Value		Divide total equity value with the total outstanding shares. This will give the per share intrinsic value, which we can use it as a gauge to compare with the current market price of this company which is currently trading in the open market.

Illustration

Step 1- Forecast Next 10 years' FCF (Using estimated growth rate based on past FCF growth)

➢ Here's the snapshot of the FCF of Reliance for the past 10 years. (Unit ₹)

Year	1	2	3	4	5	6	7	8	9	10	11
FCF	60.5	87.3	162.5	208.5	290.4	335.4	349.2	450.5	604.1	680.0	

➢ Compound annual growth for the past 10 years in Reliance is 27.28%.

➢ Further FCF for the next 10 years the company can generate need to be estimated

Step2 - Discount these FCF to Present Value (using a discounted growth rate value)

➢ Calculate the FCF that will be generated for the next 10 years using 27.37 growth rate.

➢ Calculate Present Value of FCF (ie DFCF) using Discount Rate of 15 %.

➢ Here is the snapshot of Forecated FCF and their discounts values for next ten years (Unit ₹)

Year	10	11	12	15	16	17	18	19	20	21	
FCF	680.0	865.5	1101.6	1402.1	1784.6	2271.4	2891.0	3679.7	4683.5	5961.2	
DFCF	591.3	654.4	724.3	801.6	887.3	982.0	1086.8	1202.9	1331.3	1473.5	9735.4

Step 3 - Calculate the Discounted Perpetuity Value (using a perpetuity growth rate)

Perpetuity Value = year 10 FCF × (1 + g) / (R - g)

where,

g = perpetuity growth rate (3%)

R = Discounted rate (15%)

Perpetuity Value = ₹ 5961.2 × (1 + 0.03) / (0.15 - 0.03)

= ₹ 6140.0 /0.12

= ₹ 51166.9

Discount it back to Present value, with the 15% discounted rate (using the compound rate), and we get a Discounted Perpetuity Value = ₹ 12648.2

Step 4. Calculate Total Equity Value (which can be also briefly assumed as the Enterprise Value)

Total Equity Value = Discounted Perpetuity Value + Total Discounted FCF

= ₹ 12648.2 + ₹ 9735.4

= ₹ 22383.6

This will be the Enterprise Value of Reliance. If someone were want to acquire Reliance right now, this will be the value to take over this company.

Step 5. Calculate Per Share Value

To get intrinsic value, divide the total equity value by the total outstanding shares:

Intrinsic Value = ₹ 22383.6 / 160.0 = ₹ 139.9

This intrinsic value that is reached based on 10 year model DCF on Reliance. Reliance is currently trading at ₹ 71 which is like a 50% discount to it's Intrinsic Value.

In general the DCF Model is used in the following cases:

➤ When the investor wants to estimate what is the maximum price he must pay to achieve a minimum or required rate of return. This price can be estimated by discounting the cash flows expected from the property over the holding period using as discount rate to have the required or minimum rate of return. This is a present value, not a net present value, calculation since the initial cash outlay is not known and is to be determined.

➤ When the investor wants to evaluate the return on investment over the investment horizon if it is acquired at a given price. This is calculated by including the acquisition price in the cash flows to be discounted, and estimating the discount rate that sets the NPV equal to zero. The estimated discount rate is actually the internal rate of return (annual, monthly, quarterly, etc.) depending on the length of the period to which the cash flows refer to.

METHODS OF APPRAISAL

For valuation purposes, a number of different DCF methods are used today. The variations are due to different capital structure of the companies. However, the assumptions used in the appraisal (especially the equity discount rate and the projection of the cash flows to be achieved) are likely to be at least as important as the precise model used. Both the income stream selected and the associated cost of capital model determine the valuation result obtained with each method. Refer Exhibit 2.2 for different approaches to DCF analysis:

Exhibit 2.2: Different approaches to DCF analysis

Approaches	Description	Advantages	Disadvantages
Flows to equity approach (FTE)	Discount the cash flows available to the holders of equity capital, after allowing for cost of servicing debt capital	Makes explicit allowance for the cost of debt capital	Requires judgment on choice of discount rate
Adjusted present value approach (APV)	Discount the cash flows before allowing for the debt capital (but allowing for the tax relief obtained on the debt capital)	Simple to apply if a specific project is being valued which does not have earmarked debt capital finance	Requires judgment on choice of discount rate; no explicit allowance for cost of debt capital, which may be much higher than a "risk-free" rate
Weighted average cost of capital approach (WACC)	Derive a weighted cost of the capital obtained from the various sources and use that discount rate to discount the cash flows from the project	Overcomes the requirement for debt capital finance to be earmarked to particular projects	Care must be in the selection of the appropriate income exercised stream. The net cash flow to total invested capital is the generally accepted choice.
Total cash flow approach (TCF)	Can be used to determine the value of various business ownership interests. These can include equity or debt holders.	Can be used to value the company based on the value of total invested capital.	Total cash flow to total invested capital and WACC are appropriate when valuing a company based on the market value of all invested capital

Flipside - DCF Analysis

It has high dependence on the chosen assumptions. Outcome of the DCF analysis is highly dependent on several key assumptions. Some of the most important assumptions where judgment is exercised include the WACC components, the Free Cash Flow growth rate after the terminal year, the revenue growth rate, the EBIT, EBITDA and Net Income margin assumptions and the Working Capital assumptions. This limitation can be addressed by running sensitivity analysis. DCF Analysis requires preparation of a comprehensive financial model of a company being valued. It is an intensive and labour consuming process which requires a considerable technical expertise.

DCF valuations can fluctuate wildly depending on the assumptions. If the inputs - free cash flow forecasts, discount rates and perpetuity growth rates - are much off the mark, the fair value generated for the company won't be accurate, and it won't be useful when assessing stock prices. Hence, the inputs into the model should be correct to get right picture.

DCF works best when there is a high degree of confidence about future cash flows. But results are worst if a company's operations experiences difficulty to predict sales and cost trends with much certainty. While forecasting cash flows a few years into the future is hard enough and pushing results is nearly impossible. The investor's ability to make good forward-looking projections is critical and that's why DCF is susceptible to error.

Valuations are particularly sensitive to assumptions about the perpetuity growth rates and discount rates. DCF model is not suited to short-term investing. DCF focuses on long-term value. A well-crafted DCF may help investor avoid buying a wrong stock, but it may also make him miss short-term share price run-ups that can be profitable. In addition, focusing too much on the DCF may cause investors overlook unusual opportunities. Hence, investors should be conservative about their inputs.

The other disadvantage of DCF is that it is not suitable for start-ups, growth companies or capital intensive companies where the cash flow cannot be accurately determined. The error of prediction and assumptions must also be dealt with in the DCF, which is covered with margin of safety.

Commercial banks have widely used discounted cash flow as a method of valuing commercial real estate construction projects. This practice has two substantial shortcomings. 1) The discount rate assumption relies on the market for competing investments at the time of the analysis. This may change over a time, and 2) straight line assumptions about income increasing over ten years are generally based upon historic increases in market rent. This is never factored in the cyclical nature of many real estate markets. Most loans are made during booming real estate markets and these markets usually last fewer than ten years. Using DCF to analyze commercial real estate during any but the early years of a boom market will lead to over valuation of the asset.

DCF is a mechanical valuation tool. Small changes in inputs can result in large changes in the value of a company. Instead of trying to project the cash flows to infinity, terminal value techniques are often used. Here a simple annuity is used to estimate the terminal value past 10 years. This is done because it is harder to come to a realistic estimate of the cash flows as time goes on it involves calculating the period of time likely to change the initial outlay.

Cash Flow

The problem with discounting dividends is that the company's dividends needs to be forecasted and guess its future dividend policy. Profits do necessarily bring in cash to the company (as profits are calculated using the accrual principle). Therefore, it makes sense to discount cash flows instead. Financial theory would also suggest that unless a company has very high return opportunities for expansion, then the difference in valuation between a dividend discount valuation and a free cash flow discount valuation will be comparatively small. Many discounted cash flow valuations do not explicitly include all cash flows a holder of a security may receive.

Two companies with the same growth prospects, similar profitability, similar debt levels (relative to profits) and trading at a price which reflects the same discount rate, would then be on similar PE ratios. Even if debt levels were different they would have similar EV/EBITDAs. This is why companies in the same sector should have similar valuation ratios unless there are differences in the risks they face or their growth prospects. Investors should understand the reasons for differences in rating between a company and its industry rivals and decide whether there are sufficient reasons to justify the difference - or whether the difference should be bigger.

Differences in valuation ratios should ultimately reflect differences in growth or risk that would also be reflected the same way by a DCF. Even investors who do not use DCF valuations should keep them in mind.

The Discounted Cash Flow (DCF) model is a model that is used widely in the analysis of real estate investment properties and specifically for the estimation of the Present Value (PV) or the Net Present Value (NPV) of cash flows associated mainly with commercial real estate investment. The latest mortgage rate forecast is an important input in the DCF model when there is borrowing with adjustable-rate loans.

The DCF model consists of a series of periodic cash flows associated with the ownership of a particular property investment, which are discounted to the present time (time 0) using a discount rate. The present value model estimates the present value of anticipated cash flows from a commercial property without taking into account the initial cash outlay or investment cost for the acquisition of the property. In the net present value model, however, the initial cash outlay in time zero is taken into account. Thus, the two important things that determine the net present value of a investment in the discounted cash flow model are the series of cash flows used and the discount rate.

Periodic cash flows that are used in the discounted cash flow model have to refer to periods of the same length (annual, semi-annual, quarterly, monthly). All cash flows that are used in the discounted cash flow model refer to the future. These forecasts need to be adjusted to take into account the position of the building under consideration *vis a vis* the market average. The discount rate used must represent the discount rate that corresponds to the length of period in which the cash flows refer to. For example, if quarterly cash flows are used then a quarterly discount rate needs to be used.

The formula for the discounted cash flow model for the calculation of NPV, which takes into account investment costs (cash outlays) at time 0, is the following:

NPV = CF0 + CF1/(1+d) + CF2/(1+d)2 + ...+ CFn/(1+d)n

Where CF represents the cash flow of each period within the investment analysis horizon, d the discount rate and n the last period of the investment horizon. As indicated earlier, the first cash flow CF0 represents the initial cash outlay or investment cost. The last cash flow CFn includes any income expected to be received during the last period of the investment plus the market value or sales price of the property at that point in time. This is calculated as the ratio of the expected Net Operating Income (NOI) in the last period of the investment horizon over an expected exit cap rate.

Here to keep in mind that the d is the periodic discount rate that corresponds to the length of period that cash flows refer to. For example, if cash flows are quarterly then the quarterly discount rate needs to be entered in the formula. Caution is needed here because discount rates are usually quoted in annual terms, and one might be tricked to use an annual discount rate with quarterly cash flows, in which case a very incorrect result will be obtained. Furthermore, caution is needed when deriving quarterly or other periodic discount rates from annual discount rates to take into account the compounding effect. The correct formula for deriving the quarterly discount rate (dq) from the annual discount rate (da) is:

$$dq = (1+ da)1/4 - 1$$

The correct formulas for deriving the monthly discount rate (dm) and the semi-annual discount rate (ds) from the annual discount rate (da) are:

$$dm = (1+ da)1/12 - 1$$

$$ds = (1+ da)1/2 - 1$$

Key Considerations

The discounted cash flow model is widely used in investment decisions especially for the calculation of the NPV or the internal rate of return (IRR). The internal rate of return of an investment is actually the discount rate that renders the NPV of the expected cash flows equal to 0. The following things apply when using the discounted cash flow model for the evaluation of an investments:

- Use of after-tax cash flows
- Cash flow at time '0' is negative as it represents investment costs (asset acquisition costs, plus any pre-acquisition costs for due diligence, such as market studies, feasibility studies, legal, environmental studies, etc., or other expenses). Subsequent cash flows might be negative as well, especially in the case of real estate development projects.
- Cash flows represent the sum of all anticipated revenues and costs in each period; notice that such costs and revenues will differ by property type and for each property depending on its idiosyncrasies. Special attention is needed when projecting property income and expenses in order to estimate these cash flows. Reliable projections of a property's net operating income (NOI) need to take into account the property's lease rollover schedule, expiring leases and vacancy durations, as well as potential changes in current market rents, which will affect income from new leases. Projecting market rents is not an easy task. Most reliable projections of market rents can be derived through advanced econometric models that take into account most likely changes in demand, supply and the way these changes affect rent adjustments. There are a number of vendors specialized in real estate forecasting that provide rent forecasts for the largest metropolitan areas in the country and the major property types, such as office, retail, industrial and apartments.

Value Of Cash and Cross Holdings

Companies with significant operating cash flows, accumulate a very large cash balance; it amounts to 20% or greater of the overall value of the firm. They are not an exceptions. Companies such as Apple and Microsoft, have also been avid cash accumulators. While the conventional valuation practice with cash has been to add the cash balance to the value of operating assets, thus adopting the common sense rule that a rupee in cash has to be worth a rupee, there is substantial evidence that markets do not always treat cash as a neutral asset. Investors view companies that generate poor returns on their operating assets (less than the cost of capital) and accumulate cash with disfavor, while being much more hopeful about companies with good investment track records and substantial cash. In many cases, one of the concerns may be raised was that the company's return on capital has lagged its cost of capital. It is therefore possible that the market may be discounting the cash holdings and therefore cash may be valued at less.

As regards cross holdings, investing in any company for example a Tata company is a joint investment in that company and a portfolio of 25-30 other Tata companies. While one reason for this cross holding structure is corporate control - it allows the family to preserve its control of the group companies - there are also more other reasons, rooted in history. In the decades before the 1990s, Indian investors had little access to financial information from the company, let alone analyst reports or investment analysis. In that period, these investors had to essentially buy companies based on how much they trusted the promoters of the company, and a trusted family name became a proxy for research. In addition, when capital markets are undeveloped, having an internal family group capital market, where excess cash at some companies can be redirected to other companies that need the cash can be a competitive advantage. The cross holdings at family group companies can become a valuation problem for two reasons:

(1) To value one company, many companies have to be valued. Consider a firm with holdings in 25 other companies. Even if we could access information on these companies (because they are public), a thorough analysis of the firm would require a valuation of 26 companies. (Using the book value of these holdings, which are not marked to market, will yield skewed estimates. Using the market values of these holdings risks feeding any market will create error in your valuation).

(2) Some cross holdings cannot be valued: With many family group companies, some of the companies in the group are privately owned and never go public. As a consequence, there is little or no information that can be used to value companies. In such cases there is no choice but to use book value.

If these concerns are carried through to their logical conclusion, it is possible that investors either unconsciously (by using book value) or consciously (by discounting the market value of the cross holdings) will reduce the values of family group companies below what they would have been worth as independent companies.

WARRANTS AND CONVERTIBLES

Warrants are call options that give the holder the right, but not the obligation, to buy shares of common stock directly from a company at a fixed price for a given period of time. Warrants tend to have longer maturity periods than exchange traded options. Warrants are generally issued with privately placed bonds. They are also called as an "equity kicker". Warrants are also combined with new issues of common stock and preferred stock, given to investment bankers as compensation for underwriting services. Both warrants and options are call options on the equity of the firm. Both are usually protected against stock dividends and stock splits. However, neither is protected against cash dividends. Exercise period of a warrant is usually several years. Warrants are issued by the firm. Options are issued by individuals. When a warrant is exercised the firm receives the exercise price from the investor and the firm simultaneously issues new shares. When a warrant is exercised, a firm must issue new shares of stock. This can have the effect of diluting the claims of existing shareholders.

A convertible bond is similar to a bond with warrants. The most important difference is that a bond with warrants can be separated into different securities and a convertible bond cannot. The value of a convertible bond has three components:

(1) Straight bond value (SBV)

(2) Conversion value (CV) is the value if converted into common stock at the current price.

(3) Option value is the value of a convertible bond exceeds both SBV and CV. It is the value for waiting since the value in the future is greater.

When the value of all equity in a firm is estimated, it is generally divided by the number of shares outstanding to arrive at the value of equity per share. This is appropriate if there are no other claims on equity. When such claims exist, they have to be subtracted out before dividing by the number of shares outstanding. Steps Involved are;

Step 1: Value the firm, using discounted cash flow or other valuation models.

Step 2: Subtract out the value of the outstanding debt to arrive at the value of equity.

Step 3: Subtract out the market value (estimated market value) of other equity claims.

Value of Warrants = (Market Price per Warrant) x (Number of Warrants)

Value of Conversion Option = (Market Value of Convertible Bonds) - (Value of Straight Debt Portion of Convertible Bonds)

Step 4: Divide remaining value of equity by the number of shares outstanding to get value per share.

DCF FOR BORROWING

The discounted cash flow model needs to be modified when borrowed money are used to finance part of the asset acquisition. What it does change is how the cash flows used in the DCF formula are calculated. In particular, if the analyst wants to take into account the effect of borrowing on the project's PV or IRR the mortgage loan payments over the holding period need to be appropriately and fully incorporated in the project's after-tax cash flows. In particular, this would include replacing any capital costs that are financed through borrowed money, with the respective periodic loan payments. For example, if construction costs of ₹ 10 Cr are financed by 50%, then the negative cash flow of ₹ 5 Cr be replaced by a negative cash flow of ₹ 5 Cr (50% of ₹ 10 Cr) and a negative cash flow equal to the payment for a loan of ₹ 5 Cr (plus any other incurred costs in association with obtaining the loan, such as bank fees, etc.).

In the case of construction loans, banks will allow only interest payments during the construction period with principal payments starting after project completion. Also in incorporating the effect of borrowing in the discounted cash flow model, the remaining loan balance needs to be subtracted from the last cash flow, which should also incorporate a positive cash flow representing the property at anticipated market value or resale price. The return that incorporates the effect of borrowing is referred to as leveraged return. This represents a typical use of the Discounted Cash Flow model since borrowing is commonly used in real estate investing due to the large capital required to acquire property.

SUMMARY

The concept of DCF valuation is based on the principle that the value of a business or asset is inherently based on its ability to generate cash flows for the providers of capital. To that extent, the DCF relies more on the fundamental expectations of the business than on public market factors or historical precedents, and it is a more theoretical approach relying on numerous assumptions. A DCF analysis yields the overall value of a business (i.e., enterprise value), including both debt and equity. The key components of DCF are, one the free cash flow which is cash generated by the assets of the business (tangible and intangible) available for distribution to all providers of capital. It is also called as unlevered free cash flow, as it represents cash flow available to all providers of capital and is not affected by the capital structure of the business. The second one is terminal value, which at the end of the free cash flow projection period (horizon period) and last discount rate, which is used to discount projected free cash flow and terminal value to their present values. The DCF method of valuation requires projecting free cash flow over a period, calculating the terminal value at the end of that period, and discounting the projected free cash flow and terminal value using the discount rate to arrive at the NPV of the total expected cash flows of the business or asset.

Review Questions

1. Explain the time value concept of money.
2. Differentiate between the calculation of present and future value of the asset.
3. How would you select explicit forecast period in DCF valuation?
4. You are valuing several companies firms using discounted cash flow (DCF) analysis. The following data is provided to you. The following historical data for the equity market during the period from 1950-2010. If you use only this information to determine the market risk premium for use in your valuation model, which estimate would be most appropriate?

Avg Risk Premium	Arithmetic Avg	Geometric Avg
Relative to 3o days T-Bills	7.87%	6.01%
Relative to 30 yrs T-Bonds	6.57%	4.91%

(a) 7.87% , (b) 6.57%, (c) 6.01%, (d) 4.91%

5. You are performing a valuation of a retail firm based on free cash flow to the firm (FCF). FCF in the most recent 12 months (year 0) was ₹ 40 crs. The firm is in a declining industry. As a result, you expect cash flows to grow at an annual rate of 5 % for the next five years and then decrease at 1.5% per year in perpetuity thereafter. The firm's cost of equity is 11.2% and its weighted average cost of capital is 9.5 %. The firm also has debt with a book value of ₹ 82 Crs and a market value of ₹ 61 Crs.

(a) Find out the value of this firm based on the discounted value of FCF?

(b) If the firm has 1, 00,00,000 shares outstanding, what is your estimate of the equity value per share?

(c) If the current market price of ₹ 2000 per share, should you buy or sell the stock?

Video Linkages

1. http://www.youtube.com/watch?v=X73WplHHw4g&feature=relatedDiscounted, Cash Flow Tutorial, Understand how to use the Discounted Cash Flow method to value any asset. Get introduced to some helpful tools that make discounted cash flow easy.
2. http://www.youtube.com/watch?v=SBc6QazpPDQ&feature=relate,d Discounted Cash Flow Valuation |CFMS 4

ASSIGNMENT

Maru Ltd is profitable company in IT sector. It is expected to grow at 10 % in next 5 years and fall thereafter to 6.5 % for following 5 years. The company is expected to produce ₹ 1.35 of free cash flow per share in immediate future. Following that, free cash flow will grow at a 5% indefinitely. Value the shares assuming a discount rate of 13%. The company's shares are currently selling for ₹ 125. Discount rate may vary from 14% to 11%. Calculate the value of the company at these discount rates. Also, consider a scenario where growth rate was 2 percentage higher in first five years? And there after 6.8%. Recommend whether or not to buy a stock based on the discounted cash flow valuation.

BIBLIOGRAPHY

1. Beranek, W., & Howe, K. M. (1990). The Regulated Firm and the DCF Model: Some Lessons From Financial Theory. *Journal of Regulatory Economics,* 193.
2. Bloomberg Professional Database. (2008, August 09). Credit Derivatives and Interest Rates. New York, New York, United States of America. Retrieved August 09, 2008
3. Bodie, Kane, & Marcus. (2008). *Investments* (7th Edition ed.). McGraw Hill.
4. Brealey, R. A., Myers, S. C., & Allen, F. (2006). *Principles of Corporate Finance* (8th Edition ed.). McGraw-Hill.
5. Brigham, E. F., & Gapenski, L. C. (1997). *Financial Management - Theory and Practice* (8th Editioned.). Orlando: The Dryden Press.
6. Damodaran, A. (1996). *Investment Valuation.* New York: John Wiley & Sons, Inc.
7. Gallager, T; Andrew Jr., J., *Financial Management: Principles and Practices,* Upper Saddle River, NJ: Prentice Hall, 1996

8. Hull, J. C. (2008). *Options, Futures and Other Derivatives* (7th Edition ed.). Upper Saddle River: Pearson Prentince Hall..

9. Kieso, D; Weygandt, Jerry, *Intermediate Accounting,* 9th Ed., New York, NY: John Wiley & Sons, Inc., 1993

10. Luehrman, T. A. (1998, July). Investment Opportunities as Real Options. *Harvard Business Review*, 51-67.

11. Luehrmann, T. A. (1997). What's it worth? *Harvard Business Review*, 135.

12. Mukherjee, T. K., Kiymaz, H., & Bake, H. K. (2004, Fall/Winter). Merger Motives and Targets: A Survey of Evidence from CFOs. *Journal of Applied Finance*, 7-24. Discounted Cash Flow Valuation 17

13. Rhaiem, N., Ben, S., & Mabrouk, A. B. (2007). Estimation of Capital Asset Pricing Model at Different Time Scales. *The International Journal of Applied Economics and Finance,* 80.

14. Ross, Westerfield, & Jordan. (2008). *Corporate Finance Fundamentals.* New York: McGraw-Hill Irwin.

15. Stermole F.J. & Stermole J.M., *Economic Evaluation and Investment Decision Methods,* Sixth edition, Investment

3 CHAPTER

Relative Valuation - 'Ratio Analysis'

"Ratios as a tool of financial analysis provide symptoms with the help of which any analyst is in a position to diagnose the financial health of the unit. Financial analysis may be compared with biopsy conducted by the doctor on the patient in order to diagnose the causes of illness so that treatment may be prescribed to the patient to help him recover."[1]

Learning Objectives

To understand:

- Ratios basics
- Types of financial ratios and their usefulness
- What ratio suggests?
- Ratios used for valuation
- Limitations of ratio analysis

Mathematically ratio is a comparison of the numerator with the denominator. It is a mathematical relationship between two numerical forms. Analysis and interpretation of financial statement with the help of 'ratio' is termed as 'ratio analysis'. Ratio analysis involves the process of computing, determining and presenting the relationship of items of financial statement (balance sheet or profit and loss account). Ratio analysis was pioneered by Alexander Wall who presented a system of ratio analysis in the year1909. Alexander's contention was that interpretation of financial statement can be made establishing quantitative relationships between various items of financial statement.

---

1 http://www.accountingexplanation.com/significance_and_usefulness_of_ratio_analysis.htm

INTRODUCTION

Ratio is a relationship in quantitative terms, between numbers, which have cause and effect relationships with each other. These two quantitative terms are related with each other in some manner or the other. The ratios used in accounts indicate some relationships between two or more items of the financial statement connected with each other. Ratio analysis is an age old technique of financial analysis.

The ratio analysis is putting together of two figures to study their relationships. The financial statements like P&L A/c and Balance Sheet is in the absolute figure and the data is historic. It conveys very little meaning and also the relationship with other parameters. However, ratios show how one number is related to another number. Accounting ratios measure and indicate efficiency of an enterprise in its working and profitability.

According to J. Batty, "The term accounting ratios is used to describe significant relationships which exist between figures shown in a balance sheet, in a profit and loss account, in a budgetary control system or in any other part of the accounting organization".

As a number the relationship between female and male in county's population is expressed as 981 to 1000 respectively. Similarly entire earth planet is consisting of ¾ of water and ¼ of solid by volume. The GDP growth of a country is expressed in term of percentages (estimated at 7.0% in 2011 over last year for India). Similarly, ratio analysis in accounts facilitates the meaningful presentation of information of financial statements in simplified, concise, summarized and lucid form.

RELATIVE VALUATION

Relative valuation or ratio analysis technique for valuing firms is a system which is popular with analysts. It determines how much target firm is valued at against other companies in your industry. There are two basic methods of analyzing value. One is called discounted flow valuation, which analyses details and calculates the worth of the company based on projected earnings. The other method is used more often because it uses a technique, which determines the value of a company based on the value of similar companies. This method is more like a real estate market value for a home. The other companies that are similar help determine the value of the company being analyzed. It is none but 'relative valuation' or 'ratio analysis'.

Ratios and relative value analysis technique for valuing firms is an important part of the financial strategy for a company and for the possibility of selling the company or merging with another company. Buyers also like to see the projected value of company before they make a large investment decisions. Comparable companies' analyses involves the comparison of operating metrics and valuation multiples for companies in a comparable "universe" to those of a target company. Comparable companies may be grouped based on any number of criteria, such as industry focus, company size or growth characteristics, for example.

Comparable companies' valuation has an application in M&A advisory, fairness opinions, restructuring, IPOs and follow-on offerings, and share repurchases. Consider an IPO of a private company that does not have a public market valuation. To determine how public markets might value the company, an investment banker will establish the comparable universe. Management will use the operating metrics and valuation multiples of the comparable to determine an appropriate valuation multiple for the target company.

USEFULNESS OF RATIOS

The Balance Sheet and the Statement of Income are essential, but they are only the starting point for successful financial management. Ratio Analysis is done on the financial statements of the company to analyse the success, failure and progress of firm's business. The information presented in financial statements of a company may be difficult to understand and it may be difficult to understand the relationship between each other. It may be unintelligible and confusing. However, ratios help in highlighting the areas deserving attention and corrective action leading to proper decision making.

Ratios will help in financial forecasting and planning process of an enterprise. Ratios help in understanding the past and the present of the particular parameter indicating it's current strength and weaknesses in the present and future market context. This knowledge is very important for the management to plan and forecast the future of an enterprise. Ratios communicate the decision makers at different levels the current situation and help them to act accordingly to avoid the deviations in planned actions to result in improved coordination from all quarters of management.

Ratios provide basis for comparing actuals with the standards. It is a great help in administering an effective system of control. The investors (shareholders) in the company stocks are shareholders are fundamentally interested in the (a) long-term solvency and (b) profitability of the unit. Ratio analysis can help them by analyzing and interpreting both the aspects of a business enterprise.

Ratios will help the creditors too, which include both short and long-term. Short-term creditors are trade creditors, bills payables, creditors for expenses, etc. They are interested in analyzing the liquidity of the unit. Long-term creditors are financial institutions, debenture holders, mortgage creditors, etc. They are interested in analyzing the capacity of the unit to repay periodical interest and repayment of loans on schedule. Ratio analysis helps both types of creditors to take appropriate action.

The employees of an enterprise are interested in fair wages, fringe benefits and bonus. Ratio analysis provides them adequate information regarding efficiency and profitability of the company they are working in. This information may help labour unions to bargain with the management regarding their demands for improved wages, bonus, etc.

Lastly the government is interested in the financial information of the business enterprises both at macro as well as micro levels. Industry information is required for formulating national policies and planning.

RATIO ANALYSIS

There are basically two uses of financial ratio analysis. The first one is to track individual firm performance over time, and to make comparative judgments regarding firm performance. Firm performance is evaluated using trend analysis – calculating individual ratios on a per-period basis, and tracking their values over time. This analysis can be used to spot trends that may be cause for concern. For example, increase in average collection period for outstanding receivables or a decline in the firm's liquidity status. In this role, ratios serve as red alerts for future troubles. Ratios can also serve as benchmarks for performance measurement.

The second usage of ratios is to make relative performance comparisons. For example, comparing a firm's profitability to that of a major competitor or observing how the firm stacks up versus industry averages. This helps the analyst or decision makers to form judgments concerning key areas such as profitability or management effectiveness. Financial ratios are used by both parties, i.e., internal and external to the firm. External users include security analysts, current and potential investors, creditors, competitors, and other industry observers. Internally, managers use ratio analysis to monitor performance and pinpoint strengths and weaknesses from which specific goals, objectives, and policy initiatives may be formed.

Ratios are the means of understanding the financial health of a business organisation. Ratio analysis is not capable of providing precise answers to all the problems faced by any company. Ratio analysis is basically a technique of:

- Finding out the meaningful relationship between significant variables of financial statement
- Interpreting the relationships to form opinion regarding the financial health of a firm

Ratio analysis has its own significance in financial analysis of an enterprise. However, the usefulness of ratios depends upon the following:

- Setting objectives of ratio analysis
- Availability, collection and selection of relevant data
- Calculating appropriate ratios in line with objectives
- Comparison of calculated ratios with norms/standards
- Interpreting the ratios

Calculation of ratios is a simple mathematical process. However interpretation of ratios needs experience and judgmental skills. The success of using ratio analysis depends on the correct interpretation of the various ratios. For correct interpretation of ratios the analyst needs intelligence, training, farsightedness and judgmental skills.

LIMITATIONS OF RATIO ANALYSIS

Ratio analysis is a widely used and useful technique to evaluate the financial position and performance of any business enterprise. The ratio analysis has following limitations, which analyst should keep in mind before using this technique.

- **Data Reliability:** The data available for financial analysis is historical and collected from various sources. Accounting system has certain limitations like historical cost, going concern value, stable monetary value, etc. Hence, the quality of ratio very much depends on correctness and freshness of data.

- **No Place for Qualitative Factors:** Ratio analysis is a quantitative analysis. Sometimes qualitative factors may be important. For example, the factors like management decision in procuring particular raw material/component in large quantity due to the anticipated shortage in near future are not considered in ratio analysis. However, these factors may be explained at the time of interpreting the ratio.
- **Contextual Study:** Ratios assume importance only when studied in proper context. Ratio in itself does not convey any meaning and hence, ratios should be compared with norms or over a period.
- **Past Records:** Ratios are based on the information/data in the past records. Past may be less important or irrelevant for the management than present and future.
- **Accounting Practices:** Different accounting practices/standards permits alternative different treatment of many items like depreciation, valuation of stock, deferred expenses, etc. Ratios based on statements prepared by different practices are not comparable.
- **Price Level Changes:** Comparison of ratios over a period of time relating to same unit may be misleading. For example, sales may be static in quantity but higher in rupee value due to inflation.
- **Analytical Skills:** The analysis and interpretation depends on intelligence, past experience, analytical skills and competence of the analyst.
- **Lack of Standards:** There are no well-accepted standards or rule of thumb for all ratios. This makes interpretation of ratios subjective, difficult and to some extent arbitrary.
- **Window Dressing:** Financial statements can easily be "window dressed" to project the better picture than true picture of the company. In addition analyst uses only published financial statements, which sometimes is manipulated and he may not have access inside information.

RATIO INTEPRETATIONS

The interpretation of the ratios is subjective process and the ratios can be interpreted in different ways such as:

- **Individual Ratio:** Some individual ratio has its own significance. For example, if the current ratio of an enterprise is continuously showing down trends, it alerts probability of insolvency in future. But all single ratios may not convey any sense. In general the single ratio may be studied with reference to thumb rules, which indicates approximations.
- **Group Ratios:** Ratios interpreted by considering group of several related ratios may prove more meaningful. For example, if current ratio is studied along with liquid ratio. Similarly profitability ratios if studied along with return on investments.
- **Historical Comparison:** This means the same ratio be studied continuously over a period of years of the same enterprise. It will show the trend of increase, decline or stability of the phenomenon. In this exercise the average value of the ratio for the past number of years can serve as a norm against which current performance may be measured. During interpretation of the ratio the analyst should take into consideration changes, which might have taken place during the time in price index, managerial policies or accounting practices, etc.

- **Future Projections Comparison:** In this, ratios calculated based on budget or projected financial statements act as the standards with which the ratios calculated from the present financial statements should be compared. Variances are noted for taking necessary corrective action.
- **Inter firm/Industry Comparison:** This is enterprise-to-enterprise comparison in same industry or average of the industry. Ratios of one company are compared with the ratios of another identical company or with the industry average at the same point of time. Such comparison is useful for evaluating relative financial position of the company as against the competition or industry average. Here caution is to take a note of difference of accounting methods, policies, procedures and terminology being followed by different units.

FACTORS TO UNDERSTAND

Financial ratios represent tools for insight into the performance, efficiency, and profitability of a firm. Interpreting financial ratios should also be undertaken with care. The following are the key factors, which should be paid attention while performing the ratio analysis:

- **Quality of Data:** The reliability of ratios depends on the quality of financial statements. Generally accepted accounting principles are likely to contain reliable data. Calculation of ratios from such financial statements is bound to be more useful and correct.
- **Objective of Analysis:** Users of accounting information are different such as short and long-term creditors, owners and would-be investors, trade unions, tax authorities, competitors, etc. Each group has its own objectives towards financial analysis of a company. The object of analysis, which determines the area such as liquidity, solvency, profitability, leverage, activity, etc., the ratios in these areas are to be studied, analyzed and interpreted.
- **Selection of Ratios:** There is no end to the number of ratios, which can be calculated. The ratios selected should serve the purpose of analysis. For example, for short-term creditors' purpose is liquidity whereas owners' purpose may be served by solvency.
- **Standards/Norms:** A single ratio used in (except few) isolation is meaningless. It must be used in conjunction or compared with some standard to arrive at any logical conclusion. Selection of standards for the purpose of interpretation will also depend upon the object of the analysis and the capability of the analyst to probe hidden information.
- **Analytical Ability:** Analysis and interpretation of ratios depends on the educational background; professional skill; experience and intelligence of the individual, who is performing it.
- **Guiding Ratios:** Ratios can be used as guide taking into consideration all other relevant factors such as financial and non-financial; macro and micro including general economy condition; values of society; government priorities, etc.

KEY RATIOS

A company's capital structure is one of the most important decisions, the management has to make because it influences everything from the firm's risk profile to the financial ratios such as return on equity and interest coverage. Investors prefer to focus on financial ratios as they are Powerful Credit Risk Analysis Tools. There are five categories of financial ratios into which most calculations fall. Financial ratios measure the following:

- **Liquidity:** An ability of firm to pay its bills as they come due.
- **Leverage:** An extent to which the firm is dependent on creditors' funding
- **Efficiency:** An extent to which the resources are utilised
- **Stock Investment Attractiveness:** Returns on investments

Exibit 3.1: Ratios – What it means?

Types	Ratio	What it means?	Remarks
Profitability	Gross Profit Margin Ratio	Tends to remain stable over time.	Significant fluctuations can be a sign of bad management controls or financial irregularities.
	Net Profit Margin	Tells you how much money a company makes for every rupee in revenue.	
	Earnings Before Interest, Taxes, Depreciation and Amortization (EBITDA)	Compares profitability between companies and industries	It is a non-GAAP meansure that allows a greater amount of discretion as to what is (and is not) included in the calculation.
	Return on capital employed (ROCE)	This ratio speaks about what returns management has on the resources employed before making any disbursement	
	Return On Equity (ROE)	Measures the net return per rupee invested in the firm by the shareholder	
	Return on Investment (ROI)	Measures return on funds invested in the business by its owners.	This ratio tells whether or not all the effort put into the business has been worthwhile.
	Return on Assets (ROA)	Measures how efficiently profits are being generated from the assets employed in the business	It tells about the company's ability to effectively using its assets.
Efficiency	Asset Turnover Ratio	Calculates total sales for each rupee of asset owned by company	Measures a company's efficiency in using its assets.
	Receivable Turnover Ratio	It tells how many times a company collects its accounts receivable in a period of time.	Measures a company's efficiency in collecting the receivables from consumers.

	Inventory Turnover Ratio	This financial ratio tells an investor how many times firm turns its inventory over a period of time.	It tells of assets tied up in inventory and heading for financial trouble. It is indication of efficiency in stock management.
	Credit given/"Debtor Days"		indicates case or problem in debt collection.
	Credit taken/"Creditor Days"		Indicates whether business is taking full advantage of trade credit available to it.
	Debt-Service Coverage Ratio (DSCR)	It is the amount of cash flow available to meet annual interest and principal payments on debt, including sinking fund payments.	Ratio less than one means borrower has to look for other funds to keep the business running.
Liquidity	Current Ratio	Serves as a test of a company's financial strength and relative effciency	A current ratio less than one does not indicate that a company is insolvent unable to pay its bills. First current liabilities are those that are due within one year, and not necessarily today. Second, current liabilities may include borrowings under a revolving line of credit, which may be renewed. Third, the company may have access to funds under a line-of-credit, from the sale of assets or another source.
	Quick Test	This financial ratio is known as the quick test, acid test, or quick liquidity test.	Of all the financial ratios, it is the most difficult and stringent measure of a company's strength and liquidity. Too much liquidity may hurt a firms profitability. Current assets such as cash and accounts receivable offer little in the way of return, and assets such inventory involve carrying costs such as: storage, insurance, and risk of obsolescence. In addition, current liabilities such as accounts payable and accrued expenses are non-interest bearing and provide a cheap source of financing.
Leverage	Debt to Equity Ratio	How much of the capitalization is the owners vs. the creditors.	Measure of the total debt a company owes compared to the shareholders equity
Stability	Interest Coverage Ratio	The interest coverage ratio has huge implications for bond and preferred stock investors in particular.	This financial ratio tells the investor the number of times the earnings before interest and taxes can pay, or "cover", the interest payment the company makes on its debt

The ratios, such as liquidity, leverage, profitability, and management ratios allow the business owner to identify trends in a business and to compare its progress with the performance of others through data published by various sources. The owner may thus determine the business's relative strengths and weaknesses. These ratios are classified into five categories such as;

1. Profitability Ratios

Profitability ratios provide measures of profit performance that helps to evaluate the periodic financial success of a firm. One of the most widely used financial ratios is net profit margin, also known as return on sales.

Gross margin measures the direct production costs of the firm. A gross profit margin of 25 per cent would indicate that for each rupee in sales, the firm spent 75 paise in direct costs to produce the good or service that the firm sold.

Operating margin goes one step further, incorporating non-production costs such as selling, general, and administrative expenses of the firm. Operating profit is also commonly referred to as earnings before interest and taxes, or EBIT. An operating margin of 17 per cent would indicate that the firm spent an additional seventeen paise out of every rupee in sales on non-production expenses, such as sales commissions paid to the firm's sales force or administrative labor expenses.

Profitability ratios show a company's overall efficiency and performance. The profitability ratios are divided into two types such as margins and returns. Ratios that show margins represent the firm's ability to translate sales rupees into profits at various stages of measurement. Ratios that show returns represent the firm's ability to measure the overall efficiency of the firm in generating returns for its shareholders.

- **Gross Margin Ratio**

This ratio is the percentage of sales rupees left after subtracting the cost of goods sold from net sales. It measures the percentage of sales rupees remaining (after obtaining or manufacturing the goods sold) available to pay the overhead expenses of the company. Comparison of ratios of similar businesses will reveal the relative strengths or weaknesses in a firm.

This ratio tells us something about the company's ability to control its production costs or to manage the margins its makes on input purchases and finished products' sales. The sales in terms of volume and value may show up and down trends, however the gross profit margin is usually quite stable. A small change in profit margin causes a substantial change in overall profits.

$$\frac{[\text{Gross Profit}]}{\text{Revenue (net sales)}} \times 100 \text{ (expressed as a percentage)}$$

(Gross Profit = Net Sales – Cost of Goods Sold)

- **Net Profit Margin Ratio**

Return on sales provides a measure of bottom-line profitability. For example, a net profit margin of 8 per cent means that for every hundred rupees in sales, the firm generated eight rupees in net income. Two other margin measures are gross profit margin and operating margin. This ratio is the percentage of sales rupees left after subtracting the Cost of Goods sold and all expenses, except income taxes. It provides a good opportunity to compare your company's "return on sales" with the performance of other companies in the industry. It is calculated before income tax because tax rates and tax liabilities vary from company to company for a wide variety of reasons, making comparisons after taxes is much more difficult. This ratio is calculated as follows:

This ratio tells us about a company's ability to control its other operating costs or overheads with the assumption that the gross profit margin is constant

$$\frac{[\text{Operating Profit}]}{\text{Revenue}} \times 100\,(\text{expressed as a percentage})$$

$$\text{Net Profit Margin Ratio} = \frac{\text{Net Profit Before Tax}}{\text{Net Sales}}$$

➢ **Earnings Before Interest, Taxes, Depreciation and Amortization (EBITDA)**

EBITDA is essentially net income with interest, taxes, depreciation, and amortization added back to it, and can be used to analyze and compare profitability between companies and industries because it eliminates the effects of financing and accounting decisions. It is a non-GAAP measure that allows a greater amount of discretion as to what is covered in the calculation.

➢ **Return on Capital Employed (ROCE)**

It is also called as "primary ratio". This ratio speaks about what returns management has on the resources employed before making any disbursement.

$$\frac{\text{Net profit before tax, interest and dividends (EBIT)}}{\text{Total assets (or total assets less current liabilities)}}$$

➢ **Return On Equity - ROE'**

Return on equity (ROE) measures the net return per rupee invested in the firm by the shareholder. An ROE of 10 percent means the firm is generating ₹ 10 return per ₹ 100 of net worth. In other words, it is the amount of net income returned as a percentage of shareholders' equity. Return on equity measures a firm's profitability by revealing how much profit a company generates with the money shareholders have invested. The ROE is useful for comparing the profitability of a company to that of other firms in the same industry. ROE is expressed as a percentage and calculated as follows;

Return on Equity = Net Income/Shareholder's Equity

➢ **Return on Investment (ROI)**

The ROI is perhaps the most important ratio of all. It is the percentage of return on funds invested in the business by its owners. This ratio tells whether or not all the effort put into the business has been worthwhile. If the ROI is less than the rate of return on an alternative, risk-free investment such as a bank savings account, the investor/owner may be wiser to sell the company, put the money in such a savings instrument, and avoid the daily struggles of small business management. The ROI is calculated as follows;

$$\text{Return on Investment} = \frac{\text{Net Profit Before Tax}}{\text{Total Assets}}$$

Return on investment is a very popular metric because of its versatility and simplicity. That is, if an investment does not have a positive ROI, or if there are other opportunities with a higher ROI, then the investment should not be undertaken.

➢ **Return on Assets Ratio (ROA)**

This measures how efficiently profits are being generated from the assets employed in the business when compared with the ratios of firms in the industry. A low ratio in comparison with similar firms indicates an inefficient use of business assets. The Return on Assets Ratio is calculated as follows;

$$\text{Return on Assets} = \frac{\text{Net Profit Before Tax}}{\text{Total Assets}}$$

Return on assets (ROA) measures how effectively the firm's assets are used to generate profits net of expenses. An ROA of 8 per cent would mean that for each rupee in assets, the firm generated eight paise in profits. This is an extremely useful measure of comparison among firm's competitive performance. It is a ratio for benchmarking utilisation of company's assets of the firm to produce profits.

In each of the profitability ratios mentioned above, the numerator in the ratio comes from the firm's income statement. Hence, these are measures of periodic performance, covering the specific period reported in the firm's income statement. Therefore, the proper interpretation for a profitability ratio should be done taking into the particular financial year.

Du Pont Approach to ROI

This formula is used for analysis of returns on investment or assets made by the business corporations. The Du Pont Model can also be used for analysis of return on equity, but with little modification. Using the Du Pont Model allows the business owner to break the components of profitability and where they come from. Following are the steps in using the Du Pont Model to calculate return on investment:

1. Compute ROI of company. This ratio tells how efficiently investment is put to use or how asset base is put to generate sales. Compare your ROI with that of industry.
2. If ROI is below the industry average, to find why use the Du Pont Model and break down the ROI into its component parts.

   ROI = {Net Income/Sales} × {Sales/Total Assets}

   ROI is composed of two parts: the company's profit margin and asset turnover or its ability to generate profit and make sales based on its asset base.

3. Find out which part of ROI is causing the problem for the business - the profit margin or the asset turnover.
4. If firm is performing poorly with regard to their ROI and the industry average. The extended Du Pont Model allows us to examine return on equity in the same way.
5. Using the numbers from the example of the calculation of ROI, this is the next step in calculating return on equity or ROE:

   If firm is performing poorly with regard to ROE as well as ROI. ROE is a measure of the wealth of the shareholders of the company and is the profitability ratio shareholders look at most often.
6. The extended Du Pont equation:

   ROE = (Net Profit Margin)(Total Asset Turnover)(Equity Multiplier)

   = {Net Income/Sales} × {Sales/Total Asset Turnover} × {Total Assets/Equity}
7. Three elements interact to form the ROE of a company. These elements are the profit margin, the efficiency with which the firm uses its assets to generate sales (total asset turnover ratio), and the effect of debt on the firm (equity multiplier).

2. Efficiency Ratios

Asset utilization ratios provide measures of management effectiveness. These ratios serve as a guide to the use of the firm's assets, inventory, and accounts receivable collections in day to day operations. Asset utilization ratios serve as warning signals/benchmarks from which meaningful conclusions may be reached on operational issues.

➢ **Total Asset Turnover (TAT) Ratio.**

This ratio offers managers a measure of how well the firm is utilizing its assets in order to generate sales revenue. An increasing TAT would be an indication that the firm is using its assets more productively. For example, if the TAT for 2010 and 2011 was 2.45 and 2.46 but for 2012 it is 3, the interpretation would follow that in 2012, the firm generated ₹ 3/- in sales for each ₹ 100/- rupees of assets, an additional sales per rupees of asset investment over the previous year. This is an indication of increased managerial effectiveness.

➢ **Fixed Asset Turnover (FAT) Ratio.**

Fixed assets (plant and equipment) are often more closely associated with direct production than are current assets (cash and accounts receivable). Hence fixed assets are referred to measure of effectiveness. A FAT of 1.8 would be interpreted as the firm generated ₹ 1.8 in sales for every ₹ 1 invested in fixed assets.

➢ **Accounts Receivable Turnover Ratio**

This ratio indicates how well accounts receivable are being collected. If receivables are not collected reasonably in accordance with their terms, management should rethink its collection policy. If receivables are excessively slow in being converted to cash, liquidity could be severely impaired.

$$\frac{\text{Net Credit Sales in a Year}}{\text{365 Days}} = \text{Daily Credit Sales}$$

$$\text{Accounts Receivable Turnover (in days)} = \frac{\text{Accounts Receivable}}{\text{Daily Credit Sales}}$$

➤ **Sales/Capital Employed**

It is a measure of total asset utilisation. It is indicative of sales being generated by each rupee's worth of assets invested in the business. Sales when combined with the return on sales it generates the primary ratio - ROCE.

➤ **Sales or Profit/Fixed Assets**

This ratio is about fixed asset capacity. A reducing sales or profit being generated from each pound invested in fixed assets may indicate over capacity or poor performance of equipment.

➤ **Inventory Turnover**

This ratio reveals how well inventory is being managed. It is important because the more times inventory can be turned in a given operating cycle, the greater the profit. It helps answer questions such as "have we got too much money tied up in inventory"? An increasing stock turnover figure or one which is much larger than the "average" for an industry, may indicate poor stock management.

The Inventory Turnover Ratio is calculated as follows:

$$\text{Inventory Turnover Ratio} = \frac{\text{Net Sales}}{\text{Average Inventory at Cost}}$$

➤ **Credit Given/Debtor Days**

$$\frac{\text{(Trade debtors average)}}{\text{Sales}} \times 365$$

The 'debtor days' ratio indicates whether debtors are being allowed excessive credit. A high ratio higher than industry average may suggest problems with debt collection from customers.

➤ **Credit taken/Creditor Days**

$$\frac{\text{(Trade creditors + accruals)}}{\text{cost of sales + other purchases}} \times 365$$

A similar calculation to that for debtors, gives an insight into whether a business is taking full advantage of trade credit available to it.

➤ **Debt-Service Coverage Ratio (DSCR)**

A DSCR of less than 1 would mean a negative cash flow. A DSCR of less than 1, say 0.93, means enough net operating income to cover only 93% of annual debt payments. This would mean that the borrower would have to look for other funds to keep the project afloat.

3. Liquidity Ratios

Liquidity ratios indicate how capable a business is of meeting its short-term obligations as they fall due. These ratios indicate the ease of turning assets into cash. They include the Current Ratio, Quick Ratio and Working Capital.

➤ **Current Ratio**

This ratio indicates whether the business can pay debts due within a year from assets that it expects to turn into cash within that year. A ratio of less than one is often a cause for concern, particularly if it persists for any length of time. The Current Ratio is one of the best known measures of financial strength.

Current Ratio =

This ratio shows the availability of enough current assets to meet the payment schedule of its current debts with a margin of safety for possible losses in current assets, such as inventory shrinkage or collectable accounts. A current ratio of 1.4 indicates that for every rupee in current liabilities, the firm has ₹ 1.40 in current assets. Such assets could, theoretically, be sold and the proceeds used to service the liabilities if the firm ran short of cash. However, some current assets are more liquid than others. Obviously, the most liquid current asset is cash. Accounts receivable are usually collected within one to three months, but this varies by firm and industry. The least liquid of current assets is often inventory. Depending on the type of industry or product, some inventory has no ready market. A generally acceptable current ratio is 2 to 1. But whether or not a specific ratio is satisfactory depends on the nature of the business and the characteristics of its current assets and liabilities. The minimum acceptable current ratio is 1:1.

Low current ratio may be raised by; paying some debts, increasing current assets from loans or other borrowings with a maturity of more than one year, converting non-current assets into current assets, increasing current assets from new equity contributions and putting profits back into the business.

In general liquidity ratios are measures that indicate a firm's ability to repay short-term debt. Current liabilities represent obligations that are typically due in one year or less. The current and quick ratios are used to gauge a firm's liquidity.

➤ **Quick Ratios**

Not all assets can be turned into cash quickly. The raw materials and other stocks - must first be turned into final product, then sold and the cash collected from debtors. The Quick Ratio therefore adjusts the Current Ratio to eliminate all assets that are not already in cash or near-cash form. This ratio of less than one would means an alarming signal. The Quick Ratio is sometimes called the 'acid-test' ratio and is one of the best measures of liquidity. It is shown below:

$$\text{Quick Ratio} = \frac{\text{Cash} + \text{Government Securities} + \text{Receivables}}{\text{Total Current Liabilities}}$$

The Quick Ratio is a much more exacting measure than the Current Ratio. By excluding inventories, it concentrates on the really liquid assets, with value that is fairly certain. This ratio indicates the ability of business to meet its current obligations with the readily convertible 'quick' funds on hand in the event all sales revenues disappear. An acid-test ratio of 1:1 is considered satisfactory unless the majority of company's 'quick assets' are in accounts receivable, and the pattern of accounts receivable collection lags behind the schedule for paying current liabilities. The quick ratio is a more strident liquidity measure than the current ratio. It is a more appropriate measure for industries that involve long product production cycles.

➢ **Cash Ratio**

Cash ratio is the most conservative liquidity ratio. It excludes all current assets except the most liquid: cash and cash equivalents. The cash ratio is defined as follows;

$$\text{Cash Ratio} = \frac{\text{Cash} + \text{Marketable Securities}}{\text{Current Liabilities}}$$

The cash ratio is an indication of the firm's ability to pay off its current liabilities if for some reason immediate payment were demanded.

➢ **Working Capital.**

Working Capital is more a measure of cash flow than a ratio. The result of this calculation must be a positive number. It is calculated as shown below;

Working Capital = Total Current Assets – Total Current Liabilities

Bankers look at Net Working Capital over time to determine a company's ability to weather financial crises. Loans are often tied to minimum working capital requirements. A general observation about these Liquidity Ratios is that the higher they are the better, especially if you are relying to any significant extent on creditor money to finance assets.

3. Leverage Ratios

Leverage ratios, also known as capitalization ratios, provide measures of the firm's use of debt financing. These are important for potential creditors, who are concerned with the firm's ability to generate the cash flow necessary to make interest payments on outstanding debt. These ratios are used extensively by analysts to make decision with regards to the provisions of new credits or extension of existing credit arrangements. It is also important for management to monitor the firm's use of debt financing. The commitment to service outstanding debt is a fixed cost to a firm, resulting in decreased flexibility and higher break-even production rates. The use of debt financing increases the risk associated with the firm. Managers and creditors must constantly monitor the trade-off between the additional risk that comes with borrowing money and the increased opportunities that the new capital provides. Leverage ratios provide a means of such monitoring. In these ratios the main factors looked at include debt, equity, assets and interest expenses. The 'leverage ratios' are indicative of the long-term solvency of the firm. Unlike liquidity ratios that are concerned with short-term assets and liabilities, the leverage ratios measure the extent to which the firm is using long-term debt.

➢ Debt-to-Equity Ratio

This is perhaps one of the most misunderstood financial ratios, as many confuse it with the total debt ratio. A debt-to-equity ratio of 48 per cent would mean that for each rupee of equity financing, the firm has 48 per cents in debt financing. This does not mean that the firm has 48 per cent of its total financing as debt and that the debt and equity percentages, together, must sum to one (100 percent of the firm's total financing). A little algebra will illustrate this point. Let x = the per cent of equity financing (in decimal form), so 0.48x is the per cent of debt financing. Then x + 0.48x = 1, and x = 0.6756. So, a debt to equity ratio of 48 per cent indicates that each rupee of the firm's assets are financed with 67.56% of equity and 32.44% with debt. The point here is to caution against confusing the interpretation of the debt-to-equity ratio with that of the total debt ratio.

For example, if a company has ₹ 15 Cr in debt and ₹ 30 Cr in equity, it has a debt-to-equity ratio of 0.5 (₹ 15 Cr/₹ 30 Cr). The debt-to-equity ratio is total debt divided by total equity:

Debt-to-Equity Ratio = Total Debt/Total Equity

➢ Total Debt Ratio.

There are only two ways to finance the acquisition of any asset; debt (using borrowed funds) and equity (using funds from internal operations or selling stock in the company). The total debt ratio captures this idea. A debt ratio of 36 per cent means that, for every rupee of assets the firm has, 36 per cents was financed with borrowed money. The natural corollary is that the other 64 per cents came from equity financing. This is known as the firm's capital structure– 36 per cent debt and 64 per cent equity. Greater debt means greater leverage, and more leverage means more risk. The exact quantification is a highly subjective question. The answer depends, to a large extent, on the nature of the business or industry. Large manufacturers, who require heavy investment in fixed plant and equipment, will require higher levels of debt financing than will service firms.

The total debt of a firm consists of both long and short-term liabilities. Short-term (or current) liabilities are often a necessary part of daily operations and may fluctuate regularly depending on factors such as seasonal sales. Many creditors prefer to focus their attention on the firm's use of long-term debt. Thus, a common variation on the total debt ratio is the long-term debt ratio, which does not incorporate current liabilities in the numerator.

Two other leverage ratios that are particularly important to the firm's creditors are the 'times-interest-earned' and the 'fixed-charge coverage' ratios. These measure the firm's ability to meet its on-going commitment to service debt previously borrowed.

➢ Times-interest-earned (TIE) Ratio.

It is also known as the EBIT coverage ratio, provides a measure of the firm's ability to meet its interest expenses with operating profits. For example, a TIE of 3.6 indicates that the firm's operating profits from a recent period exceeded the total interest expenses it was required to pay. The higher this ratio, the more financially stable the firm and the greater the safety margin in the case of fluctuations in sales and operating expenses. This ratio is particularly important for lenders of short-term debt to the firm, since short-term debt is usually paid out of current operating revenue.

➤ **Fixed charge coverage Ratio.**

It is also known as the debt service coverage ratio, takes into account all regular periodic obligations of the firm. By including the payment of both principal and interest, the fixed charge coverage ratio provides a more conservative measure of the firm's ability to meet fixed obligations.

Illustration...

Rama Enterprise Ltd (REL) is in food products. The following data is available to evaluate its performance against overall performance of the food industry.

Ratio	2012	2011	2010	Industry Avg 2012
Long-term debt	0.44	0.39	0.34	0.34
Inventory Turnover (days)	59	41	36	51
Depreciation/Total Assets	0.21	0.012	0.017	0.014
Days' sales in receivables (days)	110	91	89	125
Debt to Equity	0.76	0.86	0.92	0.90
Profit Margin	0.081	0.069	0.059	0.074
Total Asset Turnover	0.55	0.66	0.71	0.45
Quick Ratio	1.027	1.029	1.031	1.032
Current Ratio	1.35	1.25	1.19	1.27
Times Interest Earned	1.9	4.2	4.5	4.8
Equity Multiplier	1.78	1.88	1.98	1.92

Inventory turnover has increased over time and is now above the industry average. This is excellent sign considering nature of the product. In 2012 for every 365/59 = 6.18 days the firm is able to sell its inventories as opposed to the industry average of 7.16 days. Days' sales in receivables has declines continuously over the time, but is still better than the industry average. This means, REL could managed to turn inventories around quickly, however they are facing more problems in collecting money from the market on the sales effected. The total asset turnover is went down over time, but it is still higher than the industry average. This means REL may face a problem in its long term investments. But they are better off as compared to their peers in the industry.

Solvency and leverage is captured by converting D/E ratio into the D/V ratio by dividing D/E ratio by equity multiplier: 2012: 42.7%, 2011: 45.7%, 2010: 46.4%, and the industry-average is 46.8%. With these numbers it is difficult to give a qualitative judgment beyond observing the drop in leverage. The number indicates 2012 is bad for REL as regards its ability to pay interest. However, times interest earned uses EBIT as a proxy for the ability to pay for interest and here cash flow should be considered instead of earnings. Based on a relatively large amount of depreciation in 2012, it seems that REL is doing well.

4. Stability Ratios

These ratios concentrate on the long-term health of a business-particularly the effect of the capital/finance structure on the business:

➢ **Gearing**

Gearing indicates the proportion of assets invested in a business that are financed by borrowing. In general, the higher the level of borrowing (gearing) the higher are the risks to a business, since the payment of interest and repayment of debts are not 'optional' in the same way as dividends. However, gearing can be a financially sound part of a business's capital structure particularly if the business has strong, predictable cash flows.

Borrowing (all long-term debts + normal overdraft)/Net Assets (or Shareholders' Funds)

➢ **Interest cover**

This measures the ability of the business to "service" its debt. Are profits sufficient to be able to pay interest and other finance costs?

Operating profit before interest/Interest

5. Investor Ratios

Investors are interested in market ratios, which are used in valuing the firm's stock. The price-earnings ratio and the market-to-book value ratio are often used in valuation analysis. The price/earnings ratio, universally known as the PE ratio, is one of the most heavily quoted statistics concerning a firm's common stock.

In general analysts use two different components in the denominator; historical earnings and forecast earnings. Historic earnings refer to the firm's reported earnings, per share, over the last twelve months of operation. Forecast earnings are based on security analyst forecasts of what they expect the firm to earn in the coming twelve-month period. A PE ratio of sixteen can be interpreted as investors are willing to pay ₹ 16 for ₹ 1 worth of earnings. PE ratios are used extensively, on a comparative basis, to analyze investment alternatives. A high PE is often indicative of investor's belief that the firm has very promising growth prospects, while firms in more mature industries often trade at lower multiples.

A related measure used for valuation purposes is the market-to-book value ratio. Technically, the book value represents the value of the firm if all the assets were sold off, and the proceeds used to pay all debt. The remainder would represent the equity that would be divided, proportionally, among the firm's shareholders.

A net profit margin of 10 per cent may be outstanding for one type of industry and mediocre to poor for another. This highlights the fact that individual ratios should not be interpreted in isolation. Ratios used for performance evaluation should always be compared to some benchmark, either an industry average or perhaps the identical ratio for the industry leader.

Another factor in ratio interpretation is for users to identify whether individual components, such as net income or current assets, originate from the firm's income statement or balance sheet. The income statement reports performance over a specified period of time, while the balance sheet gives static measurement at a single point in time. This should be taken into consideration at the time of interpretation of results of ratio calculations. Despite of their limitations, financial ratios remain useful tools for both internal and external evaluations of key aspects of a firm's performance.

Taken by itself, the P/E ratio doesn't mean much, but when compared to its industry, it provides a meaningful indicator of valuation according to earnings. The P/S ratio (price to sales) is used by some analysts in lieu of the P/E ratio, especially in industries where sales are more indicative of a company's valuation than earnings. The P/B ratio (price to book) gives an idea of the company's valuation relative to its book value, which is derived, by dividing its net worth by the number of shares, which are outstanding. Finally, the P/CF ratio (price to cash flow) gives an idea of the company's health in terms of its cash flow. A cash rich company, relative to its competitors, will have a better chance of surviving a downturn in the economy.

➢ Price to Sales (P/S) Ratio

In some cases, a target company does not have any current earnings. In other cases the company is very young or might be experiencing a cyclical low in their earnings cycle. Additionally, a variety of accounting rules can make a profitable company appear to have no earnings due to special write-offs specific to that industry. For all of the above-mentioned reasons, some prefer to use a ratio of current price to sales of the company.

P/S Ratio = (current price per share x shares outstanding)/revenue

As with most ratios, the lower the ratio the better the expected value of those companies' shares. However, much like the P/E ratio, it fails to account for future growth and therefore can give investors misleading results if used alone.

➢ Price to Cash Flow Ratio (P/CF)

Price to cash flow takes into consideration the many accounting rules that can hide a company's earnings, while focusing on the company's ability to be profitable. The purpose of the Statement of Cash Flows produced by companies is to show the actual cash generated by the company by removing non-cash related expenses and determining the actual uses and sources of cash of the company being evaluated.

Price to Cash Flow Ratio = Current price / Cash flow from operations per share

or

Price to Cash Flow Ratio = Market capitalization / Cash flow from operations

As mentioned before, a lower ratio is generally considered desirable if other factors lead to believe the company has bright future prospects. Some analysts will remove from cash flows from operations the capital expenditures of the company in order to calculate Free Cash Flow, which would be the funds that the company has in excess of what is necessary to run the firm. At this point, the firm could choose to reinvest those funds or pay them as a dividend to shareholders. It is calculated using the same methods as price to cash flows and is interpreted in the same fashion.

➤ **Price to Book Value (P/B Ratio)**

It is calculated by dividing the current price of the company by the reported book value per share. As with other ratios, a high ratio could indicate the firm is overvalued relative to the equity of the company. A low ratio could indicate the firm is undervalued relative to the equity of the company.

➤ **Earnings per share (EPS) Ratio**

It is an earning (profits) attributable to ordinary shareholders/weighted average ordinary shares in issue during the year. EPS measures the overall profit generated for each share in existence over a particular period.

➤ **Price/Earnings Ratio (P/E Ratio)**

P/E ratio is an indication of how highly the market 'rates' or 'values' a business. A P/E ratio is best viewed in the context of a sector or market average to get a feel for relative value and stock market pricing.

Market price of share/Earnings per share

A valuation ratio of a company's current share price compared to its per-share earnings. For example, if a company is currently trading at ₹ 120/- a share and earnings over the last 12 months were ₹ 16 per share, the P/E ratio for the stock would be 7.5 (₹ 120/₹ 16). EPS is usually from the last four quarters average, but sometimes it can be taken from the estimates of earnings expected in the next four quarters (projected or forward P/E). A third variation uses the sum of the last two actual quarters and the estimates of the next two quarters.

In general, a high P/E suggests that investors are expecting higher earnings growth in the future compared to companies with a lower P/E. It's usually more useful to compare the P/E ratios of one company to other companies in the same industry, to the market in general or against the company's own historical P/E.

A high P/E ratio may signify that the company is overvalued, which means that eventually market forces will drive the price down. A high P/E could indicate great earning power and the possibility that profitability will increase over time, justifying the higher price. A low P/E may indicate the potential for strong future performance. Companies with low P/Es may be undervalued, or trading at a price lower than the company's fundamentals. In that case, earnings may increase dramatically in future. Otherwise a low P/E could indicate a faltering company wherein investment is not advisable.

➤ **Price/Earnings Growth (PEG) Ratio**

To counter the shortfalls of the traditional P/E ratio, PEG Ratio was developed. Growth in earnings is what helps determine whether a high or low P/E is justified. So, the formula for PEG ratio is;

PEG Ratio = (price/earnings)/earnings growth rate

By taking into consideration growth of the company's earnings, investor can see that a low PEG ratio means that the company is trading at a low price relative to its earnings growth potential. A high PEG ratio means that the company's stock is trading at a high price relative to its earnings growth potential. Thus PEG ratio became a quick measure of valuation. In general a ratio of 2 or higher is considered overvalued, with PEG ratios of around 1 or lower considered to signal an undervalued investment.

➢ **Dividend Yield**

It is also called as payout ratio. It provides a guide to assess the ability of a business to maintain a dividend payment. It also measures the proportion of earnings that are being retained by the business rather than distributed as dividends.

$$\frac{(\text{Latest dividend per ordinary share})}{\text{Current market price of share}} \times 100$$

SUMMARY

Financial ratios indicate about a company's activities and its financial health. The basic source of these ratios is the company's profit & loss account and balance sheet that contain financial information about that company. The ratios help to bring those details to light and identify the financial strengths and weaknesses of the company. When assessing ratios, it is important that the results are compared with other companies in the same industry and not to be taken in isolation. What may seem like a poor ratio at first glance may well be normal for that industry and, of course, the *vice versa*. What may seem a good ratio on its own could be below average for that industry. Ratio Analysis enables the business analyst to spot trends in a business and to compare its performance and condition with the average performance of similar businesses in the same industry. Analyst compares target company's ratios with the average of similar companies in the industry for several successive years, watching especially for any unfavourable trends that may be observed. Ratio analysis may provide early warning indications that allow management to solve company's problems before business gets into serious trouble.

Review Questions

1. "Financial Ratio Analysis is a tool for assessing the health of a company"; explain
2. What financial ratios convey and how are they classified?
3. What are the limitations of ratio analysis? Discuss various ratios used for:
   (i) short-term investment in company's security and
   (ii) considering an enterprise for an acquisition
4. Explain 'Du Pont' approach to ROI and discuss issues in computation of ROI.
5. Which ratios will you consider for monitoring the day to day operations of the company?
6. How will you judge asset performance of a business enterprise?

Video Linkages

1. Ratio Analysis, http://www.youtube.com/watch?v=5haBO2slVJM
2. Financial Ratio Analysis Part I, http://www.youtube.com/watch?v=0kcdFHWcXjw&feature=related

3. Financial Ratio Analysis Part II, http://www.youtube.com/watch?v=0hlAX7W51Q8&feature=related
4. ACCA P3: Introduction to Ratio Analysis, http://www.youtube.com watch?v=3MOSVV2qirk&feature=rela

ASSIGNMENTS

1. Select two companies (one each with highest and lowest market share) in each of the following industries and perform ratio analysis for the same year to find out the 'operational efficiency'.

- FMCG
- Engineering

2. Consider two companies in one industry sector and find out through ratio analysis their liquidity position.

BIBLIOGRAPHY

1. Eugene F. Brigham, Joel F.(2007), *Fundamentals of Financial Management,* South-Westen Cengage Learning, Houston, USA
2. Fridson, Martin, and Fernando Alvarez. (2002), *Financial Statement Analysis: A Practitioner's Guide,* New York: John Wiley,
3. Harrington, Diana R. (1993), *Corporate Financial Analysis: Decisions in a Global Environment,* 4th ed. Chicago: Richard D. Irwin, Inc., 1993.
4. Helfert, Erich A. (1997), *Techniques of Financial Analysis: A Modern Approach,* 9th ed. Chicago: Richard D. Irwin, Inc.,
5. Pamela P. Peterson, Frank J. Fabozzi, (2012), *Analysis of Financial Statements,* John Wiley NY
6. Krishna G Palepu, Paul M. Healy, (2008) *Business Analysis & Valuation: Using Financial Statements,* Thomson Learning, OH USA
7. H. Kent Baker, Gary Powell, (2005), *Understanding Financial Management: A Practical Guide,* Blackwell Publising, Auatralia,

4
CHAPTER
Private Company Valuation

> *"Erroneous assumptions can be disastrous"*
>
> **— *Peter F. Drucker***

Learning Objectives

To understand:

- Private vs public company
- Need for private company valuation
- Private co.s valuation approaches and methods
- Issues in valuation of private company

Valuation is a process used to determine what a business is worth. Determining a private company's worth and knowing what drives its value is a prerequisite for deciding on the appropriate price to pay or receive in an acquisition, merger transaction, corporate restructuring, sale of securities, and other taxable events. Private companies may include small family-owned enterprises, divisions/subsidiaries of larger private companies or large corporations. Private companies are not required to regularly file with the Securities and Exchange Board of India. Hence, private companies financial data can be incredibly elusive. A private company is one that is privately-owned and the members of the general public cannot purchase stock in a private company unless that company chooses to go public and become a public company. There are a number of factors that are considered differently in the valuation of privately held vs. public companies in the same industry sector. A direct comparison for valuation purposes is difficult and in some cases it's like comparing apples to oranges.

INTRODUCTION

Both public and private companies engage in M&A transactions, but there are several differences between the valuation processes for each. These differences are explained subsequently in the following pages. Due to the high liquidity of publicly traded stock, public firms may more easily use their shares as trump card in M&A transactions. Although in some cases, a private company may use its stock as currency for an M&A transaction, however, liquidity factor crops in. A valuation method that consists primarily of discounted cash flow and asset valuation is most likely to apply and the private firm will most often use cash to acquire a given target. A public company can raise money from the public market to help finance an M&A transaction. Private company cannot raise money from the public market and must resort to debt financing, venture capital, or other private forms of funding. Public M&A transactions must be approved by the SEBI for anti-trust purposes and also require regulatory compliance.

TYPES OF PRIVATE COMPANIES

The privately owned companies can be classified as follows;

- **Family Owned Private Companies:** Many large private companies have been family owned and operated for generations. Such private companies include Haldirams, Nerulas, Godrej and Kirloskar Group.

- **Private with a Pending IPO:** Private companies that file for an initial public offering must go through an audit process in order to meet the stringent guidelines set by the SEBI to become a publicly traded company. Private companies with a pending IPO status are required to file quarterly updates with the SEBI until further notice.

- **Private Companies that were Formerly Public:** Due to the costs of being a publicly-traded company, many firms go private or are taken private. The companies that were formerly under public category went private through bankruptcy or restructuring or buyout.

- **Private Companies as a part of Public Companies:** L & T Special Steels and Heavy Forgings Private Limited and Spectrum Infotech Pvt. Limited are private companies wherein L&T Ltd, has major financial stake.

- **Private Companies with Public Subsidiaries:** Private companies that have a majority stake in a public company can consider the company as a subsidiary. For example, Cargill, the major agribusiness conglomerate, owns a majority stake in Mosaic Co., a publicly traded company.

BUY-SELL ACTIVITY

In order to adapt to competitive pressures, advancements in technology, and economic conditions, privately-held companies are often forced to adapt their business by acquiring or partnering/merging with another company in order to remain competitive or simply to grow their business. A private company may also sell itself to a larger public company for the same reasons. Private companies may reconfigure their assets, operations, and relationships with the stockholders in search of higher growth, new technology, business expansion, and greater revenues.

Mergers, acquisitions and corporate restructuring often enable a private company to develop a competitive advantage by increasing flexibility, growth, and shareholder value. Common M&A motives include; strategic growth, talent growth, preparation for an IPO or exit, and entering a new geographic or demographic market.

A private company may plan for expansion too. There are a variety of reasons private companies choose to expand through an expansion transaction rather than naturally. In expansion process, growth happens much faster, virtually overnight in some cases, whereas natural organic growth takes time as its sales grow. A privately held company may want to eliminate a competitor, enter a new geographic market, introduce a new product line, or bring on the talent and management team that results from an expansion transaction. Expansion can be accomplished through mergers, asset acquisitions, tender offers or joint ventures. The following methods can be used to help a private company grow without having to create a whole other business entity.

➢ **Merger:** A private company merger takes place, when two or more private companies combine to form a single entity under a consolidated management and ownership. A merger can take place through an amalgamation or absorption. There are three types of mergers. The first one is 'Horizontal Merger'. It is when two private companies from the same business class or market enter into a merger agreement. In a horizontal merger, the merged private companies benefit from economies of scale and increase total market share by consolidating facilities, combining operations, increasing working capital, reducing competition or reducing advertisement costs, etc. The second one is 'Vertical Merger' It occurs when two firms from different stages of the same business class, activity or operation enter into a merger agreement. These types of private companies typically have buyer-seller or supply chain relationships before the merger. Generally, private companies attempt vertical mergers or hostile takeovers of other firms to maximize backward or forward integration along their supply chain. The acquiring private company reaps the benefits of a reduced inventory and more efficient allocation of working capital. The third one is 'Conglomerate Merger'. It occurs when two private companies that operate in different or unrelated business lines enter into a merger agreement. Firms choose to enter into a conglomerate merger to benefit from the access to greater financial resources. Firms, by expanding into new markets and different businesses, create a diverse portfolio of products that balance business risk.

➢ **Amalgamation:** An amalgamation is when two or more private companies enter into the merger agreement to form a completely new entity. In this type of merger both private companies lose their identity and a new private company is formed to manage the consolidated assets. Amalgamation tends to occur when both private companies are of equal size.

➢ **Absorption:** Absorption is when the merger occurs between a two entities of dissimilar size. In such a case, the larger private company would absorb the smaller one. The fusion dissolves the smaller private company and places all its assets in control of the larger private company. Absorption may also take a smaller private company and make it a stand-alone operating division or subsidiary of a larger private company.

➢ **Acquisition:** A private-market acquisition is when a company (public or private) buys up the stock of a private company. An acquisition may also take the form of an 'asset acquisition', where rather than buying the stock, the buyer simply buys the entirety or a portion of the assets of another private company. The assets may be tangible such as plants and machinery, or intangible assets such as patents and trademarks. The target private company may then continue as a smaller company or dissolve.

➢ **Acquisition-by-hire:** It may occur especially when the target private company is quite small or is in the start-up phase. In this case, the acquiring company simply hires the staff of the target private company, thereby acquiring its talent (if that is its main asset and appeal). The target private company simply dissolves and little legal issues are involved.

➢ **Tender Offer:** A tender offer is an offer by an acquiring company to the general shareholders of a target private company to purchase a majority of the equity at a premium to market value. Tender offers are an attempt to gain management control through holding the majority of voting equity. The tender offers are more common public companies rather than private companies.

➢ **Joint Venture:** A joint venture is when two or more private companies enter into an agreement to allot a portion of resources towards the achievement of a particular goal over a designated period of time. Synergies occur when businesses capitalize on joint opportunities or other combined efforts to obtain an effect greater than working alone, whether it is increased revenue or decreased costs.

The mergers and acquisitions are two distinctly separate types of transactions. However, 'merger' refers to a merger of equals: two companies of the same size come together, surrender their shares, and issue new shares for a new, combined company. In a merger, the merging organizations surrender their shares and issue new shares for a new, combined company. In practice a merger of equals is actually quite rare since most deals that are reported as a merger are actually acquisitions, where one firm actually purchases and assumes ownership of the other. In some acquisitions, the acquirer will create a 'Merger', which will be a non-operating legal entity that acts as an investment vehicle for the acquirer, allowing it to merge the target labeling the acquisition as a merger.

There are two types of buyers and investors for private company, financial buyer and strategic buyers. Financial buyers include private equity firms (also known as financial sponsors), venture capital firms, hedge funds, family investment offices and ultra high net worth individuals. These firms and executives are in the business of making investments in private companies and realizing a return on their investments. Financial buyers look to identify private companies with attractive future growth opportunities and durable competitive advantages, invest capital in their operations, and realize a return on their investment upon exit via a direct sale or an IPO. The strategic buyers search for operating private companies that offer products or services similar to their own. Targets of strategic buyers are often competitors, suppliers or customers of the original firm. Strategic buyers can also aim to acquire firms that have operations that are unrelated to their core businesses. Such an acquisition would be considered as an attempt of a strategic buyer to diversify their revenue sources. Their goal is to identify private companies whose products or services can synergistically integrate with their existing businesses to create long-term shareholder value.

PRIVATE VS. PUBLIC COMPANY

Following are the major differentiating factors between private and public companies with regards to company valuation process.

➢ **Access to Capital:** One of the main advantages that public companies have is that fund raising is significantly easier for a public company than for a privately-held firm. A public company can merely file to issue new shares and then sell them on the stock market. A private company must go through an often long venture capital, bank loan, or other funding process. For private company access to capital is rather difficult.

➢ **Mergers & Acquisitions:** On the buy-side, publicly traded stock has the advantage of using the market's valuation and can more easily be used to acquire other companies, thus preserving the firm's cash position in the event of an acquisition. Public companies are also better positioned to finance an M & A deal due to their ability to tap public markets and more easily raise capital.

➢ **Liquidity of Shares:** Publicly held companies enable their shareholders to sell their stock. Therefore, equity participation devices such as management and employee stock options have more value at a public company and thus can be more useful in attracting and retaining talent. Even if public stockholders do not exercise their right to sell, publicly traded stock can be used as collateral to secure loans. This is not possible with privately held company.

➢ **Discount Factor for Absence of liquidity:** Depending on a private company's industry, location, and transparency, illiquidity discounts may cascade up to a proposed 20-30%. The reason for the private firm 'illiquidity discount' is the difficulty involved in cash flow estimation due to the less complete accounting than that found with a public firm. Private firms are more likely to mix personal-related expenses with corporate spending and thus, upon a sale, the financials must often be re-aligned to account for a proper bottom line and proper fair value. All else being equal, a public company enjoys a higher valuation than a similar private company because of its liquidity. Further, public companies generally have a decentralized or less concentrated equity ownership. Due to the greater dispersion of stock ownership, the threat of a hostile takeover may be less likely than for many private companies.

➢ **Visibility in Market:** A public company has a readily accessible share market price, which gives it an advantage in proposing a merger with a target company. Moreover, in a stock-for-stock acquisition, where the target company receives some or all of the purchase price in the buyer's stock, a target seller would much rather receive the liquid currency of public stock versus illiquid private buyer's stock.

➢ **Brand Image:** An initial public offering is a high visibility mark of success and prestige and public companies are more likely to receive attention from the media as compared to private company.

➢ **Takeover Risk:** A private company has little risk that it will be subject to a takeover against its will. Public companies are exposed to hostile takeover attempts through tender offers to shareholders and suddenly find themselves sold essentially against their will.

➢ **Control:** Public limited companies are less flexible as they have reporting requirements, shareholder expectations, and market pressures. However, private firms have greater operational flexibility by being able to focus on long-term growth rather than quarterly earnings. The private company executives without shareholder approval take significant action at the proper time.

➢ **Exemption from Reporting and Investor Relations Requirements:** Regulatory filings with the Securities and Exchange Commission are necessary to comply with securities laws, which can be expensive, time consuming, and their total effects on company productivity are difficult to predict.

➢ **Shareholder Activism:** By gaining a major stake, shareholders may influence the firm's restructuring or operation or decision making process. Private firms offer no scope for such activism.

PRIVATE COMPANY VALUATION

Private and public companies are different in many ways. Company and stock specific factors make key differences. They may impact valuation methods and assumptions for private company valuations. Private companies are typically at the earliest stages of development, while public companies are well developed and further advanced. They are typically smaller in size, have less management depth, lower quality of financial and other information, less pressure from short-term investors and tend to report less taxable income and tax payments (tax concerns). The characteristics of the stock of a private company are different from that of public companies. These factors are generally negative for private company valuation. Private companies usually have less liquid equity and concentrated control. Private company valuations are typically performed for three different reasons as follows;

➢ **Transaction-related:** Valuations are performed when there are transactions that affect the ownership or financing of a private company. These transactions include private financing, initial public offering (IPO), acquisition, bankruptcy, and share-based payment (compensation).

➢ **Compliance-related:** Sometimes valuations are performed for compliance purposes. An example of financial reporting valuation is the business valuation required for goodwill impairment tests. Tax- related reasons for valuations include corporate and individual tax reporting.

➢ **Litigation-related:** Many legal proceedings require valuations. Examples are shareholder disputes, property damages, and divorce.

In general there are following three approaches for the valuation of private companies.

In **income-based approach** - Value of a private company is computed as the present value of future income discounted at a rate of return that reflects the riskiness of the investment. The result is generally the fair market value.

In **market-based approach** - Price to earnings or similar multiples of a return of the latest historical period rather than an estimate of the future are use. The difficulty lies in identifying public companies that are sufficiently comparable to the subject private company for this purpose. Also, as for a private company, the equity is less liquid than for a public company, its value is considered to be slightly lower than such a market-based valuation would give.

In **asset-based approach** - Value of a business is equal to the sum of its parts. Instead of making subjective judgments about capitalization or discount rates, the adjusted net book value method is relatively objective.

Each approach has advantages and drawbacks, which must be considered when applying those techniques to a particular private company.

VALUATION TECHNIQUES

Many of the same techniques used to value public companies can be used to value private companies as well. However, finding the true intrinsic value of a private company is a tricky task. It involves calculations and assumptions based on industry-wide and company specific statistics. It includes key planning, adjusting of financial statements and applying the appropriate business valuation methodology. There are many factors that make impact on the valuation. The factors covered are size of company, lack of operational history, management and operational control, difficulty quantifying earnings and cash flow, capital structure, and risk in the business. There are many valuation method used and each will have different results based on the sensitivity of inputs. In addition, there are certain modifications necessary to adjust for the private company. The cost of capital for private companies is different since they do not have access to capital via equity markets. A privately held company is owned either by non-governmental organizations or by less than 50 shareholders so as not to require reporting with the SEBI. The private company's owners do not publicly issue or trade shares of the private company instead they keep ownership and associated transactions discreet.

FACTORS INFLUENCING VALUATION

Private company valuation is not an entirely objective matter. Subjective estimates for different motives impact valuation outcomes. Valuation of a private company may be required for the following reasons;

- Selling the company
- Raising the capital
- Divorce settlement
- Management buyout
- Taxation purposes

The factors that may influence a private company's valuation are its size, operating history, management and operational control, quantification of earnings and cash flow, capital structure, business risk, and breadth of liquidity in the market for private company's stock. These are discussed as follows:

- **Market Liquidity:** The lack of liquidity discounts the value of a private company by as much as 50% since there is no benchmark for valuing private companies on a daily basis as with a publicly traded exchange. Most commonly, a liquidity discount of 20-30% is applied. There are many factors that go into determining the discount factor in a private valuation including size, operating history, quality of earnings/cash flows, management, industry profile, and business risks.

- **Size:** Privately held companies are generally much smaller than their publicly traded comparables. Small private companies may be good acquisition targets for larger competitors and publicly traded companies. Size contributes to the discount of the valuation since it reflects the industry. Small industries may not be as attractive or may have undesirable growth rates, which could influence the valuation discount. Smaller sized may have more risk than larger ones.

➢ **Growth History:** Operating history is important to determine a track record for revenue growth, profitability and earnings growth. The shorter operating history of a private company has the greater risk for inconsistent cash flows, which leads to a greater valuation discount.

➢ **Product Mix:** The product mixes can impact the valuation discount and market share and product concentration add to business risk.

➢ **Operational Control:** Private companies have a very small pool of shareholders that often act as managers. This limits the pool of talent that runs the private company. In addition there may be no succession plan placing the business in considerable risk if the principal manager is no longer able to work. Finally, family controlled enterprises may have considerable internal conflict over the operational control. These risks lead to increased valuation discount.

➢ **Earnings:** The private companies in general are managed for tax minimization, long-term growth, or cash flow. Different operational motives make it difficult to measure true earnings and cash flows of the private company. It is important to normalize financials, when trying to value a private company to determine what the private company would be earning if it was operated like a public company.

➢ **Capital Structure:** Private companies do not have access to capital and therefore are unable to be as selective of their funding sources. Public companies are able to choose from both equity and debt sources to minimize their cost of capital while private companies are primarily dependent on bank loans, which are relatively expensive and weaken the internal cash flows.

➢ **Financial Risk:** Private companies are generally riskier than their public comparables,. The reasons are that they are smaller in size, absence of demonstrable financial track record and face risk of business concentration in an expansive industry.

Private company valuations are discount-based on several risk factors associated with private sector investing, which results in a marked difference between the valuation of a privately held company, subsidiary or a division and a publicly traded corporation. There are number of distinctions between private and public companies that have an impact on the private company's value. An accurate valuation of privately owned companies largely depends on availability and reliability of the private company's historic financial information. Public company financial statements are officially audited, documented and overseen by a government regulator. This is not the case with private companies.

The private companies in general manage their operations for different purposes than profit. The private firms often prepare their financial statements to minimize profits and, therefore, taxes. However, the public firms tend to want higher profits to increase their stock price. As a result, a firm's historic financial information may not be accurate and can lead to over or undervaluation. In view of this when it comes to private companies, some nontraditional valuation techniques may be appropriate such as analysis of invested capital, replacement cost, asset appraisal and capitalization of earnings.

METHODS FOR VALUATIONS

When it comes to private companies, the following three techniques are most commonly used:

➢ Peer Group Analysis

- Historical Transaction Analysis
- Discounted Cash Flow (DCF) Analysis

There are other valuation methods used by the analysts and which are;

- Asset Valuation
- Break-up Analysis
- Leveraged Buyout (LBO) Analysis
- Internal Rate of Return
- Replacement Cost
- Invested Capital

➢ **Peer Group Analysis:** It is the valuation of similar or comparable publicly traded companies to value a target private company. Peer grouping can be based on criteria, such as industry focus, private company size, or growth. The multiples can be Enterprise Value (EV) based multiples like EV/Sales, EV/EBITDA or EV/EBIT, and Equity based multiples like Price to Earnings (P/E). The multiples derived from this type of analysis are at a given point in time and generally change over time. It is important to note that trading multiples do not reflect control premiums or potential synergies. The following steps are applied to compare target private company to a similar public company:

➢ **Step I:** The process start with selecting companies in the comparable universe or peer group for a given private company target falling in similar industry, business, and financial characteristics with the target. The sources that can provide insight in identifying accurate public comparables are annual reports.

➢ **Step II:** This step consists of calculating relevant financials ratios. It requires normalizing the financials to adjust for one-time / non-recurring items that temporarily distort earnings. Income statement items (denominator) should be adjusted for one-time or non-recurring items. Consequently create a list of ratios and values need to be compared. These can include price, shares outstanding or market capitalization, earnings per share (EPS), growth rate (five-year), price-to-earnings ratio (P/E), price-to-sales ratio (P/S), EV (enterprise value) and EBITDA etc.

➢ **Step III:** Next step is to calculate multiples. Multiples are the heart of the comparable companies analysis as it is hinged on both the comparable company's risk profile and operating performance. Multiples that are used should be relative to the industry and appropriate in relating the public and private companies.

➢ **Equity Multiples** - These are applicable to equity holders only. The following equity multiples are used to derive an implied equity value.

- Price/Earnings - market equity value/net income to common shareholders
- Price/Book - market equity value/book value of equity
- Price/Cash Flow - market equity value/after-tax cash flow
- PEG Ratio - PE Ratio/Annual EPS Growth

➢ **Enterprise multiples** - Other flows apply to all capital providers (debt & equity). The balance sheet and income statement values utilized are before the effects of discretionary debt payments. Hence, enterprise multiples are used to derive an implied enterprise value. Relevant multiples:

➢ Enterprise value/Sales

➢ Enterprise value/EBITDA

➢ Enterprise value/EBIT

In the final analysis compared are several multiples to determine which one(s) the market uses to value the universe of comparable private companies.

➢ **Step IV:** Here one must determine relevant valuation ranges. It's important to pay careful attention to the selection of companiess, how one spreads the financial for each private company, and selection of favorable multiples.

➢ **Step V:** One has to apply private company discount here. It is not merely enough to simply use the same multiple as that of another publicly traded company. In most cases, the multiples that the company universe is trading at, must be adjusted as public companies will in general receive higher valuations than the private companies due to a lack of liquidity and the potential restructuring or accounting reorganization issues that may cropup in the event of an exit. Valuation discounts for liquidity should be applied to the private company that best reflects the target private company's risk and often varies up to 30%.

A major disadvantage of this valuation method is that it is often difficult to find comparable private companies and adjustments are required to reflect differences, such as business mix, geographic spread and capital structure.

➢ **Historical Transaction Analysis:** Comparable transactions analysis (selected acquisitions) is very similar to trading company except deal company utilize actual transaction multiples instead of trading multiples from the universe of comparable private companies. The analysis uses multiples and premiums paid in comparable transactions to value target private companies. The attributes required to this application are:

➢ Industry group

➢ Latest transactions

➢ Products, markets served, distribution channels

➢ Geographic location

➢ Size - revenues, assets, market cap

The disadvantage of this method is the only commonly available metric is sales, and value is not always clearly tied to sales or even profit. Moreover old transactions are rarely directly comparable as every transaction has its own set of unique circumstances and valuation multiples.

➢ **Discounted Cash Flow Analysis:** This method uses the forecasted free cash flow of the target private company discounted by the firm's weighted average cost of capital, plus a risk factor measured by beta. Since risks are not always easy to determine precisely, Beta uses historic data to measure the sensitivity of the private company's cash flow through business cycles. Key Components of a DCF are:

- **Free Cash Flow (FCF)** - Cash generated by the assets of the business (tangible and intangible) available for distribution to all providers of capital. FCF represents cash flow available to all providers of capital and is not affected by the capital structure of the business.
- **Terminal Value (TV)** - Here the rate used to discount projected FCFs and terminal value to their present values.
- **Estimating Beta** - Here to note that since private companies do not have equity traded on any exchange, there is no concrete method for determining the 'beta' of a private company's equity. Therefore the estimation of beta is based on the trading volatility of comparable public companies. It is important to calculate the unlevered betas of the universe of comparable private companies.

$$\beta \text{ unlevered} = \beta \text{ levered} / (1\text{+Debt / Equity}) (1\text{-T})$$

After the calculation of unlevered beta, then that you must re-lever the average unlevered beta for the private company using the optimal capital structure.

$$\beta \text{ levered} = \beta \text{ unlevered} / (1\text{+Optimal Debt / Equity}) (1\text{-T})$$

- **Problems with Equity Risk Premium** - Equity risk premium is the return that investors seek to obtain by investing in the stock market. Equity risk premium is the difference between the risk free rate and the demanded rate of return from the stock market. The equity risk premium for private companies needs to be adjusted to reflect a higher return for a riskier investment.
- **Estimating Cost of Equity** -The cost of equity of a private company is calculated as a function of the risk free rate, beta, and the market premium (MP).

$$\text{Cost of Equity} = \text{RFR} + \text{Beta (MP)}$$

The risk free rate is often known as the interest rate associated with what is considered a 'riskless' security (typically the yield on the highest rated government bonds in the 10-20 year maturity range).

- **Estimating Cost of Debt** -The problem with the cost of debt of private companies is that many private companies rely on bank loans as their primary source of funding. Bank loan rates are outdated and term structures are long-term. Therefore bank debt does not reflect the current debt cost of capital and is usually offered at a premium to public debt.

Calculating the current cost of debt capital would require analysis of comparable public company cost of debt or the approximation of the cost of acquiring new funding as of the valuation date.

$$\text{After-Tax Cost of Debt} = \text{Cost of Debt} \times (1 - \text{Tax Rate})$$

- **Estimating Cost of Capital** - Per cent of debt and equity is obtained from the capital structure.

$$\text{WACC} = (\text{Per cent of Debt}) \times (\text{Cost of Debt}) + (\text{Per cent of Equity}) \times (\text{Cost of Equity})$$

- **Cash Flow Problems with Private Company** - It is important to normalize cash flows to reflect an arm's-length approach to management. Recasting cash flows for the private company is to determine the true value of the private company based on 'real' cash flows.

- **Terminal Value Calculations Issues -** The two main ways of calculating the terminal value of a private company is through comparable multiples or perpetuity growth method. Considerations must be made in both methods that appropriate recast cash flows are used and growth rates are inline with potential growth opportunities for the private company based on management discussion and industry analysis.

Using the comparable multiples method requires that the private company's financial statements are recast to reflect the style of their public comparables. Valuing a private company using a discounted cash flow analysis requires consideration to be given to recasting financial statements to mirror public counterparts and adjusting components of the WACC to mirror current cost of capital in an illiquid market. Here all adjustments should be reasonable and defensible.

The major disadvantage of this method is that the valuation is not always accurate. The outcome of the valuation is highly dependent on the quality of the assumptions made regarding FCF, TV, and the discount rate. As a result, DCF valuations are usually expressed as a range of values rather than a single value by using a range of values for key inputs.

The other methods for valuation of private companies are:

- **Asset Valuation:** Asset valuation applies to companies that have heavy fixed assets, such as manufacturing plants or refineries; it is appropriate to value the assets independently from the firm. An asset appraisal will yield a more accurate valuation than a discounted cash flow analysis in private companies such as these. In this method, the fair market value of fixed assets and equipment (FMV/ FA) is calculated as a means of evaluating the business.

- **Break up Analysis:** It is a sum of parts valuation based on different business lines. Each part is valued separately employing above methodologies and then summed together.

- **Leveraged Buyout (LBO) Analysis:** Leverage is simply the use of debt; an LBO is the purchase of a private company through the use of borrowed funds, or debt. This method is used to determine the range of prices that a financial buyer would be willing to pay for a company based on target rates of return to equity and leveraged capital structure. In general, the target company of an LBO analysis is public. The public equity is being bought out by a small number of investors, thus taking the public company private. In some cases, an LBO involves strong management support and participation. In such a case, management, with the help of a private equity firm, employ their own funds to take the public company private.

- **Internal Rate of Return:** Internal Rate of Return is a valuation methodology that can be used to calculate the entry price, exit price, or average cash flows in an investment. Given the high risk on investment in venture capital and private equity, the firms require a high IRR in their target companies. In this case, the IRR represents the percentage of profits made on an investment in a specific period of time. Technically, the internal rate of return is the discount rate that generates a zero net present value.

- **Replacement Cost:** Similar to the total invested capital valuation; replacement cost valuation considers the total cost of reproducing the operations of the business in today's environment. This accounts for start-up expenses, real estate, equipment, and inventory and labor costs.

➢ **Invested Capital:** Cash generated by the assets of the business (tangible and intangible) available for distribution to all providers of capital. FCF is often referred to as unlevered free cash flow, as it represents cash flow available to all providers of capital and is not affected by the capital structure of the business.

ISSUES IN VALUATION

Basically there are many issues in assessing the value of a private company as follows:

➢ **Earnings Normalization:** The income statement of a private company is adjusted to show the prospective purchaser, the return from normal operations of the business and show a 'public equivalent' income stream. These adjustments eliminate one-time gains or losses, other unusual items, non-recurring business elements, and the like. Here, the compensation to employees and owner is also normalized and as other discretionary expenses that would not exist in a publicly traded company.

➢ **Cash Flow Estimation:** The issue is about reliability in estimation of the cash flow under different scenarios. The question is whether to use a single discount rate for all future cash flows, or to use one discount rate in each scenario. These biases crop in cash flow forecasts depending on who makes the analysis. The income approach methods determine fair market value by multiplying future income/cash flows by a discount or capitalization rate. The discount or capitalization rate converts the future economic benefits into a present value. There are three forms of income approach. They all involve estimating the required rate of return.

In the **Required Rate of Return Approach** the issues are premium company size, smaller company's earnings or cash flow be discounted or capitalized at a higher rate because the private company is smaller than most public companies. Secondly, cost of debt of private firms have limited access to public debt markets, and are therefore not rated. Thirdly, most debt on the books is bank debt, and the interest expense on this debt might not reflect the rate at which they can borrow.

Free Cash Flow Method, project the future free cash flows and discount them to present rupee to estimate their present value. The discount rate should be the company's WACC. A terminal value needs to be calculated when a stable growth rate is expected.

Capitalized Cash Flow Method is often used for the valuation of small private companies that are expected to grow at a constant rate.

In Excess Earnings Method the tangible and intangible values are calculated. The tangible value of the company is simply calculated as the value of the company's net worth (working capital + fixed assets). However, the intangible part is calculated by capitalizing those earnings that are calculated to be in 'excess' of what a reasonable amount of earnings would be on the company's tangible net worth. Thus adding the tangible and intangible values of the company together results in the value of the entire company.

In **Market Approach Methods** of private company valuation a comparison is done between the subject company with similar public companies. The key assumption is that these comparable public companies do exist. The problem, however, is how to find them and assess their pricing. Analysts should consider the liquidity of equities, size of the firms, company lifecycles, availability of financial data, etc. Within the market approach following three methods are used:

➢ **Guideline Public Company Method (GPCM) –** Here market multiples are derived from market prices of stocks of companies that are engaged in the same or similar lines of business, and that are actively traded on stock market.

➢ **Guideline Transactions Method (GTM) –** It considers market transactions involving the acquisition of the total equity of similar companies. The pricing multiple more accurately reflects the value of total companies. The multiple may need to be adjusted for a number of reasons are; synergies, contingent consideration, non-cash considerations, availability of meaningful transactions and changes between transaction date and valuation date.

➢ **Prior Transaction Method –** This method considers actual transactions in the stock of the subject private company, if such transactions are available and frequent.

In **Asset-based Approach** to private company valuation, the value of asset of a business is equal to the sum of its parts. The rationale is that investor will not pay more for the business assets than the cost of procuring assets of similar economic utility. This is due to the fact that profitable going firms have a variety of intangible assets that should be discretely valued in order to properly estimate total asset value. The approach is appropriate for the valuation of holding companies, very small companies with limited intangible value or early stage companies.

In assessing the value of private companies valuation discounts and premiums are applied. Control and marketability issues are important and challenging elements in the valuation of private companies and equity interests therein. If publicly traded companies are used as the basis for pricing multiples, control premiums may be appropriate in measuring the value of the total equity of a private company. Control premiums have also been used to estimate lack of control discounts. Evidence of the adverse impact of the lack of control is an important consideration in assessing this discount.

Secondly, 'Lack of Marketability Discounts' is important for shareholders, who own a minority interest in a closely held company, their stock tends to be much less marketable and its value is reduced accordingly. The marketability (liquidity) of stock shares is a concept that is distinct from the level of control, but related to it. Discounts for lack of marketability (DLOM) are used in the valuation of non-controlling equity interests in private companies.

The other issues in general in private company valuations are:

➢ **Liquidity of Stock:** A lack of market liquidity is usually the biggest factor contributing to a discount in the value of companies. One can switch his investment to the stock of a different public company on a daily basis. The stock of privately held firms, however, is more difficult to sell quickly, making the value drop accordingly.

➢ **Profit measurement:** While private companies look for mostly to minimize taxes, public companies seek to maximize earnings for shareholder reporting purposes. Therefore, the profitability of a private firm may require restatement in order for it to be directly comparable to that of a public firm. In addition, public company multiples are generally calculated from net income (after taxes), while private-company multiples are often based on pre-tax (and many times, pre-debt) income. This discrepancy can result in an inaccurate formula for the valuation of a private company.

➢ **Capital structure:** Public companies within a specific industry generally maintain capital structures (debt/equity ratio) that are fairly similar. That means the relative price/earnings ratios (earnings include the servicing of debt) are usually comparable. Private companies within the same industry, however, can vary widely in capital structure. The valuation of a privately held business is therefore frequently based on 'enterprise value' or the pre-debt value of a business rather than the value of the stock of the business, like public companies. This is another reason why private company multiples are generally based on pre-tax profits and may not be directly comparable to the price/earnings ratio of public firms.

➢ **Risk profile:** Public companies in general provide an assurance of continuing operations above that of smaller, privately held firms. Downturns in the economy or a change in the environment (such as an increase in competition or regulatory changes) often have a greater impact on private firms than public firms in terms of performance and market positioning. The higher risk if accounted may result in a discount in value for private firms.

➢ **Differences in operations:** Public companies typically have operations spanning a broader range of products and services than do private companies. In addition, even if the products and services are the same, the revenue mix is often different.

➢ **Operational control:** The sale of a private company usually results in the purchase of the controlling interest in the business, ownership of public-company stock generally consists of a minority share ownership, which may be construed to be less valuable than a controlling interest position.

VALUATION STANDARDS

The purpose of valuation standards is to protect users of valuations and the community at large. Standards typically cover the development and reporting of a valuation. A number of organizations have released valuation standards or guidance. Typically there is no mandatory compliance, and very often buyers and sellers are not even aware of these standards. No single set of valuation standards covers the valuation of private companies.

SUMMARY

Among the techniques used for valuation of private companies; break-up analysis, asset valuation and DCF models are less feasible options as they require detailed financial information from inside the private company. Since private companies manage their balance sheet and earnings for different end goals than public companies, using discounted cash flow or comparable valuation techniques require additional insight. Due to lack of liquidity and increased risk in business, the discount rates used in DCF analysis needs to be modified accordingly. Therefore, a more feasible approach is to find comparable public companies whose values are known. Comparable companies' analysis is mostly used in M&A advisory, fairness opinions, restructuring, IPOs and follow-on offerings, and share repurchases. Furthermore, the trade-competition approach is pertinent if there are publicly traded competitors; in its absence deal-competition approach is used.

Each valuation approach has its own particular use and should be used in that respect. It is doubtful that any one analysis by itself will yield a result that can be relied upon. Hence, it is likely that one will need to use multiple approaches to yield a range of values for a private company. Each methodology provides additional clarity on the other valuations. Evaluating the results of numerous methods provides a better understanding of a business' true worth. It is also important to note that different people will have different ideas on the value of a company depending on factors such as public status of the seller and buyer, nature of potential buyers, nature of the deal, market conditions and tax position of buyer and seller. A fair amount of experience, judgment and corporate finance and equity market knowledge is required. In each case straightforward tools contain several hidden layers of complexity and restraints.

Review Questions

1. Discuss the similarities and contrasts of closely held company and public limited company
2. What are the different approaches for the valuation of closely held company?
3. What are the different reasons for performing valuation for privately held companies?
4. Discuss the valuation discounts and premiums in valuating privately held companies.

Video Linkages

1. Is Overvaluation Of Stock A Problem For Private Companies? http://www.youtube.com/watch?v=lURwTmq8NIQ
2. 2012 CFA Level 2 Online Lecture R43 Private Company Valuation Part 1.mp4, http://www.youtube.com/watch?v=SNTtDsG5Og0

ASSIGNMENTS

1. Select a closely held company and get the financial data from 'annual reports' of the company available at 'Registrar of Companies' office and work on the valuation of share of that closely held company considering guideline data on companies in competition.

BIBLIOGRAPHY

1. Aswath Damodaran, (2008) *Domaodaran on Valuation,* John Wiley and Sons, NY, USA
2. Chris M. Mellen and Frank C.Evas, (2010) *Valuation for M&A for Building Value for Private Co,* John Wiley and Sons, NY, USA
3. Jerald E.Pinto, Elquine Henry ,Thomas R.Robinson, John D.Stowe, (2010) *Equity Assets Valuation,* John Wiley and Sons, NY, USA
4. Leslie Matuson, (1981) *The Theory and Practice of Private Co Valuation,* University of Witwaterand.
5. Luis F.Pereiro, (2010) *Valuation of Companies in Emerging Markets-A Practical Approach,* John Wiley and Sons, NY, USA

6. Practicing Law Institute, Acquiring or Selling the Privately Held Company Vol I, 1988

7. Rawley Thomas, Benton E.Gup, (2009) *The Valuation Handbook, Valuation Techniques for Today's Top Practitioners.* John Wiley and Sons, NY, USA

8. Robert D.Feder, (2010) *Valuation Strategies in Divorce,* Vol1, Aspen Publisher, (4 Edn)

9. Shannon P. Pratt, (2001) *Business Valuation Discount and Premium,* John Wiley and Sons, NY, USA

10. Stanley J.Feldman, (2005) *Principles of Private Firm Valuation,* John Wiley and Sons, NY, USA

> *"Stock valuation is not an estimate of the fair value of stocks, but rather a convention, which serves to provide the necessary stability and liquidity for investment, so long as the convention does not break down"*[1]
>
> **— John Maynard Keynes**

Learning Objectives

To understand:

- Securities - equity, debt and derivatives
- Why valuation of securities?
- Approaches to security valuations.
- Security valuation methods.

In Security Valuation the aim is to maximise the worth/value to the individual/company over a period of time. As a company grows and acquires additional assets, the company liquidity position changes, and the likelihood of future earnings also increase, which should have a positive impact on share price and security valuation. These additional assets allow the company to select from a wider range of projects from which to maximise future wealth. Security Valuation also impacts on the credit rating of a company, which in turn changes the real return required on projects, and the discount rate, which should be applied to the Net Present Value calculations.

---

1. The Uncomfortable Dance Between V'ers and U'ers, McCulley

INTRODUCTION

In general, the value of an asset is the price that a willing and able buyer pays to a willing and able seller. If either the buyer or seller is not both willing and able, then an offer does not establish the value of the asset. There are three types of value, of which we are concerned with and these are Book Value (The asset's historical cost less its accumulated depreciation), Market Value (The price of an asset as determined in a competitive marketplace), Intrinsic Value (The present value of the expected future cash flows discounted at the decision maker's required rate of return). There are two parameters, which determines the intrinsic value of an asset to an individual. These are the size and timing of the expected future cash flows and individual's required rate of return. Hence security analysis is necessary. Securities valuations are used in the finance industry for a wide variety of purposes. Tasks such as price discovery and formation, portfolio valuation, fund unit exchanges, securities lending, risk management, and treasury functions rely heavily on clear and current market prices.

Security analysis is about valuing the debt, warrants, bond and equity of companies from the perspective of outside investors. The publicly available information is used for this analysis. There are several types of value, of which we are concerned with four, book value (carrying value on the balance sheet of the firm's equity ie. total assets less total liabilities, tangible book value (book value minus intangible assets), market value (the price of an asset as determined in a competitive marketplace) and intrinsic value (the present value of the expected future cash flows discounted at the decision maker's required rate of return). The security analyst must have a thorough understanding of financial statements, which are an important source of this information. As such, the ability to value equity securities requires cross-disciplinary knowledge in both finance and financial accounting. Security analysis tends to take the perspective of potential investors, whereas corporate finance tends to take an inside perspective.

TYPES OF SECURITIES

Securities are a form of ownership that can be easily traded on a secondary market. Securities allow investor to own the underlying asset without taking possession. Securities are very easily traded, as they are very liquid. They are easy to price, and so are a great indication of the underlying value of the asset. There are three types of securities as indicated below;

- **Equity Securities:** These allow the investor to own shares of a corporation. The most direct way is to buy shares of a company. You can also profit by buying shares of mutual funds, which invests in the shares for you. The secondary market for equity is the stock market such as the Bombay Stock Exchange and National Stock Exchange, NASDAQ.

- **Debt Securities:** These are also known as 'fixed-income securities'. The debt instrument can be bought or sold between two parties at notional amount (amount borrowed) with fixed interest rate and repaid on maturity date or can be further renewed. Debt securities include government bonds, corporate bonds, certificates of deposits, commercial papers, debentures, municipal bonds, preferred stocks. The interest rate on a debt security is largely determined by the perceived repayment ability of the borrower. The higher risks of payment default almost always lead to higher interest rates to borrow capital.

➢ **Derivative Securities:** A derivative security, also known as a derivative stock, is a financial instrument. the price of which is dependent on one or a number of financial assets. In itself, the derivative security is an agreement between two contracted parties to buy or sell an asset at a fixed price pre-decided on or before a date of expiration. The value of the security is dictated by the value of the underlying asset, which is usually stock, commodity, bond, currency, interest rate or markets indexes. Derivative securities usually are valued by using a version of the Black-Scholes Option Pricing Model.

A derivative security is particularly appealing to those investors looking to offset or hedge their risk when investing. Many investors in derivative have different motives such speculation and arbitration wherein interest is lessening or off-setting or hedging risk. They are instead motivated by the prospective profit that stock derivative speculation can bring. The other players who participate in the stock derivatives market are brokers, banks and financial institutions etc. Stock Options allow investor to trade in stocks without actually buying them upfront. Investor can buy a call option to purchase the stock at a certain date at a certain price. If the stock price goes up, he exercises option and purchase the stock at lower negotiated price, then immediately resell it for the higher actual price. Put option gives investor the right to sell the stock at an agreed upon price. If the stock price is actually lower that day it is purchased then profit is made by selling it at the agreed upon higher price.

Future Contracts are derivatives based on commodities such as oil, groceries or even currencies. Like options, investor pays a small fee (called a margin) to get the right to buy or sell the commodities for an agreed-upon price in the future. However, futures are more dangerous because, rather than buying options that can be chosen to ignore, investor is entering into an actual contract that he must fulfill.

Securities help the economy by making it easier for those with money to find those who need capital for investment. On the other hand, securities also create wider, more destructive swings in the business cycle. Since securities are so easy to buy, individual investors can purchase them impulsively, without being fully informed or diversified. When stock prices fall, they can lose their entire life savings. Derivatives can make volatility even worse. All these new products create too much liquidity.

SELECTING STOCK VALUATION METHOD

When trying to find out which valuation method to use to value a stock for the first time, most investors will come across many valuation techniques in practice. These include simple ones, such as the 'comparables' method, and the more involved methods, such as the discounted cash flow model. There is no one method that is best suited for every situation. Each stock is different, and each industry sector has unique characteristics that may require varying valuation approaches.

In general valuation methods fall into two main categories: absolute and relative valuation models. In absolute valuation method the attempt is to find the intrinsic value of an investment based only on fundamentals. Here the focus is on dividends, cash flow and growth rate for a company. The models that fall into this category include dividend discount model, discounted cash flow model, residual income models and asset-based models.

The relative valuation models compare the target company to other similar companies. These methods generally involve calculating multiples or ratios, such as the P/E and comparing them to the other comparable firms. For instance, if the P/E of the firm investor are trying to value is lower than the P/E multiple of a comparable firm, that company may be said to be relatively undervalued. Relative valuation is easier and quicker to do than the absolute valuation methods.

➤ **Dividend Discount Model (DDM):** This model calculates the 'true' value of a firm based on the dividends the company pays its shareholders. The justification for using dividends to value a company is that dividends represent the actual cash flows going to the shareholder, thus valuing the present value of these cash flows should give an investor value for how much the shares should be worth. Here one has to first see that the company actually pays a dividend. Secondly, it is not enough for the company to just a pay dividend; the dividend should also be stable and predictable. The companies that pay stable and predictable dividends are mature ones and fundamentally strong in the industries. For instance, take a look at the dividends and earnings of company XYZ below and see if you think the DDM model would be appropriate for this company.

	2007	2008	2009	2010	2011	2012
Dividends Per Share (₹)	6.2	6.4	6.6	6.8	7.0	7.2
Earnings Per Share (₹)	49.6	51.2	52.8	54.4	56.0	57.6

In this example, the earnings per share are consistently growing at an average rate of 3%, and the dividends are also growing at the same rate. This means the firm's dividend is consistent with its earnings trend, which would make it easy to predict for future periods. In addition, the payout ratio is consistent, i.e., 0.125 for all six years which is good. Hence the future cash flow can be worked out using the dividend model.

With these assumptions, a model, which is known as the Dividend Discount Model, or the Gordon Model is derived. This model gives investors the present value of an infinite stream of dividends that are growing at a constant rate:

$$\text{Value of Stock} = \frac{\text{Dividend per Share}}{\text{Discount rate} - \text{Dividend growth rate}}$$

Example:

Dividend paid in the current year is ₹ 7.2 per share. Dividends were growing at 8% per year, and your required return was 15%. The value of the stock must be:

$$\text{Value of Stock} = \frac{7.2}{0.15 - 0.08} = ₹\ 102.86$$

➤ **Discounted Cash Flow Model (DCFM):** This method is used when company does not pay dividend or payment of dividend is irregular. DCFM uses a firm's discounted future cash flows to value the business. The big advantage of this approach is that it can be used with a wide variety of firms that don't pay dividends, and even for companies that do pay dividends, such as company XYZ in the previous example. The DCF model has several variations, but the most commonly used form is the

Two-Stage DCF Model. In this variation, the free cash flows are generally forecasted for five to ten years, and then a terminal value is calculated to account for all the cash flows beyond the forecast period. This method is used where the company is having predictable free cash flows, and for the free cash flows to be positive. See the following example of ABC company;

	2007	2008	2009	2010	2011	2012
Operating Cash Flow	335	586	1278	990	2230	1850
Capital Expenditures	289	786	1450	880	1890	1980
Free Cash Flow	46	–200	–172	110	340	–130

Here, ABC has produced increasing positive operating cash flow. But there is high level of capital expenditures as company investing a lot of its cash back into the business in order to grow. This results in negative free cash flows for three of the six years, and would make it extremely difficult to predict the cash flows for the next five years period. So, in order to use the DCFM most effectively, the target company should generally have stable, positive and predictable free cash flows. Companies that have the ideal cash flows suited for the DCFM are typically the mature firms that are past the growth stages.

➢ **Comparables Method:** In this method an intrinsic value for the stock like the previous two valuation methods is not calculated. It simply compares the stock's price multiples to a benchmark to determine if the stock is relatively undervalued or overvalued. The rationale for this is based on the criteria that the two similar assets should sell for similar prices. This method can be used in almost all circumstances as many multiples can be used for valuation process. These are price-to-earnings (P/E), price-to-sales, (P/S), price-to-cash flow (P/CF), and others. Of these ratios though, the P/E ratio is the most commonly used one because it focuses on the earnings of the company, which is one of the primary drivers of an investments value.

Here, the company should be public limited generating positive earnings because a comparison using a negative P/E multiple would be meaningless. Also the earnings should not be too volatile and the accounting practices used by management should not distort the reported earnings drastically.

VALUATING COMMON STOCKS

A share of common stock represents an ownership position in the firm. Here, the owners are entitled to vote on important matters regarding the firm, to vote on the membership of the board of directors, and (often) to receive dividends. In the event of liquidation of the firm, the common shareholders will receive a pro-rata share of the assets remaining after the creditors and preferred stockholders have been paid off.

Firms obtain their long-term sources of equity financing by issuing common and preferred stock. The payments of the firm to the holders of these securities are in the form of dividends. Unlike interest payments on debt, which are tax deductible, dividends must be paid out of after-tax income.

Preferred stock, on the other hand, is a hybrid form of financing, sharing some features with debt and some with common equity. For example, preferred dividends like interest payments on debt are generally fixed. In addition, the claims against the assets of the firm of the preferred stockholders, like those of the debt holders, are also fixed.

The common stockholders have a residual claim against the assets and cash flows of the firm. That is, the common stockholders have a claim against whatever assets remain after the debt holders and preferred stockholders have been paid. Moreover, the cash flow that remains after interest and preferred dividends have been paid belongs to the common stockholders.

The priority of the claims against the assets of the firm belonging to debt holders, preferred stockholders, and common stockholders differ. The owners of the firm's debt securities have the first claim against the assets of the firm. This means that the debt holders must receive their scheduled interest and principal payments before any dividends can be paid to the equity holders. If these claims are not paid, the debt holders can force the firm into bankruptcy. The preferred stockholders have the next claim. They must be paid the full amount of their scheduled dividends before any dividends may be distributed to the common stockholders.

Just like with bonds, the first step in valuing common stocks is to determine the cash flows, which are two, such as dividend payments and future selling price. Finding the present values of these cash flows and adding them together will give the final value.

Illustration

Assume that you are considering the purchase of a stock, which will pay dividends of ₹ 4 next year, and ₹ 5 the following year. After receiving the second dividend, you plan on selling the stock for ₹ 105. What is the intrinsic value of this stock if your required return is 16%

$$\text{Value of Stock} = \Sigma \frac{Dn}{(1+RR)^{n}} + \frac{D1+n+SP}{(1+RR)^{1+n}}$$

$$\text{Value of Stock} = \frac{4}{(1+0.16)^{1}} + \frac{5+105}{(1+0.16)^{2}} = 2.50 + 52.88 = ₹\ 55.38$$

In valuing the common stock, two assumptions are kept in mind, i.e., dividends will be paid in the future and selling price of the stock for in the future. Both of these assumptions are unrealistic, especially knowledge of the future selling price. If the following assumptions are taken, a simple model can be derived for common stock valuation; holding period is infinite (i.e., investor will never sell the stock) and dividends will grow at a constant rate forever.

➢ **'Stock option' or 'phantom stock':** It is an employee benefit plan that gives selected employees (senior management) many of the benefits of stock ownership without actually giving them any company stock. Sometimes referred to as "shadow stock". Phantom stock is a compensation tool that can be used by companies to motivate and incentivize key employees to help build the value of the business without diluting the owner's equity position. For private companies, a phantom stock plan, also 'shadow' stock, provides a value-based compensation approach that functions in a similar way to public company stock option plans. There are also similar plans described as stock appreciation rights or SAR plans.

Although many variations exist, the typical plan creates deferred compensation units and tax deferral advantages that are assigned a base value equivalent to the value of a company's common stock. The participant does not "purchase" underlying phantom shares; rather the individual is granted phantom shares with a vesting schedule and receives the upside increase in value over the original value at grant. Triggering events for the payout of the change in value from the issuing value include an employee's retirement or a change in controlling ownership of the company.

Phantom share value is calculated based on changes in the equity value of the company determined by an independent valuation. Value can increase or decrease based on actual financial performance. The participant is not taxed until there is an actual receipt of benefit payments. Similarly, the corporation will receive a deduction for the payment in the year the payment is actually made. The value of phantom stock is established on the books at the time it is credited and is adjusted annually to reflect the change in its value. To determine the value of phantom stock units, the equity of the company must be valued.

➤ **Preferred Stocks:** Preferred stock pays a fixed dividend periodically and the preferred stockholders are usually not entitled to vote as are the common shareholders. Preferred stock is very much like common stock, except that the dividends are constant (i.e., the growth rate is 0%). Peferred stock is an equity with priority over common stock with respect to the payment of dividends and the distribution of assets in a liquidation. Preferred stock is a hybrid security, which shares features with both common stock and debt. Preferred stock is similar to common stock in that it entitles its owners to receive dividends, which the firm must pay out of after-tax income. Moreover, the use of preferred stock as a source of financing does not increase the probability of bankruptcy for the firm. The preferred dividend rate is expressed as a percentage of the par value of the preferred stock. The annual preferred dividend is determined by multiplying the preferred dividend rate times the par value of the preferred stock. Since the preferred dividends are generally fixed, preferred stock can be valued as a constant growth stock with a dividend growth rate equal to zero. Thus, the price of a share of preferred stock can be determined using the following equation:

$$Pv = \frac{Dp}{r}$$

where,

➤ Pv = the preferred stock value,

➤ Dp = the preferred dividend, and

➤ r = the required return on the stock.

Illustration

Suppose that you are interested in purchasing shares of a preferred stock, which pays a ₹ 5 dividend every year. If your required return is 6%, what is the intrinsic value of this stock?

The price of a share of preferred stock with par value is ₹ 100 per share, the preferred dividend rate 8%, and the required return is 10%. shall be :

Pv = (8 × 100)/10 = ₹ 80

Preferred stock is similar to common stock in that it entitles its owners to receive dividend, which the firm must pay out of after-tax income. Preferred shares generally have a dividend requirement that makes them appear similar to debt. The dividend structure usually has rights attached to it, such as whether the shares participate in enterprise earning. Moreover, the use of preferred stock as a source of financing does not increase the probability of bankruptcy for the firm. However, like the coupon payments on debt, the dividends on preferred stock are generally fixed. Also, the claims of the preferred stockholders against the assets of the firm are fixed as are the claims of the debt holders. The classic version of preferred stock is a share that pays a fixed amount of dividend and never matures. It is, therefore a perpetuity.

Preferred stock is an equity. However, technically it is a perpetuity. To value a preferred stock simply take the annual return in rupees and divide by the appropriate required discount rate. The formula for the value of a share of preferred stock is:

$$\text{Value of Preferred Stock, Pv} = \frac{D}{K}$$

Where:

D = Dividend

K = Required Discount Rate

Illustration

A share of preferred stock pays a 8% dividend has a par value of ₹ 100. If the required rate of return by investors is 10%, what would be the price?

$$\text{Pv} = \frac{8}{0.10} = ₹\ 80$$

STOCK VALUATION METHODS

Stocks have two types of valuations. One is a value created using some type of cash flow, sales or fundamental earnings analysis. The other value is dictated by how much an investor is willing to pay for a particular share of stock and by how much other investors are willing to sell a stock for (in other words, by supply and demand). Both of these values change over time as investors change the way they analyze stocks and as they become more or less confident in the future of stocks.

The fundamental valuation is the valuation that people use to justify stock prices. The most common example of this type of valuation methodology is P/E ratio, which stands for Price to Earnings Ratio. This form of valuation is based on historic ratios and statistics and aims to assign value to a stock based on measurable attributes. This form of valuation is typically what drives long-term stock prices. There are many different ways to value stocks. The key is to take each approach into account while formulating an overall opinion of the stock. If the valuation of a company is lower or higher than other similar stocks, then the next step would be to determine the reasons.

➤ **Earnings Per Share (EPS):** EPS is the total net income of the company divided by the number of shares outstanding. The most important thing to look for in the EPS figure is the overall quality of earnings. Make sure the company is not trying to manipulate their EPS numbers to make it look like they are more profitable. Also, look at the growth in EPS over the past several quarters/years to understand how volatile their EPS is, and to see if they are an underachiever or an overachiever. In other words, one has to see that whether they have consistently beaten expectations or are they constantly restating and lowering their forecasts. The EPS number that most analysts use is the forecast future EPS. To compute this number, the net income that excludes any one-time gains or losses are used. Also excluded are non-cash expenses like stock options or amortization of goodwill. Then divide this number by the number of shares outstanding. Historical EPS figures and forecasts for the next 1-2 years can be found from information available on free financial sites. Through fundamental investment research, one can determine their own EPS forecasts and apply other valuation techniques below.

➢ **Price to Earnings (P/E):** To compute this figure, take the stock price and divide it by the annual EPS figure. For example, if the stock is trading at ₹ 200 and the EPS is ₹ 5, the P/E is 40 times. To get a good feeling of what P/E multiple a stock trades at, investor should look at the historical and forward ratios.

Historical P/Es are computed by taking the current price divided by the sum of the EPS for the last four quarters or for the previous year. Investor should also look at the historical trends of the P/E by viewing a chart of its historical P/E over the last several years to find out what range the P/E has traded in to determine if the current P/E is high or low versus its historical average.

Forward P/Es reflect the future growth of the company into the figure. Forward P/Es are computed by taking the current stock price divided by the sum of the EPS estimates for the next four quarters, or for the EPS estimate for next calendar of fiscal year. P/Es change constantly. If there is a large price change in a stock or if the earnings (EPS) estimates change, the ratio is recomputed.

➢ **Growth Rate:** Valuations rely very heavily on the expected growth rate of a company. One must look at the historical growth rate of both sales and income to get a feeling for the type of future growth expected. However, companies are constantly changing, as well as the economy, so solely using historical growth rates to predict the future is not an acceptable form of valuation. However, they are used as guidelines for what future growth could look like in future, if similar circumstances are faced by the company. Although companies are in the best position to forecast their own growth, they are far from accurate, and unforeseen events could cause rapid changes in the economy and in the company's industry.

Before starting valuation exercise, it's important to look at a range of forecast values. For example, if the company being valued has been growing earnings between 5 and 10% each year for the last 5 years, but expects that it will grow 15-20% this year, a more conservative growth rate of 10-15% would be appropriate in valuations. Another example would be for a company that has been going through restructuring. They may have been growing earnings at 10-15% over the past several quarters/ years because of cost cutting, but their sales growth could be only 0-5%. This would indicate that their earnings growth will probably slow when the cost cutting has fully taken effect. Therefore, forecasting an earnings growth closer to the 0-5% rate would be more appropriate rather than the 15-20%. The growth rate method of valuations relies heavily on gut feel to make a forecast. Hence, there may be error in making forecasts.

➢ **Price Earnings to Growth (PEG) Ratio:** This valuation technique has really become popular over the past decade. It is better than just looking at a P/E because it takes three factors into account; the price, earnings, and earnings growth rates. To compute the PEG ratio, divide the Forward P/E by the expected earnings growth rate (you can also use historical P/E and historical growth rate to see where it's traded in the past). This will yield a ratio that is usually expressed as a percentage. The theory goes that as the percentage rises over 100% the stock becomes more and more overvalued, and as the PEG ratio falls below 100% the stock becomes more and more undervalued. The theory is based on a belief that P/E ratios should approximate the long-term growth rate of a company's earnings. It is a thumb rule to use this in the overall valuation process.

For example two stocks that investor is thinking about buying. Stock A is trading at a forward P/E of 15 and expected to grow at 20%. Stock B is trading at a forward P/E of 30 and expected to grow at 25%. The PEG ratio for Stock A is 75% (15/20) and for Stock B is 120% (30/25). According to the PEG ratio, Stock A is a better purchase because it has a lower PEG ratio, or in other words, you can purchase its future earnings growth for a lower relative price than that of Stock B.

➢ **Return on Invested Capital (ROIC):** This valuation technique measures how much money the company makes each year on per rupee of investment, which is the amount of money invested in the company by both stockholders and debtors. This ratio is expressed as a per cent and investor should look for a per cent that approximates the level of growth that he expects. This ratio measures the investment return that management is able to get for its capital. The higher the number, the better the return.

To compute the ratio, take the net income (same one used in the EPS figure mentioned above) and divide it by the invested capital. Invested capital can be estimated by adding together the stockholders equity, the total long and short-term debt and accounts payable, and then subtracting accounts receivable and cash. This ratio is much more useful when investor compares it with other companies that he is valuing.

➢ **Return on Assets (ROA):** Similar to ROIC, ROA, expressed as a per cent, measures the company's ability to make money from its assets. To measure the ROA, take the net income divided by the total assets. This ratio is not always a good indicator of the company's potential because of common irregularities in balance sheets due to things like Goodwill, write-offs, discontinuations, etc.

➢ **Price to Sales (P/S):** This ratio compares the current stock price to the annual sales. In other words, it tells investor how much the stock costs per rupee of sales earned. To work it out, take the current stock price divided by the annual sales per share. The annual sales per share should be calculated by taking the net sales for the last four quarters divided by the fully diluted shares outstanding. The price to sales ratio does not take into account any debt the company has. For example, if a company is heavily financed by debt instead of equity, then the sales per share will seem high. This ratio is best looked at when comparing multiple companies.

➢ **Market Cap:** Market Cap, which is short for Market Capitalization, is the value of all of the company's stock. To measure it, multiply the current stock price by the fully diluted shares outstanding. Remember, the market cap is only the value of the stock. To get a more complete picture, investor should look at the Enterprise Value.

➢ **Enterprise Value (EV):** Enterprise Value is equal to the total value of the company, as it is trading for on the stock market. To compute it, add the market capitalization and the total net debt of the company. The total net debt is equal to total long and short-term debt plus accounts payable, minus accounts receivable, minus cash. The Enterprise Value is the best approximation of what a company is worth at any point in time because it takes into account the actual stock price instead of balance sheet prices. Enterprise Value fluctuates with changes in stock price.

➢ **EV to Sales:** This ratio measures the total company value as compared to its annual sales. A high ratio means that the company's value is much more than its sales. To compute it, divide the EV by the net sales for the last four quarters. This ratio is especially useful when valuing companies that do not have earnings or that are going through unusually rough times. In the event, a company currently losing money, then the P/E ratio would be irrelevant. Then EV to Sales ratio will tell what that company could trade for when its bad time is over and its earnings are back to normal.

➢ **EBITDA:** EBITDA stands for earnings before interest, taxes, depreciation and amortization. It is one of the best measures of a company's cash flow and is used for valuing both public and private companies. To compute EBITDA, use a company's income statement, take the net income and then add back interest, taxes, depreciation, amortization and any other non-cash or one-time charges. This leaves investor with a number that approximates how much cash the company is producing. EBITDA is a very popular figure because it can easily be compared across companies for comparison

➢ **EV to EBITDA:** This is one of the best parameter, which helps to decide whether or not a company is cheap or expensive. To compute, divide the EV by EBITDA The higher the number, the more expensive the company is. However, remember that more expensive companies are often valued higher because they are growing faster or because they are a higher quality company.

➢ **Average growth approximation:** Assuming that two stocks have the same earnings growth, the one with a lower P/E is a better value. The P/E method is perhaps the most commonly used valuation method in the stock brokerage industry. By using comparison firms, a target P/E ratio is selected for the company, and then the future earnings of the company are estimated. The valuation's fair price is simply estimated earnings times target P/E.

➢ **Constant Growth Sock Valuation:** Stock Valuation is more difficult than bond valuation because stocks do not have a finite maturity and the future cash flows, i.e., dividends, are not specified. Therefore, the techniques used for stock valuation must make some assumptions regarding the structure of the dividends.

A constant growth stock is a stock whose dividends are expected to grow at a constant rate in the near future. The value of a constant growth stock can be determined using the following equation:

$$P_0 = \frac{Dv(1+g)}{(r-gw)} = \frac{D1(1+gw)}{(r-gw)}$$

where,

➢ P_o = the stock price at time 0,

➢ Dv = the current dividend,

➢ D1 = the next dividend (i.e., at time 1),

➢ gw = the growth rate in dividends, and

➢ r = the required return on the stock, and

➢ gw < r.

Illustration

Find the stock price, given that the current dividend is ₹ 4 per share, dividends are expected to grow at a rate of 8 % in the near future, and the required return is 12%.

$$P_0 = \frac{4(1+0.08)}{(0.12-0.08)} = ₹\ 108$$

➢ **Non-Constant Growth Stock Valuation:** Many firms have rapid growth in certain periods. This may result from the introduction of a new product, a new technology, or an innovative marketing strategy. However, the period of rapid growth cannot continue indefinitely. In future competitors will enter the market and catch up with the firm.

These firms cannot be valued properly using this valuation constant growth stock valuation approach. Then, it assumes that dividends will grow from that point on at a constant rate, which reflects the long-term growth rate in the economy. The value of a non-constant growth stock can be determined using the following equation:

$$P_0 = \sum_{t=1}^{t} \frac{Dt}{(1+r)^t} + \frac{Dt+1}{(r-gc)}(1+r)^{-t}$$

where,

➢ P_0 = the stock price at time 0,

➢ Dt = the expected dividend at time t,

➢ t = the number of years of non-constant growth,

➢ gc = the long-term constant growth rate in dividends, and

➢ r = the required return on the stock, and

➢ gc < r.

Illustration

Dividend paid currently on a stock is ₹ 4 per share and investors require a rate of return of 12%. Dividends are expected to grow at a rate of 20% per year over the next three years and then at a rate of 5% per year from that point on. Find the price of the stock.

There are 3 years of non-constant growth, thus, period P = 3. Before substituting into the formula given above it is necessary to calculate the expected dividends for years 1 through 4 using the provided growth rates.

Dv1 = 4.00 (1+0.20) = ₹ 4.80

Dv2 = 4.80 (1+0.20) = ₹ 5.76

Dv3 = 5.76 (1+0.20) = ₹ 6.91

Dv4 = 6.91 (1+0.20) = ₹ 8.29

$$Sv = \frac{4.80}{(1+.12)^1} + \frac{5.76}{(1+0.12)^2} + \frac{6.91}{(1+0.12)^3} + \frac{8.29}{(0.12-0.05)}(1+0.12)^{-3}$$

Sv = 4.28 + 4.59 + 4.91 + 84.29 = ₹ 98.07

➢ **Implied Growth Models:** One can use the Gordon model or the limited high-growth period approximation model to calculate an implied growth estimate. To do this, one takes the average P/E and average growth for a comparison index, uses the current P/E of the stock in question, and calculates what growth rate would be needed for the two valuation equations to be equal. This gives investor an estimate of the "break-even" growth rate for the stock's current P/E ratio.

VALUATING DEBT SECURITIES

Debt securities are investments in debentures, bonds, perpetuities, deposits or commercial papers depending on their maturity. Debt securities are generally issued for a fixed term and redeemable by the issuer at the end of that term. Debt securities may be protected by collateral or may be unsecured. The holders of debt securities have a priority in a bankruptcy of the issuer.

➢ **Bond:** A bond is a tradable instrument that represents a debt owed to the owner by the issuer. Most commonly, bonds pay interest periodically (usually semi-annually) and then return the principal at maturity. Most corporate, and some government, bonds are callable. That means that at the company's option, it may force the bondholders to sell them back to the company. Ordinarily, there are restrictions on the timing of the call and the amount that must be paid. There are two types of cash flows that are provided by a bond investments; periodic interest payments (usually every six months, but any frequency is possible), repayment of the face value (also called the principal amount, which is usually ₹ 1,000) at maturity. The following timeline illustrates a typical bond's cash flows:

	1st yr	2nd yr	3rd yr	4th yr	5th yr
0	100	100	100	100	100 + 1000

Bond valuation includes calculating the present value of the bond's future interest payments, also known as its cash flow, and the bond's value upon maturity, also known as its face value or par value. Because a bond's par value and interest payments are fixed, an investor uses bond valuation to determine what rate of return is required for an investment in a particular bond to be worthwhile.

A bond or a debenture is a long-term debt instrument or security. It is issued by business enterprises or government agencies to raise long-term capital. A bond usually carries a fixed rate of interest. It is called as coupon payment and the interest rate is called as the coupon rate. The coupon payment can be either annually or semi-annually.

A bond can be irredeemable or redeemable. Redeemable bonds have a fixed maturity date and irredeemable bonds have perpetual life with only interest payments periodically.

Basically, the value of a bond is the present value of all the future interest payments and the maturity value, discounted at the required return on bond commensurate with the prevailing interest rate and risk.

$$\text{Bond Value} = \frac{\text{Interest 1}}{(1+r)^1} + \frac{\text{Interest 2}}{(1+r)^2} + \text{-------} + \frac{(\text{Interestn} + \text{MaturityValue})}{(1+r)^n}$$

$$\text{Bond Value} = \sum_{t=1}^{t=N} \frac{\text{Interest}}{(1+r)^t} + \frac{\text{Par}}{(1+r)^N}$$

= Interest (PVIFA) + Par (PVIF)

= Present Value of the Interest Payments + Present Value of the Par

Where:

Interest 1 to n = Interests in periods 1 to n.

r = Expected return

The maturity value of the bond is the face value. When the required rate of return is equal to the coupon rate, the bond value equals the par value. When the required rate of return is more than the coupon rate, the bond value would be less than its par value. The bond in this case would sell at a discount. When the required rate of return is less than the coupon rate, the bond value would be more than its par value. The bond in this case would sell at a premium.

Illustration

Face value of the bond is ₹ 1,000 (maturity value ₹ 1,000). The bond has a 10% coupon rate payable semi-annually and the yield to maturity (return) is 8%. The bond matures in 5 years period from now. What is the value of the bond?

Interest 1 till 10 intervals = ₹ 50 per semi-annual period. (₹ 100 annually)

n = 10 because 5 years × 2 payments per period.

Yield to maturity = 8%, therefore, semi-annual YTM (return) =8/2 = 4% or 0.04

$$\text{Bond Value} = \frac{₹ 50}{(1+0.04)^1} + \frac{₹ 50}{(1+0.04)^2} + \text{------} + \frac{₹ (50+1000)}{(1+0.04)^{10}} = ₹\ 1040$$

= Present Value of Interest Payment + Present Value of Maturity Payment

= 339.27 + 680.58 = 1079.85

A bond selling at less than par is said to be selling at a discount. Any time the market rate of interest is less than the coupon rate of interest, the bond will sell at a premium. Similarly, when market rates of interest are greater than the coupon rate, the bond will sell at a discount. The value of a bond depends on several factors such as time to maturity, coupon rate, and required return. Higher required returns lead to lower bond prices, and vice-versa. Higher coupon rates lead to higher bond prices, and vice versa.

➢ **Perpetuities:** There is a type of bond that never matures called 'perpetuity'. Canada issued some perpetuities in the late 1970s. If long-term bonds are more sensitive to changes in interest rates than short-term bonds.

When N is infinity, the value of a perpetual bond reduces to

$$\text{Value of a prepetuity} = \frac{\text{Interest}}{K}$$

There are not a lot of perpetuities that trade in the marketplace today.

➢ **Debentures:** A debenture is a document that either creates a debt or acknowledges it, and it is a debt without collateral. It is used as medium to long-term debt instrument used by large companies to borrow money. A debenture is like a certificate of loan or a loan bond evidencing the fact that the company is liable to pay a specified amount with interest and although the money raised by the debentures becomes a part of the company's capital structure, it does not become share capital. Debentures are generally freely transferable by the debenture holder. Debenture holders have no rights to vote in the company's general meetings of shareholders. There are also options for 'convertibility', which means a creditor may turn their debentures into equity in the company as per the issue terms of debentures. There are two types of debentures; convertible debentures, which can be converted into equity shares of the issuing company after a predetermined period of time. 'Convertibility' is a feature that firms may add to the bonds they issue to make them more attractive to buyers. Non-convertible debentures, which are simply regular debentures, cannot be converted into equity shares of the liable company. They are debentures without the convertibility feature attached to them. As a result, they usually carry higher interest rates than their convertible counterparts. The valuation of debenture is done as follows:

Dv = I (PVIFAkn) + M (PVIF kn)

Where:

Dv = Debenture Market Value

I = Annual Interest Payment (Coupon Rate)

M = Face Value of Debentures

PVIFA = Present Value Interest Factor for an Annuity

PVIF = Present Value Interest Factor for Lump Sum

k = Discount Rate

n = Intervals

DERIVATIVE SECURITIES VALUATION

Derivative securities include stock options, warrants, rights, convertible debt, and convertible preferred stock. These securities confer a right to buy or sell an underlying asset, typically a financial security like a stock or bond, at a fixed price within a designated period of time. Derivative securities are typically valued using a version of the Black-Scholes Option Pricing Model.

The two key inputs in valuing derivative securities are the price of the underlying asset and the volatility of the asset's return. If a stock option is being valued, for example, the price of the underlying asset is the stock price. If a public firm issued the stock, then the price of the underlying asset, that is the stock price, can be easily determined from the public exchange where the stock is traded. The volatility of the asset's return is generally measured as the standard deviation of the stock's return. The inputs needed to implement this model are often difficult to calculate and, therefore, the calculation requires careful and diligent analysis to ensure consistency between the value of the derivative in question and the value of its underlying asset.

Additional complexity is introduced when valuing derivative securities where the underlying assets consist of stock in a privately held firm because of lack of liquidity for a private firm's stock.

The contract specifies the rights and obligations between the writer of the security and the holder to receive or deliver future cash flows based on some future event. The future value of a derivative is a stochastic process due to its uncertainty. The main groups of underlying assets are stocks, foreign currencies, interest rates, stock indices and commodities.

➢ **Futures:** A futures contract is an agreement that one places in advance to buy or sell an asset or commodity at a certain date for a certain price called the delivery price. As time passes, the forward price is liable to change but the delivery price remains the same. The price is fixed when the order is placed but the payment is not made until the delivery date. The contract can be reversed before expiration by taking an equal and opposite position in the same futures contract. The holder of the long (short) position gains, if the futures price at which the position is reversed is above (below) the initial futures price.

Futures contracts are highly uniform and with a well specified commitments describing the good to be delivered at a certain time and in certain manner. The contract also stipulates the minimum price fluctuation and the daily price limit.

At the start of a futures contract, the prospective trader must deposit funds referred to as an initial margin. It is the minimum amount of money that must be in an investment account on the day of transaction. This amount acts as a financial safeguard to ensure that traders will fulfill their contract obligations. Traders know their daily price changes through a process referred to as marking-to-market In this process the daily price changes are paid by the parties incurring losses to the parties making profits.

A trader receives a margin call when the value of the initial margin falls below maintenance margin. A maintenance margin is the minimum amount of money that must be kept in a margin account on any day other than the day of a transaction. The margin call requests the trader to replenish the account to bring it back to its initial level. This additional amount brought by the trader is called the variation margin.

The variation margin is the money added to or subtracted from a futures account that reflects profits or losses accruing from the daily settlement or the marking-to-market. The parties in the contract have an obligation to the clearing house, which in turn ensures that the parties concerned honor the contract.

➢ **Forwards:** A forward contract is an agreement between two parties, a buyer and a seller, to purchase or sell an asset at a later date at a price agreed upon today. Forward markets have no formal corporate body organized as the market. They trade in an over-the-counter market among major financial institutions. An over-the-counter is trading in financial instruments off organized exchanges with the risk that performance by the counter parties is not guaranteed by an exchange. The parties in a forward contract incur the obligation to ultimately buy or sell the asset.

Forward contracts are tailor made to meet the specific needs of the parties involved. The futures and forward contracts have differences and similarities, in that; they differ in the institutional setting in which they trade but the principles of pricing are the same. While the profit or loss from a futures contract is evaluated everyday; that of the forward contract is only realized at the expiry date. It costs nothing to enter into a forward contract but there is an initial margin for the futures contract. Both the futures and forward contracts are linear instruments. This implies that the contract price changes have a direct relationship with the price changes of the underlying asset. The forward and the futures contracts do not contain the element of choice, the parties concerned are obligated to honor the contract.

➢ **Options:** An option gives the holder the right but not the obligation to buy or sell an asset in the future at a price that is agreed upon today. Every option has the exercise date or expiration date, exercise price or strike price and command a premium, also called the price of the option. The option is said to be exercised when the holder chooses to buy or sell the underlying stock. The writer of the option is the other party to the contract. The holder (writer) is said to be in the long (short) position of the option contract. The standard derivatives or 'plain vanilla options' are the European and American options. Other options are called Exotic or non standard derivatives. Examples include; Asian, Lookback, Barrier options among others.

A European call (put) option gives the holder the right but not the obligation to buy (sell) the underlying asset with an initial price S, at a given maturity date T and for a fixed price K, called the strike price. Let the price of European call (put) option be denoted by c(p). Then the pay-off of a European call at maturity time T is;

$$c = \max (ST - K, 0)$$

If $ST < K$, the call will be worthless and the holder will not exercise the right. The pay-off of a European put is;

$$p = \max (K - ST, 0)$$

If $ST > K$, the put will be worthless and the holder will not exercise the right. The call-put parity is the relationship between a European call and put, given by;

$$c + Ke - rt = p + S$$

where r denotes the risk free interest rate and S the initial stock price.

American call (put) option gives to its holder the right but not the obligation to buy (sell) the underlying asset at any time t ($0 < t < T$), up to maturity date T, for a strike price K. Let the price of the American call (put) option be denoted by C(P). The pay-off of an American call at maturity time T is;

$$C = \max (ST - K, 0)$$

The pay-off of an American put is

$$P = \max (K - ST, 0)$$

If $ST > K$, the put will be worthless and the holder will not exercise the right.

SUMMARY

The process of determining how much a security is worth is of critical importance in various situations. Such as buy and sell of an enterprise, M & A deals, regulatory compliance, taxation, etc. There are three types of securities such as equity, debt and derivatives. Security valuation is highly subjective, but it is comparatively easier, when one is considering the value of tangible assets, level of debt, and other quantifiable data of the company issuing a security. For example, determining a company's earnings for the current year is easier than determining what the value of the company's brand recognition might be in 10 years. Valuation is important in fundamental analysis, the practitioners of which usually consider a company's earnings to be indicative of its value. Fundamental analysis is one of two main methods for analyzing a stock's potential return. Fundamental analysis involves assessing a corporation's financial history and current standing, including earnings, sales, and management. It also involves gauging the strength of the corporation's products or services in the marketplace.

An analyst uses the details as well as the current state of the economy to assess whether the stock is likely to increase or decrease in value in the short and long-term and whether the stock's current price is an accurate reflection of its value. A valuation method that measures the intrinsic value of a security by examining related economic, financial, and other qualitative and quantitative factors. An analysts study everything that could possibly affect a security's value, including macroeconomic factors (such as the overall economy and industry conditions) and specific factors (such as the financial condition and management of companies). The end goal of fundamental analysis is to produce a value that an investor can compare with a security's current price in an attempt to figure out whether the security is underpriced or overpriced.

The most theoretically sound stock valuation method, called income valuation or the discounted cash flow (DCF) method, involves discounting of the profits (dividends, earnings, or cash flows) the stock will bring to the stockholder in the foreseeable future, and a final value on disposal. The discounted rate normally includes a risk premium, which is commonly based on the capital asset pricing model.

Typically debt security covers bonds, perpetuities, debentures etc. Valuating debt securities is comparatively simpler due to fixed rate of returns. Derivative securities include stock options, warrants, rights, convertible debt, and convertible preferred stock. These securities confer a right to buy or sell an underlying asset, typically a financial security like a stock or bond, at a fixed price within a designated period of time. Derivative securities are typically valued using a version of the Black-Scholes Option Pricing Model.

Review Questions

1. What are the different types of securities and explain their features?
2. How are the different categories of common stocks valuated?
3. What is 'Bond' and how is its valuation done?
4. Discuss the various methods for valuation of equity stocks?
5. How are derivative securities valued?

Video Linkages

1. http://www.youtube.com/watch?v=SvHLx0Wsxz4, Security Valuation
2. http://www.youtube.com/watch?v=Qmb8CzZ9B4Y&feature=related, Bond Valuation
3. http://www.youtube.com/watch?v=rSNNBrt-XfE&feature=related, Introduction to Valuation

ASSIGNMENT

Consider three leading public limited companies in different industry segments and do a valuation excise for their different securities.

BIBLIOGRAPHY

1. Arnold Kleinstein and Steven Allen, (1991), Valuing Fixed-Income Investments and Derivative Securities: Cash-Flow Analysis and Calculations, New York Institute of Finance
2. Aswath Damodaran, (2009), *Damodaran on Valuation,* Wiley India.
3. Avellaneda M. and Laurence P. (2000). *Quantitative Modeling of Derivative Securities: From Theory to Practice.* Chapman and Hall. UK
4. Baxter M. and Rennie A. (1996). *Financial Calculus: An Introduction to Derivative Pricing.* Cambridge University Press, Cambridge.
5. Baz J. and Chacko G. (2004). *Financial Derivatives: Pricing, Applications and Mathematics.* Cambridge University Press, Cambridge.
6. Bodie, Zvi, Alex Kane, and Alan J. Marcus, (2003) *Essentials of Investments,* 5th Edition, Irwin/McGraw-Hill,
7. Gordon V. Smith, (1988) *Valuation: A Business and Professional Guide,* Wiley,
8. Imam, Shahed, Richard Barker and Colin Clubb. (2008), The Use of Valuation Models by UK Investment Analysts. *European Accounting Review.* 17(3):503-535
9. KennethS. Hackel, (2010) *Securty Valuation and Risk Analysis,* McGraw Hill.
10. Reed Lajoux, Robert A.G., G.Monk (2010), *Corporate Valuation for Portfolio Investment: Analyzing Assets, Earnings, Cash Flow, Stock Price, Governance, and Special Situations,* John Wiley & Sons,
11. Stephen Penman, (2009) *Financial Statement Analysis and Security Valuation,* McGraw-Hill/Irwin;
12. Stephen Ross, Randolph Westerfield, and Jeffery Jaffe, (1990) *Corporate Finance,* Irwin, 1990, pp. 115-130.
13. Tim Koller, Marc Goedhart, David Wessels,, (2005) McKinsy & Co Inc, *Valuation: Measuring and Managing the Value of Companies,* John Wiley & Sons, 2005
14. William F. Sharpe, *"Investments",* Prentice-Hall, 1978, pp. 300.

6
CHAPTER
Option Price Valuation

"Options are fairly priced. If you think you see money lying on the floor, don't pick it up. Chances are you're getting into a trade that you understand a lot less than a market maker does."

— Tony Battista

Learning Objectives

To understand:

- Options basics
- Options types
- Option value
- Option pricing models

Options enable investors to adapt or adjust their position according to any situation that arises. Options can be as speculative or as conservative as desired by investor. Options involve risks and are not suitable for everyone. Option trading can be speculative in nature and carry substantial risk of loss. Whether it is to hedge the risk of foreign-exchange transactions or to give employees ownership in the form of stock options, most leading global companies today use options in some form or another. Early examples include agricultural futures contracts dating back to 2000 B.C. in India and option contracts on ship cargoes created by ancient Phoenicians and Greeks. Options and futures contracts were used in 17th century markets in Amsterdam as well as in Osaka. Such securities have helped manufacturers, farmers, mining companies, traders and transporters manage a multiplicity of risks ranging from stock market volatility to borrower default. The markets for options are crucial to business for the management of many types of risks. Risk factors frequently hedged with derivatives include, but are not limited to uncertainties associated with interest and exchange rates, client default, economy-wide and industry specific output.

INTRODUCTION

An option is a contract to buy or sell a specific financial product in security market known as the option's underlying instrument or underlying interest. For equity options, the underlying instrument is a common stock. The contract establishes a specific price, called the strike price at which the contract may be or acted on before the expiry date. When an option expires, it carries no value. If, over the life of the contract, the asset value decreases, the buyer can simply elect not to exercise his/her right to buy/sell the asset. In general there are two types of option contracts; call options and put options. A call option gives the buyer the right to buy the underlying asset, while a put option gives the buyer the right to sell the underlying asset.

This can be illustrated as follows; Rama buys a Call option contract from Shiva. The contract states that Rama will buy 100 Tata shares from Shiva on the 01 October 2012 (5th May for ₹ 225) for ₹ 225. The current share price for TATA is ₹ 250. This is an example of a Call option as it gives Rama the right to buy the underlying asset.

If the share price of TATA is trading above ₹ 225 on 01 Oct 2012, then Rama will exercise the option and Shiva will have to sell him TATA shares for ₹ 225. With TATA trading anywhere above ₹ 225, Rama can make an instant profit by taking the shares from Shiva at the agreed price of ₹ 225 and then selling the shares on the open market for whatever the current share price is and making a profit.

The ₹ 225 value, which is stated in the agreement, is referred to as the Exercise (or Strike) Price. This is the price at which the asset will be exchanged.

The date (in this case 01 Oct 2012) is known as the Expiry (or Maturity) Date. This date is the deadline for the option contract. At this date, the option buyer is to decide if a transaction of the underlying asset is to occur. Let's imagine that at the expiration date, TATA is trading at ₹ 250, then Rama will buy the shares from Shiva at the agreed ₹ 225 and then he can sell them back on the open market for ₹ 250 and make an instant ₹ 25.

Alternatively, if TATA is trading at ₹ 200, then buying the shares from Shiva at ₹ 225 is too expensive as he can buy them on the open market for ₹ 200 and save ₹ 25. In this situation, Rama would choose not to exercise his right to buy the shares and let the options contract expire worthless. His only loss would be the amount that he paid to Shiva when he bought the contract, which is called the option premium. Shiva would, however, keep the option premium received from Rama as his profit.

In the real world of exchange traded options, transactions don't really take place between two people like as above. The process actually removes the identity of who is on the other side of the trade. One simply buys or sells an options contract from the 'Stocks Exchange' without knowing who is on the other side.

As an investor, one has to choose call or put option, i.e., whether to buy or sell and whether to choose a call or a put is based on what you want to achieve as an options investor. If you buy a call, you have the right to buy the underlying instrument at the strike price on or before the expiration date. If you buy a put, you have the right to sell the underlying instrument on or before expiration. In either case, as the option holder, you also have the right to sell the option to another buyer before it expires.

The simple examples so far have only been call options, i.e., giving you the right to buy the underlying asset. You're probably already thinking "what if I want to sell the shares instead of buy them at ₹ 225? That is why these two types of option contracts (Calls and Puts) exist. In the previous example, Rama bought a call option from Shiva. Rama also could have bought a put option from Shiva. Buying a put option means that Rama buys the right to sell TATA shares at ₹ 225 on the 01 Oct 2012. Therefore Rama will make a profit if the market is below ₹ 225 on the day of expiration. Buying put options enables investors to profit when the markets fall without having to sell short stock. Buyers of put options have unlimited profit potential if markets begin to sell off. Put option holders also have limited risk if the market goes against them, i.e., up.

The situation is different if you "sell to open", an option. Selling to open a short option position obligates you, the writer, to fulfill your side of the contract if the holder wishes to exercise. When you sell a call as an opening transaction, you're obligated to sell the underlying interest at the strike price, if you're assigned. When you sell a put as an opening transaction, you're obligated to buy the underlying interest, if assigned. As a writer, you have no control over whether or not a contract is exercised, and you need to recognize that exercise is always possible at any time until the expiration date. But just as the buyer can sell an option back into the market rather than exercising it, as a writer you can purchase an offsetting contract, provided you have not been assigned, and end your obligation to meet the terms of the contract. When offsetting a short option position, you would enter a "buy to close" transaction.

When an investor buys an option, the purchase price is called the premium. If you sell, the premium is the amount you receive. The premium is not fixed and changes constantly. Hence, so the premium investor pays today is likely to be higher or lower than the premium yesterday or tomorrow. What those changing prices reflect is the give and take between what buyers are willing to pay and what sellers are willing to accept for the option. The point at which agreement becomes the price for that transaction, and then the process begins again.

If investor buys options, he spent money which he will never recover if he does not sell option at a profit or exercise it. And if investor does make money on a transaction, he must subtract the cost of the premium from any income he realizes to find his net profit. On the other hand, as a seller, investor collects the premium. If the option is never exercised, investor keep the money. If the option is exercised, he still get to keep the premium, but are obligated to buy or sell the underlying stock if he is assigned.

A call option is in-the-money if the current market value of the underlying stock is above the exercise price of the option, and out-of-the-money if the stock is below the exercise price. A put option is in-the-money if the current market value of the underlying stock is below the exercise price and out-of-the-money if it is above it. If an option is not in-the-money at expiration, the option is assumed to be worthless.

An option's premium has two parts: an intrinsic value and a time value. Intrinsic value is the amount by which the option is in-the-money. Time value is the difference between whatever the intrinsic value is and what the premium is. The longer the amount of time for market conditions to work to, investor benefits the greater on the time value.

OPTION VALUE

The price of an options can be broken down into two parts: extrinsic value and intrinsic value. Intrinsic value is the portion of the option that can be realised if the option is exercised. Therefore, only in-the-money options have intrinsic value. This can be illustrated with the following example;

Underlying: TATA

Underlying Price: ₹ 250

Type: Call Option (Indian)

Strike Price: ₹ 225

Expiry Date: 01 Dec 2012

Now, imagine that this particular call option is currently trading at ₹ 50. How can we better understand this price?

Well, the first part we can look at is it's Intrinsic Value: the value of the option that, if exercised, would result in a profit. We know that the call option's strike price is ₹ 225 and with TATA trading at ₹ 250 it is already worth at least ₹ 25.

This is what's known as Intrinsic value - the value that can be made by exercising the option.

When an option is trading at more than the intrinsic value, the difference is known as Extrinsic Value, or more commonly known as Time Value. Looking at the previous example, we have already determined that the option is worth at least ₹ 25 its Intrinsic Value. However, it is actually trading at ₹ 50. The remaining ₹ 25 is called Extrinsic Value and represents the markets view of how far the underlying could trade as high as by the time the contract expires.

Sometimes an option can have zero Intrinsic Value but can still be worth something in the market. This is because traders believe that there is still some chance that the underlying could trade in a favorable direction, which would make the option profitable.

An option that has zero Intrinsic Value is said to be out-of-the-money, i.e., if you bought this call option and you exercised it, you would lose money by being assigned Tata shares at the exercise price ₹ 300, which is actually worth only ₹ 275 on the open market, leaving you with a loss of ₹ 25.

So, the call option has zero Intrinsic Value. Yet it's price in the market is ₹ 300. It simply means that because the option still has 6 months until expiry, there is still plenty of time for the option to exceed the hurdle of ₹ 300.

If the option expired tomorrow, it would have almost zero Extrinsic Value and zero Intrinsic Value - therefore being considered worthless. This is because the call option only has one day left for it to trade higher than ₹ 300 to give the trader a chance at making money from it. However, because the option doesn't expire for another 6 months, there are approximately 120 days (or 120 chances) that TATA has to trade another rupee higher and therefore turn this option into an in-the-money option.

Unlike stock investing, options have to take into account time and volatility. That's why valuing options premiums can seem difficult. The premium of a stock option depends partly on its relation to the underlying stock. This is signified by the option's strike price as related to the market price of the stock at the time of the option purchase. If the strike price of the option is equal to the current market price, the option is considered at the money. A call with a strike price above the market price or a put with a strike price below the market value is considered out of the money. It is out of the money because it would be worthless if it expired today.

For example, if investor buys a Reliance Ind ₹ 1200 call, but the price is ₹ 1100, it is out of the money. If investor buys a Reliance at ₹ 1200 put when the stock is at ₹ 1300, it is also out of the money, because he would not exercise either option. After all, why would an investor want to pay ₹ 1200 for a stock when he could get it for ₹ 1100. Conversely, why would an investor sell a stock for 1200 when people were willing to pay ₹ 1300 for it.

Investor buys an out-of-the-money option because he believes that given the volatility of the shares and the time he is guaranteed until expiration, the shares will move above ₹ 1200 and be in the money. That's when the call's strike price is below the current market price or the put's strike price is above the market price. The option now has intrinsic value – a calculable worth.

In-the-money-options usually have a higher premium than out-of-the- money options. But out-of-the-money options move far more rapidly in favor of the buyer, percentage-wise, than do in-the money options when the underlying price moves way investor wants. They also deteriorate more slowly than in the-money options if the underlying stock moves adversely, depending on the time until expiration.

If option prices were based on their intrinsic value alone, there would no reason to buy options other than for insurance or hedging purposes. An option's premium would be fixed. But beyond an option's intrinsic value is its extrinsic value, the worth of the premium represented by time and volatility.

Options have a fixed term of life and die a little everyday until they reach their expiration date. Unlike stock investors, option investors may not have time to recoup losses in a sudden turnaround. That risk can be reflected in the premium.

For example, in March an Investor is looking to buy more Reliance Ind. options. Currently the stock is at ₹ 1200, and he thinks it will go up to at least ₹ 1300, but he is not sure when. Well, he could buy a March ₹ 1300 call, or a December ₹ 1300 call. Both are calls on the same stock at the same strike price, but the premiums could still be different.

An option has no intrinsic value unless it is in the money. For the Reliance Ind ₹ 1300 call option to be in the money, it must go up by ₹ 100. The options now have three months (March) for the stock to go up ₹ 100 or 11 months, i.e., December. Most people would pick 11 months and would buy the December ₹ 1300 call, but it depends on when you expect the price to move and how much you are willing to pay for the extra time.

Options are speculative investments, and their value depends on supply and demand as just about anything you can buy and sell. Also, investor is willing to accept, more risk the more they're going to get paid for.

With more investors clamoring for the same option-and with writers having to accept greater risk-anything can happen in 11 months; less is likely to happen in three months so you can expect the premium on the longer-dated option to be higher. In, the longer the time until expiration, the more time the option has to meet investor's profit target. That's less risk for investor and that means a higher premium.

Investor has to keep in mind the break-even price while targeting for profit. That's the price the underlying investment must reach for to recoup his premium. He calculates the distance to the break-even price based on the price of the underlying instrument's shares, not the price he paid for the option.

For example, investor buy a Reliance in March ₹ 1300 call option for ₹ 50 a share (a premium of ₹ 5000). In order to recoup the premium, the stock would have to go up by ₹ 50 (above ₹ 1300 a share), so the break-even price is ₹ 1350 per share. Since investor has the right to buy 100 shares of Reliance at ₹ 1300 per share, a price of ₹ 1350 would gain investor ₹ 50 per share, or ₹ 5000 (₹ 50 times 100 shares). This equals the ₹ 5000 premium investor paid to buy the option. Any further increase in the stock price is profit, ₹100 for every rupee rise in the stock.

However, for a put, the opposite is done. Divide the premium by 100 and subtract it from the strike price. Once you figure out the break-even point, it's time to decide if the risks outweigh the potential rewards.

OPTIONS PRICING

There are many factors which affects the option prices. Factors such as supply and demand in the market where the option is traded, impacts the price of an option. The other factor is overall economic situation in the country. The identity of the underlying instrument, how it traditionally behaves, and what it is doing at the moment are more specific ones. Its volatility is also an important factor, as investors attempt to gauge how likely it is that an option will move in-the-money.

Option pricing models allow to value assets that otherwise would not be able to value. The examples are equity in deeply troubled firms with no revenues and profits are difficult to value using discounted cash flow approaches or with multiples. They can be valued using option pricing. Option pricing models provide a fresh insights into the drivers of value. For example more risk or variability can increase value rather than decrease it.

When an option is bought or sold, a profit or loss results from that trade. If investor were to make that same trade under identical conditions many times, then the theoretical value (fair value) of the option is the price that would result into investor's breaking even. The value of an option is based on several factors. A pricing model is then applied to these factors (assigning the numerical value) to calculate the theoretical value. One such pricing model for equity option was developed by Myron Scholes and Fisher Black developed. This model over the years is quite popular but needs the following inputs:

- **Stock price:** Higher the stock price, the more a call is worth. If stock price is lower a put is advisable.

- **Strike price:** Higher the strike price, the less a call (the more a put) is worth. The right to purchase the stock for a cheaper price is worth more than the right to buy it at a higher price.
- **Time to expiration:** Worth of an option is proportional to length of its expiry period left. With larger expiry period, the more any option is worth.
- **Interest rate:** Higher the interest rate, the more the call (less the put) is worth. This is because a call buyer uses less cash to buy the call than he would use to buy stock, and the difference can be invested to earn interest. The more interest earned, the more a call buyer is willing to pay for the option.
- **Dividend:** Dividends reduce the price of the stock. In general ex-dividend, stock price is decreased by the amount of the dividend. The higher the dividend, the less a call is worth, and the more a put is worth.
- **Volatility:** Volatility used in the model is an forecast of the potential price movement that will occur during the life of the option. The higher the volatility, the more any option is worth because a high volatility increases the probability that the option will make a large favorable move for the holder of the option. In case of unfavorable loss to option holder is limited to the price paid for the option. The change in the volatility estimate changes the value of an option by a large amount as volatility is a difficult factor to estimate. There is more than one type of volatility. 'Historical Volatility' is calculated by measuring the stock's past price movements. When dealing with options, you want to know the volatility the stock is going to have from the time the option is purchased (or sold) until expiration. That volatility can never be known, because the time frame is the future. Thus, the best we can do is estimate that future volatility. That estimate is based upon more than the volatility history of the stock. The term used to describe the estimated future volatility is forecast volatility. When we look at option prices, we use a different term: implied volatility. It is the estimate, made by professional traders in the marketplace, of the future volatility of the stock.

In options pricing it is important to distinguish between an option premium and the theoretical or fair value of an option. An option premium is the price which an option buyer and seller agree to when they enter into an option contract; it is a function of supply and demand. The fair value of an option is a price derived from a mathematical model. It is the price at which both the buyer and the seller of an option should expect to break even. Therefore, fair value is an estimate of where an option should sell in an efficient market.

OPTION PRICING MODELS

An option pricing model is a mathematical formula or model wherein the value against each of the following is inserted to get the theoretical fair value of the option:

- underlying stock or index price;
- exercise price of the option;
- expiry date of the option;
- expected dividends to be paid over the life of the option

- expected risk free interest rate over the life of the option;
- expected volatility of the underlying stock or index over option life;

When the formula is applied to these variables, the resulting figure is called the theoretical fair value of the option.

The models that are commonly used for pricing derivative might be divided into two main classes. The first classes is the models that provide analytical formula to get the risk neutral price under some reasonable assumptions. The Black-Scholes formula is in this group. The formulae that we have to price the derivatives are quite limited. The reason is that an attempt is done to solve a partial differential equation at the end of the day. But mathematician could manage to solve just some of the partial differential equations; therefore, analyst is bounded to find some limited solutions.

The second classes of models provide numerical procedures to price the option. Binomial trees that first suggested by Cox, Ross and Rubenstein, is in this group, because one needs to follow a procedure called "backwards induction" to get option price. Monte Carlo simulations are another type of models that belongs to this class. Also finite differencing methods are a type of numerical class.

The Black-Scholes model and the Cox, Ross and Rubinstein binomial model are the primary pricing models used in option pricing. Both models are based on the same theoretical foundations and assumptions (such as the geometric Brownian motion theory of stock price behaviour and risk-neutral valuation). However, there are also some important differences between the two models is discussed below.

- **Black-Scholes Model**

The Black-Scholes model, for European options (options exercisable only at maturity) on non-dividend paying stocks, was published in 1973. Black and Scholes determined that, under certain assumptions, it is possible to set up a perfectly hedged or riskless position consisting of a long position in an underlying stock and a short position in options on that stock (or vice versa) such that any profit resulting from an instantaneous increase in the stock price would be exactly offset by a loss on the option position, or vice versa. The option premium at which this equilibrium condition obtains is the fair value of the option.

In 1973, Fischer Black and Myron Scholes developed a precise model for determining the equilibrium value of an option. Until this model, analysts were unable to develop a method of putting an accurate price on options, the future right to buy or sell assets. The problem was how to evaluate the risk associated with options, when the underlying stock price changes from moment to moment.

According to Black and Scholes, the risk of the option is reflected in the stock price itself. The stock price includes market participants' expectations about the future of the company that issued the stock. The insight allowed Black and Scholes to create a pricing formula that included the stock price, the agreed sale or 'strike' price of the option, the stock's volatility, the time until the option's expiration, and the risk-free interest rate offered on an alternative investment. Black and Scholes model is based on assumption that an option can be exercised only at maturity, with no transaction costs or market imperfections, on a stock which pays no dividend and whose stock price follows a random pattern. The model is as follows:

$$C = SN(d_1) - Ke^{[-rt]}(d_2)$$

Where:

C = Value of the option

S = Current price of stock

t = the length of time in years to the expiration of the option

K = Option striking price

r = the short-term interest rate continuously compounded

N = Cumulative Standard Normal Distribution

e = Exponential constant (2.7183)

$$d_1 = \frac{\ln(S/K) + (r + sd^2/2)t}{sd\sqrt{t}}$$

$$d_2 = d_1 - sd\sqrt{t}$$

sd = Standard deviation of stock returns

ln = Natural Logarithm

The fair value of an option has two components: intrinsic value and time value. Intrinsic value is the sum of money that would be realized if the option were exercised today. Time value reflects the potential risky changes in the price of the underlying instrument from today until expiration. Fair value is a function of five variables: price of the underlying instrument, time to expiration, strike price, interest rate and volatility.

For a call option, intrinsic value is the amount by which the price of the underlying instrument exceeds the option striking price; for a put option, it is the amount by which the price of the underlying instrument is less than the striking price. For a fixed striking price, the intrinsic value and fair value of a call option increase, rupee for rupee, with increases in the underlying instrument price; conversely, the intrinsic value and fair value of a put option increase as the underlying instrument price declines. Intrinsic value may not be less than zero, as the option buyer is under no obligation to exercise at a loss. An option that has some intrinsic value is said to be in-the-money; an option that has no intrinsic value is said to be out-of-the-money. An option whose strike price is equal to the market price is said to be at-market. Time value is determined by the interrelationship of all the key option variables:

- Time to expiration.
- Underlying instrument price vs. strike price.
- Interest rates.
- Volatility.

Volatility has the largest impact on time value and fair value of any of the variables mentioned. Yet, it is the one variable which cannot be stipulated from contract terms or inherent market prices. It is relatively easy to calculate a volatility based on a history of underlying prices, but history, while a good reference, may not always be an adequate predictor of the future. The ideal volatility is that which will correctly predict the magnitude of price fluctuations during the life of an option. Ultimately, this is a matter of judgment.

One of the preferred methods of determining volatility is to look to the option market itself. For an actively traded option with a strike price at or near the market, arbitrage opportunities will keep the market price generally in line. It is reasonable to assume that the market price for such a liquid option is "fair". Then by iterative solution, it can be determind the value of volatility that will cause an option model to yield a fair value equal to the observed market price. This volatility is called the implied volatility. If the implied volatility is then used to calculate fair values of all options, the resultant fair values will be consistent with the originally selected liquid option's fair value, and market opportunities relative to the selected option will be apparent. The hedge equilibrium condition which is the basis for the Black-Scholes model leads to two additional significant relationships: the hedge ratio or delta, and put-call parity.

➢ Hedge Ratio/Delta

The delta is the first derivative of option value with respect to underlying price and describes how much the option value will move for each unit move in the price of the underlying instrument. A delta of 0.5 means that for each one cent move of the underlying instrument, the option will move a half cent in the same direction. Thus, a delta-neutral position appropriate for a 0.5 delta consisting, say, of two short IMM DM options and one long IMM DM futures contract will change very little in value if the futures contract goes up or down one cent. Large moves of the underlying commodity change the delta, however; so, to maintain a neutral hedge, it is necessary periodically to re-balance options and underlying contracts. The option seller should use the delta to manage his short option position so that he is covered if he receives an unexpected assignment.

➢ Put/Call Parity

The hedge equilibrium condition also leads to the put/call parity relationship. Put/call parity provides that a put option can be converted to a call option having the same strike and expiration if it is combined with a long underlying instrument position (for the same quantity). Conversely a call option can be converted to a put option if combined with a short underlying instrument position.

For example, a put option on 1 million Swiss francs with a strike of 55 cents and expiration date of January 1st plus a sale of 1 million Swiss francs for January 1st at a price of 55 cents, is equivalent to a call option on 1 million Swiss francs with a strike of 55 cents and expiration date of January 1st.The reciprocal nature of this relationship means that for European cash options, the deltas for a put and call option for the same strike and maturity will always add up to exactly one. It should also be noted that the deltas for an at-market European cash call and put option pair, while summing to 1.0, nevertheless are not each 0.5. That is, they are not equally likely to be exercised. There are two reasons for this: first, the lognormal price distribution assumed in the model assumes an upward bias; that is, prices can move up infinitely, but cannot move below zero. Second, any non-zero interest rate has the effect, over time, of pushing underlying prices up because of the costs of financing the underlying instrument.

For European options on futures, the deltas add up to less than one. This is so because the expected value of a futures contract is today's futures price and, in taking the first derivative of the option value formula, a present value term is applied to the delta, discounting the value from maturity to the present time. (At maturity, then, the deltas will add up to one.)

For American options, which may be exercised early, and for which both the call and put for a given strike and maturity may yield a profit and be exercised at different times, the deltas may add up to more or less than one. Strictly speaking, because of early and independent exercise, put/call parity does not apply to American options.

If there are payouts against the underlying instrument, such as stock dividends, bond coupon yields or commodity interest rate differential (domestic vs. foreign), fair value, delta calculations and parity relationships are even more complex. With currencies, for example, both the spot and forward price must be taken into consideration; so long as the interest rate differential is not zero, these prices will be different. If forward prices for a commodity are at a premium to spot, calls will be based on the forward prices while puts will be based on spot. Conversely, if forward prices for a commodity are at a discount to spot, calls will be based on spot and puts will be based on the forward prices.

➢ Noreen-Wolfson Option Model

The Black-Scholes Option Model does not account for dividends or for the dilution associated with the issuance of new stock. In 1981, Eric Noreen and Mark Wolfson adapted the Black-Scholes Model for use in valuing executive stock options.

➢ Other European Models

The Black-Scholes model has been the foundation for most other option valuation models that have been developed subsequently. The model has been adjusted for stocks with dividends and physical commodities with carrying costs. Black adapted the model to European options on futures on the basis of the spot/forward price relationship in a full carry market. More recently, Garman and Kohlhagen described an adaptation of the Black-Scholes model for options on foreign currencies, wherein the foreign interest rate, domestic interest rate, and the interest rate differential are appropriately used in the calculation. Thus, with appropriate modifications to account for dividends, interest rates, or carrying costs, the Black-Scholes model has proven to be an appropriate basis for valuing European-type options on physical commodities, financial instruments, and currencies, as well as stocks.

With regard to futures options, the futures prices contain the statistical information about foreign interest rates (or dividends, or coupon, or physical carrying cost) as well as subjective and intuitive factors that do not need to be modeled. Therefore, the appropriate underlying futures price can be used directly, and no correction for dividends, coupon, or foreign interest rate needs to be provided for. Black's 1976 futures option model is appropriate for valuation of European options on futures.

➢ American Options

In the commodity markets, over-the-counter options are usually European. But nearly all exchange-traded options are American-type options. An American-type option allows the option holder to exercise the option at any time prior to expiration. This characteristic produces additional risks for the option writer, and additional opportunities for the option buyer.

For American put options on physical instruments, and for both American calls and puts on futures, early exercise may be advantageous. It may be worth more to the option holder to take a certain profit early and invest the proceeds than to forego the use of the funds until expiration.

Whereas the Black-Scholes European option model and most of its derivatives can easily be programmed, American-type option valuation is much more complex. In fact, there has been no accepted closed-form solution to the general case of valuing American options. The mathematical approaches generally used, such as the binomial method, involve extensive iteration and require substantial computational power.

But American call options on physical (cash) instruments are rarely exercised early. It has been shown that the value of an American physical call option is always at least as great as the value it would have if exercised immediately. This has given rise to the expression that an American physical call option is "worth more alive than dead". Thus, a rational investor will not exercise an American physical call option early.

To handle American option pricing in an efficient manner other models have been developed as follows:

Roll, Geske and Whaley (RGW) analytic solution: The RGW formula can be used for pricing an American call on a stock paying discrete dividends. Because it is an analytic solution it is relatively fast.

Black's approximation for American calls: Although the RGW formula is an analytic solution it involves solving equations iteratively and thus it is slower than Black-Scholes. Black's approximation basically involves using the Black-Scholes model after making adjustments to the stock price and expiration date to take account of early exercise.

Barone-Adesi and Whaley quadratic approximation: An analytic solution for American puts and calls paying a continuous dividend. Like the RGW formula it involves solving equations iteratively so whilst it is much faster than the binomial model it is still much slower than Black-Scholes.

➢ Binomial Option Pricing Model

First proposed by Cox, Ross and Rubinstein in a paper published in 1979, this solution to pricing an option is probably the most common model used for equity calls and puts today.

The model divides the time to an option's expiry into a large number of intervals, or steps. At each interval it calculates that the stock price will move either up or down with a given probability and also by an amount calculated with reference to the stock's volatility, the time to expiry and the risk free interest rate. A binomial distribution of prices for the underlying stock or index is thus produced.

At expiry the option values for each possible stock price are known as they are equal to their intrinsic values. The model then works backwards through each time interval, calculating the value of the option at each step. At the point where a dividend is paid (or other capital adjustment made) the model takes this into account. The final step is at the current time and stock price, where the current theoretical fair value of the option is calculated.

The number of steps in the model determines its speed, however most home PCs today can easily handle a model with 100 or so steps, which gives a sufficient level of accuracy for calculating a theoretical fair value.Both of the previous models value "European" options. They are applicable where the holder of the option can exercise the option only on its maturity date. However, most executive stock options ("ESOs") are "American" options where the option holder can execute the option at any time up to and including the maturity date. Also, executive stock options normally are not transferable and can be exercised only while the executive is employed by the firm.

The binomial model breaks down the time to expiration into potentially a very large number of time intervals, or steps. A tree of stock prices is initially produced working forward from the present to expiration. At each step it is assumed that the stock price will move up or down by an amount calculated using volatility and time to expiration.

This produces a binomial distribution, or recombining tree, of underlying stock prices. The tree represents all the possible paths that the stock price could take during the life of the option. At the end of the tree - i.e. at expiration of the option - all the terminal option prices for each of the final possible stock prices are known as they simply equal their intrinsic values.

European option with an underlying stock price of ₹ 100 and an exercise price of ₹100. Taking into account the volatility and risk-free rates, over five years the price may be between ₹ 57.20 and ₹ 174.90.

Next the option prices at each step of the tree are calculated working back from expiration to the present. The option prices at each step are used to derive the option prices at the next step of the tree using risk neutral valuation based on the probabilities of the stock prices moving up or down, the risk-free rate, and the time interval of each step.

The main advantage of the binomial model as compared to the Black-Scholes Option Model is that it can be used to accurately price American options. It's possible to check at every point in an option's life (e.g. at every step of the binomial tree) for the possibility of early exercise. Where an exercise point is found it is assumed that the option holder would elect to exercise, and the option price can be adjusted to equal the intrinsic value at that point.

The same underlying assumptions regarding stock prices underpin both the binomial and Black-Scholes models - that stock prices follow a stochastic process described by geometric Brownian motion. As a result, for European options, the binomial model converges to the Black-Scholes formula as the number of binomial calculation steps increases.

FAIR VALUE AND MARKET PRICE

Although the fair value may be close to where the market is trading, other pricing factors in the marketplace mean fair value is used mostly as an estimate of the option's value.

Moreover, fair value will depend on the assumptions regarding volatility levels, dividend payments and so on that are made by the person using the pricing model. Different expectations of volatility or dividends will alter the fair value result. This means that at any given time there may be many views held simultaneously on what the fair value of a particular option is.

In practice, supply and demand will often dictate at what level an option is priced in the marketplace. Traders may calculate fair value on a option to get an indication of whether the current market price is higher or lower than fair value, as part of the process of making a judgment about the market value of the option.

VOLATILITY

The volatility figure input into an option pricing model reflects the assumptions of the person using the pricing model. Volatility is defined technically in various ways, depending on assumptions made about the underlying asset's price distribution. For the regular option trader it is sufficient to know that the volatility a trader assigns to a stock reflects expectations of how the stock price will fluctuate over a given period of time. Volatility is usually expressed in two ways: historical and implied.

Historical volatility describes volatility observed in a stock over a given period of time. Price movements in the stock (or underlying asset) are recorded at fixed time intervals (for example every day, every week, or every month) over a given period. More data generally leads to more accuracy.

Be aware that a stock's past volatility may not necessarily be reproduced in the future. Caution should be used in basing estimates of future volatility on historical volatility. In estimating future volatility, a frequently used compromise is to assume that volatility over a coming period of time will be the same as measured/historical volatility for that period of time just finished. Thus if you want to price a three month option, you may use three month historical volatility.

Implied volatility relates to the current market for an option. Volatility is implied from the option's current price, using a standard option pricing model. Keeping all other inputs constant, you can put the current market price of an option into any theoretical option price calculator and it will calculate the volatility implied by that option price.

This is one of the key figures traders watch to assist them in assessing the value of an option. It is also commonly fed back into the option pricing model to calculate the option's theoretical fair value.

"GREEKS" - IN OPTION PRICING

Options prices and changes in these prices are measured by six indicators called GREEKS. The six Greeks are DELTA, GAMMA, THETA, VEGA, RHO and ZETA.

- **DELTA** - measures the rate at which an option price will change relative to the stock price. It represents speed.
- **GAMMA** - measures the rate at which DELTA changes. It is equivalent to acceleration.
- **THETA** - measures the rate of change of time value
- **VEGA** - measures the historical volatility.
- **RHO** - measures the sensitivity of the option price relative to changes in the Risk Free Interest Rate. This factor does not need to interest option traders.
- **ZETA** - is a measure of implied volatility

For selling options investor should understand the concept of Time Value and Time Decay. Investor can keep an eye on Theta, but if he can count the number of weeks on one hand until expiration, he is in a good place to sell options. Knowing about volatility (in general) helps because high volatility stocks give better option premiums and therefore better profits (and slightly higher risk).

If investor is buying options he needs to understand; Intrinsic Value, Time Value, Delta and Volatility. He can choose Options to maximise the leverage of DELTA or choose Options to maximise the leverage of Intrinsic Value. He needs to know about Time Decay so that he gives option enough time to move, but also to understand that as long as he holds on to that option, Time is eating away at profits. Finally, volatility (measured by VEGA and ZETA) helps investor to find a good entry point so that he buys options that are cheap or at fair value, and sell when they are expensive. If investor trade volatility trades, such as strangles and straddles, then he needs to know the working of volatility.

Stock Option Valuation (options pricing) is a complex topic and probably one of the toughest concepts investor will encounter. Stock options are very different from shares of stock. They have very specific and unique characteristics. It is these characteristics that are going to determine about making a profit from the purchase of the option.

There are several components to stock option valuation (options pricing) for investor. The option price does not always move in relationship with the price of the underlying stock. There are following factors involved that determine the price/cost of the option:

- Current market price of the stock
- Strike price of the option (in relation to the current stock price)
- Remaining life of the option (period until expiration)
- Volatility
- Interest rates
- Stock Dividends

When the stock price "increases" a Call options' premium will "increase", but a Put options' premium will "decrease". When the stock price "decreases" a Call options' premium will "decrease", and the Put options' premium will "increase". In nutshell the "Call options" their price follows the direct movement of the stock price. If the stock moves up so will the Call options premium. If the stock price moves down the Call option will begin to lose value. Put options are the exact opposite. Only two factors that an investor has any control over are time to expiration and the strike price.

SUMMARY

An option contract is an agreement between two parties to buy/sell an asset (stock or futures contract) at a fixed price and fixed date in the future. It is called an option because the buyer is not obliged to carry out the transaction. If, over the life of the contract, the asset value decreases, the buyer can simply elect not to exercise his/her right to buy/sell the asset. In general there are two types of option contracts; call options and put options. A Call Option gives the buyer the right to buy the underlying asset, while a Put Option gives the buyer the right to sell the underlying asset.

The Black-Scholes model is used to calculate a theoretical call price (ignoring dividends paid during the life of the option) using the five key determinants of an option's price: stock price, strike price, volatility, time to expiration, and short-term (risk free) interest rate. Opting Pricing Model was first proposed by Black and Scholes in a paper published in 1973. The Model is an analytic solution to pricing a European option on a non dividend paying asset. This model further formed the foundation for much theory in derivatives finance. The Black Scholes formula is a continuous time analogue of the binomial model. The Black Scholes formula uses the pricing inputs. It is analytically produce a theoretical fair value for an option. The model has many variations which attempt, with varying levels of accuracy, to incorporate dividends under American market conditions. However, with computing power these days the binomial solution is more widely used.

Review Questions

1. What do mean by 'Options'?
2. Which are the parameter's considered in Option Valuation?
3. Discuss the various option pricing model used in market.
4. Explain in details Balck-Scholes Model for option pricing with illustrations

Video Links

1. http://www.youtube.com/watch?v=_UN4s4WceOs, Stock Options
2. http://www.youtube.com/watch?v=cSFFLDA_96U&feature=related, Understanding Stock Options - Part 1
3. http://www.youtube.com/watch?v=IsuqiQZlJzc, Indian Future & Option Basic

ASSIGNMENT

Select a loss making heavy engineering firm or new biotechnology firm with heavy debts registered with stock markets and work out option price using Black Scholes Model.

BIBLIOGRAPHY

1. Alan L. Lewis, (2000), *Option Valuation Under Stochastic Volatility: With Mathematical Code,* Finance Press (February 1, 2000)
2. Desmond Higham, (2004) *An Introduction to Financial Option Valuation: Mathematics, Stochastics and Computation,* Cambridge University Press
3. Krishna G. Palepu, Paul M. Healy, Erik Peek, Victor Lewis Bernard, (2007), *Business Analysis and Valuation: Text and Cases,* Cengage Learning EMEA,
4. L. Andersen and M. Broadie (2001): *'A Primal-Dual Simulation Algorithm for Pricing Multi-Dimensional American Options',* Working paper, Columbia University.

5. Neil A. Chriss, Ira Kawaller, (1996) *Black-Scholes and Beyond: Option Pricing Models,* McGraw-Hill;

6. Sheldon Natenberg, (1984), *Option Volatility & Pricing: Advanced Trading Strategies and Techniques,* McGraw-Hill NY

7. Zhang, P., (1998). *Exotic Options,* 2nd Edition. World Scientific Publishing, River Edge, NJ.

7 CHAPTER

Valuation in Mergers and Acquisitions

> *"Acquisition valuations are complex, because the valuation often involved issues like synergy and control, which go beyond just valuing a target firm."*
>
> **— Aswath Damodaran**

Learning Objectives

To understand:

- Understanding M&A valuation
- Challenges in M&A valuations
- Key concerns during valuation
- Success factors
- Mathematics of valuation

Merger and Acquisition decision is an investment decision. This is the most important decision, which influences both the acquiring firm and the target firm, which is to be acquired. An organization cannot make that crucial decision without sharp and detailed analysis by financial planners and analyst. The acquiring firm must correctly value the firm to be acquired and the acquired firm must get the returns for the goodwill they have created over the years in the market. Growth through acquisition is occurring in an unprecedented number of companies today as strategic acquisitions replace the once-prevalent hostile takeovers by corporate raiders. In the current business environment, it is vital to understand how to blend strategic and financial concepts to evaluate potential acquisition.

INTRODUCTION

In merger one firm absorbs the assets and liabilities of the other firm. The acquiring firm retains its identity. In many cases, control is shared between the management teams of two companies. Financially an entirely new firm is created. Merger is approved by the shareholders through voting. In acquisition larger corporation purchases the assets or stocks of a smaller corporation, while control remained exclusively with the larger corporation. Transactions that bypass the management are considered hostile, as the target firm's managers are generally opposed to the deal. In reality, there is always a bidder and a target. Almost all transactions could be classified as acquisitions. There are other two transactions; one is divestiture which is a transaction in which a firm sells one of its subsidiaries or divisions to another firm. The other one is spin-off in which a firm either sells or issues all or part of its subsidiaries to its existing public investors, by issuing public equity.

In India over the years after the liberalization of Economy in 1991, the numbers as well as the average size of merger and acquisition deals are increasing. During post liberalization, increase in domestic competition and competition against cheaper imports have made organizations merge themselves to reap the benefits of a large-sized company. However, in the merger and acquisition, valuation is the building block of a proposed deal.

M&A valuation involves determining the maximum price that a buyer is willing to pay to buy the target company. From the seller's point of view, it means estimating the minimum price he wants to take against his business. If there are many buyers, then each one bids a purchase price based on his valuation. Finally, the seller will give the business to the highest bidder.

The valuation is not totally objective process. The use of different valuation techniques and principles using assumptions has made valuation a subjective process. The different techniques used in valuation processes are some time conflicting. For example, the asset value can be determined both at the market price and the cost price. Therefore, it is essential that the merging parties should first discuss and agree upon the methods of valuation.

Calculating the swap ratio is at the core of the valuation process. It is the ratio at which the shares of the acquiring company will be exchanged with the shares of the acquired company. For instance, a swap ratio of 1:2 means, that the acquiring company will provide its one share for every two shares of the other company.

MERGER AND ACQUISITION

A merger is a combination of two corporations in which only one corporation survives and the merged corporation goes out of subsistence. Alternatively, in merger two corporations combine and share their resources in order to accomplish mutual objectives and both companies bring together their own shareholders, employees, customers and the community at large. Acquisition takes place when one firm is purchasing the assets or shares of another company.

Mergers are often categorised as horizontal, vertical, or conglomerate. A horizontal merger is one that takes place between two firms in the same line of business whereas vertical merger involves companies at different stages of production. The buyer expands backwards in the direction of the source of the raw material or forward in the direction of the customer. The last one, i.e., conglomerate merger involves companies in unrelated line of business.

The scale and the pace at which merger activities are coming up are remarkable. The recent booms in merger and acquisitions suggest that the organisations are spending a significant amount of time and money either searching for firms to acquire or worrying about whether some other firm will acquire them. Also, mergers are regarded as one of the activities the purpose of business expansion or a measure of external growth in contrast to internal growths. The recent booms in mergers and acquisitions would increase at a much faster rate in near future. The reason for this is the world markets are becoming more integrated due open trade policies between countries. Hence, more and more companies are adopting and forming strategic alliances in order to compete in the competitive world and to maintain their market shares.

Acquisition refers to the process of acquiring a company at the acquisition price or acquisition premium. The price is paid in terms of cash or acquiring company's shares or both. There are two types of business acquisitions, friendly acquisition and hostile acquisition. In a friendly acquisition, a company invites other companies to acquire its business. In a hostile acquisition, the company does not want to sell its business. However, the other company determined to acquire the business takes the aggressive route of buying the equity shares of the target company from its existing shareholders.

As the motive is to takeover someone else's business, the acquiring company offers to buy the shares at a very high premium, that is, the gaining difference between the offer price and the market price of the share. This motivates the shareholders and they sell their stake to earn quick money. This way the acquiring company gets the majority stake and takes over the ownership control of the target company.

Acquiring an existing business enables a company to speed up its expansion process because they do not have to start from the very scratch. The target company is already established and has all the processes in place. The acquiring company simply has to focus on merging the business with its own and move ahead with its growth strategies. However, in reality, it is not as simple as it seems. Most of the acquisitions fail miserably due to poor implementation attitude and strategies.

There are many types of mergers and acquisitions that redefine the business world with new strategic alliances and improved corporate philosophies. From the business structure perspective, some of the most common and significant types of mergers and acquisitions are listed in the following table:

Exhibit 7.1 Types of Mergers and Acquisitions

Merger Type	What it Means?
Horizontal	It exists between two companies who compete in the same industry segment. They leverage on the two companies combined operations and skills leading to improved performance, increased capital, and enhanced profits. In this, the numbers of competitors are reduced and gives a higher edge over competition
Vertical	Vertical merger is a kind in which two or more companies in the same industry but in different fields combine together in business. In this form, the

	companies in merger decide to combine all the operations and productions under one shelter. It is like encompassing all the requirements and products of a single industry segment.
Co-generic	In this two or more companies in association are some way or the other related to the production processes, business markets, or basic required technologies. This offers great opportunities to businesses as it opens avenues to diversify around a common set of resources and strategic requirements.
Conglomerate Merger	In this two or more companies belonging to different industrial sectors combine their operations. This is just a unification of businesses from different verticals under one flagship enterprise or firm.
Amalgamation	Amalgamation is an arrangement where two or more companies consolidate their business to form a new firm, or become a subsidiary of any one of the company. Merger involves the fusion of two or more companies into a single company where the identity of some of the companies gets dissolved. On the other hand, amalgamation involves dissolving the entities of amalgamating companies and forming a new company having a separate legal entity. There are two types of amalgamations. The first one is similar to a merger where all the assets and liabilities and shareholdings of the two companies are combined together. The accounting treatment is done using the pooling of interests method. The second type of amalgamation involves acquisition of one company by another company. In this, the shareholders of the acquired company may not have the same equity rights as earlier, or the business of the acquired company may be discontinued. The accounting treatment is done using a purchase method. It involves recording assets and liabilities at their existing values or re-valuating them on the basis of their fair values at the time of amalgamation

M&A VALUATION METHODS

There are a number of company valuation methods in M & A. While the most common is discounted cash flow. It is always best to go for a number of alternative methods, and compare their results to see if finally the figure arrived is approximately is more or less same or with little deviation. However, for two types of companies DCF method is inadequate for valuating them. The first ones are the newer target companies with minimal historical results wherein the cash flow is an inadequate basis for valuation. Other ones are companies which are growing fast and all of their cash is being used for growth. Following are a few methods used in M&A company valuation.

➢ **Stock Market Price:** If the target company is publicly held, then the buyer can simply base its valuation on the current market price per share, multiplied by the number of shares outstanding. The actual price paid is usually higher, since the buyer must also account for the control premium. The current trading price of a company's stock is not a good valuation tool if the stock is thinly traded. In this case, a small number of trades can alter the market price to a substantial extent, so that the buyer's estimate is far off from the value it would normally assign to the target. Most target companies do not issue publicly traded stock, so other methods must be used to derive their valuation.

When a private company wants to be valued using a market price, it can adopt the unusual ploy of filing for an initial public offering while also being courted by the buyer. By doing so, the buyer is forced to make an offer that is near the market valuation at which the target expects its stock to be traded. If the buyer declines to bid that high, then the target still has the option of going public and realizing value by selling shares to the general public. The stock lockup periods (as per SEBI) is required for many new public companies, here the target shareholders are usually more than willing to accept a buyout offer if the price is reasonably close to the target's expected market value.

➢ **Revenue Multiple:** Another option is to use a revenue multiple or EBITDA multiple. It is quite easy to find the market capitalizations and financial information for publicly held companies. The buyer then converts this information into a multiples table, which itemizes a selection of valuations within the industry. The table should be restricted to comparable companies in the same industry as that of the seller, and of roughly the same market capitalization. If some of the information for other companies is unusually high or low, then eliminate these outlying values in order to obtain a median value for the company's size range. Also, it is better to use a multi-day average of market prices, since these figures are subject to significant daily fluctuation.

The buyer can then use this table to derive an approximation of the price to be paid for a target company. For example, if a target has sales of ₹ 120 Crores, and the market capitalization for several public companies in the same revenue range is 1.25 times revenue, then the buyer could value the target at ₹ 150 Crores. This method is most useful for a turn-around situation or a fast growth company, where there are few profits avenues. However, the revenue multiple method only pays attention to the first line of the income statement and completely ignores profitability. To avoid the risk of paying too much based on a revenue multiple, it is also possible to compile an EBITDA (i.e., earnings before interest, taxes, depreciation, and amortization) multiple for the same group of comparable public companies, and use that information to value the target.

It is advisable to use both the revenue multiple and the EBITDA multiple in concert. If the revenue multiple reveals a high valuation and the EBITDA multiple a low one, then it is entirely possible that the target is essentially buying revenues with low-margin products or services, or extending credit to financially weak customers. Conversely, if the revenue multiple yields a lower valuation than the EBITDA multiple, this is more indicative of a late-stage company that is essentially a cash cow, or one where management is cutting costs to increase profits, at the expense of revenue growth.

If the comparable company provides one-year projections, then the revenue multiple can be re-named a trailing multiple (for historical 12-month revenue), and the forecast can be used as the basis for a forward multiple (for projected 12-month revenue). The forward multiple gives a better estimate of value, because it incorporates expectations about the future. The forward multiple should only be used if the forecast is issued by a public company. The company knows that its stock price will drop if it does not achieve its forecast, so the forecast is unlikely to be aggressive.

Revenue multiples are the best technique for valuing high-growth companies, as these companies have minimal profits to report. Such companies have very high value, but it is not revealed/reflected in their profitability figure. Sometimes, multiples can be misleading. When acquisitions occur within an industry, the best financial performers with the fewest underlying problems are the choicest acquisition targets, and therefore will be acquired first. When other companies in the same area later put themselves up for sale, they will use the earlier multiples to justify similarly high prices. However, because they may have lower market shares, higher cost structures, older products, and so on, the multiples may not be valid. Thus, it is important to know some of the underlying characteristics of the companies that were previously sold, to see if the comparable multiple should be applied to the current target company.

➢ **Enterprise Value:** Another method is to work out enterprise value. The enterprise value is a company's market capitalization, plus its total debt outstanding, minus any cash on hand. In essence, it is a company's theoretical takeover price, because the buyer would have to buy all of the stock and pay off existing debt, while pocketing any remaining cash.

➢ **Valuation Based on Comparable Transactions:** Another way to value an acquisition is to use a database of comparable transactions to determine what was paid for other recent acquisitions. Investment bankers have access to this information through a variety of private databases. The information can also be collected online through public filings or press releases.

➢ **Real Estate Values:** The buyer can also derive a valuation based on a target's underlying real estate values. This method only works well in case target companies having a larger real estate portfolio. In case of retailing industry, the store at prime location fetch large cash which sometimes greater that product sales. In cases where the business is financially troubled, it is entirely possible that the purchase price is based entirely on the underlying real estate, with the operations of the business itself being valued at essentially zero. The buyer then uses the value of the real estate as the primary reason for completing the deal.

➢ **Product Development Costs:** If a target has products that the buyer could develop in-house, then an alternative valuation method is to compare the cost of in-house development to the cost of acquiring the completed product through the target. This type of valuation is especially important if the market is expanding rapidly right now, and the buyer will otherwise forgo sales if it takes the time to pursue an in-house development path. In this case, the proper valuation technique is to combine the cost of an in-house development effort with the present value of profits foregone by waiting to complete the in-house project. Interestingly, this is the only valuation technique where most of the source material comes from the buyer's financial statements, rather than those of the seller.

➢ **Liquidation Value:** The most conservative valuation method of all is the liquidation value method. This is an analysis of what the selling entity would be worth if all of its assets were to be sold off. This method assumes that the ongoing value of the company as a business entity is eliminated, leaving the individual auction prices at which its fixed assets, properties, and other assets can be sold off, less any outstanding liabilities. It is useful for the buyer to at least estimate this number, so that it can determine its downside risk in case it completes the acquisition, but the acquired business then fails subsequently.

➢ **Replacement Cost:** The replacement value method yields a somewhat higher valuation than the liquidation value method. Under this approach, the buyer calculates what it would cost to duplicate the target company. The analysis addresses the replacement of the seller's key infrastructure. This can yield surprising results if the seller owns infrastructure that originally required lengthy regulatory approval. For example, if the seller owns a chain of restaurants that are located on government property, it is essentially impossible to replace them at all, or only at vast expense. An additional factor in this analysis is the time required to replace the target. If the time period for replacement is considerable, the buyer may be forced to pay a premium in order to gain quick access to a key market.

While all of the above methods can be used for valuation, they usually supplement the primary method, which is the discounted cash flow method.

Illustration.....

Equity Valuation- Ameya Engineering Ltd (AEL) acquires Bala Metals Ltd (BML).

Assuming that market equals intrinsic value, the present value of cash flow of both the companies shall be as follows:

PV=FCF1/(r-g).

Firm AEL: Expected free cash flow FCF1 = ₹ 200 Cr

WACC = 10%

Growth g = 6%, and 100 Cr shares of common stock

AEL's estimated current (t = 0) (stand-alone) value.

FCF1/(WACC – g) = ₹ 200 cr/ (0.10-0.06)

= ₹ 5000 cr

or ₹ 5000 cr/100 cr = ₹ 50 per share

Firm BML: Expected future cash flow FCF1 = ₹ 15 Cr.,

WACC = 12%,

Growth g = 6%, and 20 Cr shares of common stock

BML's estimated current (t = 0) (stand-alone) value.

VB=FCF1/(WACC – g) = ₹ 15 cr/(0.12-0.06)

= ₹ 250 cr

or ₹ 250 cr/ 20 cr = ₹ 12.50 per share

Combined Form AEL + BML will generate a free cash flow of

A combined Firm Z will generate a estimated Free Cash Flow of FCF1 = ₹ 225 cr next year (t=1).

Therefor the incremental or Δ FCFAB.

Δ FCFAB = FCFAB – [FCFA + FCFB]

Δ FCFAB = ₹ 225 – (₹ 200 cr + ₹15 cr) = ₹ 10 cr

The combined Firm Z will produce ₹ 10 cr more FCF next year than the sum of what the stand-alone firms AEL and BML do on their on.

Weighted Average Cost of Capital or WACC of the combined Firm AEL & BML shall be assuming that AEL and BML contribute proportionally (here, weighted by existing intrinsic values AEL and BML to the new WACCAB.

WACC AEL = [V AEL/(V AEL+V BML)](WACC AEL) + [V BML/(V AEL+V BML)](WACC BML)

WACC of Z (AEL+BML) = {5000/(5000+250)} (0.10) + {250/(5000+250)}(0.12)

= 0.095 + 0.0057

= 0.1007 or 10.07 %

New firm 'Z', its worth and the price AEL should pay to acquire BML shall be as follows:

Estimated value of the combined Firm Z. Assume the FCF growth rate remains at g = 6% per year.

Value of 'Z' (AEL+BML) = FCA 'Z' /(wacc of 'Z' – g) +

= ₹ 225/ (0.1007-0.06)

= ₹ 225/.0407

= ₹ 5528.25 cr

Vsynergy = Value of 'Z' = Z – (V of AEL + V of BML)

= {₹ 5528.25 cr – (₹ 5000 cr + ₹ 250 cr)}

= ₹ 278.25 cr

The merged Firm Z is worth ₹ 5528.25 cr which is ₹ 278.25 cr more than the firms are worth as stand-alone firms.

Also the synergy or NPV of this merger is ₹ 278.25 cr Here, this merger makes economic sense.

Following will the price at which will Firm AEL be able to acquire Firm BML.

Scenario 1:

Firm AEL pays a price that allocates all of the merger NPV to the existing Firm AEL shareholders? The entire Merger Value (Mvalue) or NPV will become impounded into the Firm AEL shares.

This involves paying ₹ 250 cr or ₹ 12.50 per share for all the existing Firm BML shares. Basically, Firm BML shareholders are selling at the existing Firm BML stock price of ₹ 12.50 per share.

New Firm Z value = (V AEL + Mvalue)/100 cr shares or (5000 cr + 278.25 cr)/100

= ₹ 52.78 per share

Firm B shareholders are unlikely to approve such an offer.

Scenario 2:

Firm AEL pays a price that allocates all of the merger NPV or Mvalue to the existing Firm BML shareholders

This involves paying V BML + Mvalue = ₹ 250 cr + ₹ 278.25

= ₹ 528.25

or ₹ 528.25 /20 cr = ₹ 26.41 per share for all the existing Firm BML shares.

Firm B shareholders are very likely to approve such an offer.

Scenarios 1 and 2 represent what appear to be extremes of bidding on a target firm. Scenario 1, paying the existing ₹ 12.5 per share for Firm B, gives Firm A shareholders all of the merger NPV or Mvalue.

Scenario 2, paying ₹ 26.41 er share (more than100% premium) for Firm BML, gives Firm BML shareholders all of the merger NPV or Vsynergy. However, Firm A shareholders would receive no benefit.

In mergers the rational price would be one that allocates the merger NPV somewhat proportionally between the bidder and target firm shareholders. In this case an price similar to scenario 2 (or even more) is the more likely outcome!

SELECTING A TARGET FIRM

For acquiring a company the buyer has to two key questions to answer. The first one is how to identify a potential target firm and the other one is how to value a target firm. The answers to these question mostly depends on the motives of acquisition as follows:

- If the motive for acquisitions is under valuation. The target firm will be identified depending upon the valuation approach and model used. Here the targets firm's trades at a multiple (of earnings, book value or sales) well below that of the rest of the industry.
- If the motive for acquisitions is diversification, the target firms will be the one in businesses that are unrelated to the business of the acquiring firm.
- If the motive for acquisitions is operating synergy, the target firm will be chosen depending upon the source of the synergy. For economies of scale, the target firm should be in the same business as the acquiring firm. For functional synergy or financial synergy the target firm should be strongest in functional or financial areas where the acquiring firm is weak.
- If the motive for the merger is control, the target firm will be a poorly managed firm in an industry where there is potential for excess returns.
- If the motive is managerial self-interest, the choice of a target firm will reflect managerial interests rather than economic reasons.

The valuation of an acquisition is not much different from the valuation of any firm. However, the existence of control and synergy premiums introduces some complexity into the valuation process. Given the inter-relationship between synergy and control, the safest way to value a target firm is in steps, starting with a *status quo* valuation of the firm, and following up with a value for control and a value for synergy.

The valuation of the target firm can be started by estimating the firm value with existing investing, financing and dividend policies. This valuation basic, provides a base from which control and synergy premiums can be estimated. After all the value of the firm is a function of its cash flows from existing assets, the expected growth in these cash flows during a high growth period, the length of the high growth period and the firm's cost of capital.

In many cases the hostile takeovers are justified on the basis of the existence of a market for corporate control. Investors and firms are willing to pay large premiums over the market price to control the management of firms, especially those that they perceive to be poorly run. In general, the value of control will be much greater for a poorly managed firm that operates at below optimum capacity than for a well managed firm. The value of controlling a firm comes from changes made to existing management policy that can increase the firm value. Assets can be acquired or liquidated, the financing mix can be changed and the dividend policy reevaluated, and the firm can be restructured to maximize value. If acquiring firm can identify the changes that needs to be made to the target firm, the control can be valuated. In that case the value of control can then estimated as:

Value of Control = Value of firm optimally managed – Value of firm with current management

The value of control is negligible for firms that are operating at or close to their optimal value, since a restructuring will yield little additional value. On the other hand the value of control can be substantial for firms operating at well below optimal, since a restructuring can lead to a significant increase in value.

Many takeovers are planned based on potential for operating synergies, which differ with variants of synergy. It is very difficult to value synergy and required many assumptions to support the valuation process. In many cases acquirer pays premium if he sees potential in benefits in synergy. Valuing synergy requires to make assumptions about future cash flows and growth, to estimate final value. The synergy can be valued by answering two fundamental questions, ie form of synergy expected to take and whether it will reduce costs as a percentage of sales and increase profit margins and will it increase future growth. Secondly as to when the synergy start affecting cash flows? After answering these questions, the value of synergy using an extension of discounted cash flow techniques can be estimated. First, value the firms involved in the merger independently, by discounting expected cash flows to each firm at the weighted average cost of capital for that firm. Then, estimate the value of the combined firm, with no synergy, by adding the values obtained for each firm in the first step. Finally, build in the effects of synergy into expected growth rates and cash flows and value the combined firm with synergy. The difference between the value of the combined firm with synergy and the value of the combined firm without synergy provides a value for synergy.

ACQUISITION ANALYSIS

A buyer performs due diligence on the target company in order to assess the benefits and liabilities of the proposed acquisition. This is done by investigating all relevant aspects of the target that could present risks or opportunities to it. In general the acquisition analysis is made in following areas.

➢ **Market Analysis:** The buyer is interested in competitive environment and the target's position. If the buyer is from the same market as the target, he is extremely knowledgeable about the structure and level of competition within the target's market. However, if the target is located within a different market, the buyer should conduct a high-level overview of how the market operates. The issues under consideration by buyer will be; ease of entry, excess capacity, level of expertise, market growth trend, pricing sensitivity and market size. These are topics and have a large impact on the long-term profitability of any company. Thus, the buyer should consider these issues in his acquisition strategy.

➢ **Analysis of Culture:** The culture in the organisation involves the integration of numerous elements, such as its organizational structure, sense of community, and decision-making systems. Many buyers spend considerable time investigating this area, because some cultures are strongly resistant to subsequent integration. What they miss is that integration of the target into the buyer's organization will be extraordinarily difficult unless the buyer works within the restrictions of the buyer's culture while making changes. In some cases, the cultures of the two companies are so incompatible that a successful integration is almost impossible. Thus, a review of culture should be done first, so that the team can quickly determine if it should recommend immediately abandoning the acquisition. The some culture areas in which conflicts can lead to acquisition failure are; organizational structure, bureaucracy, innovation and employee focus. In such case the buyer can conduct a change management workshops in order to change the existing culture. Hence, acquirer should pay a greater attention to the differences between the buyer's and target's cultures, and how they will impact the post acquisition.

➢ **Analysis of Workforce:** The analysis needed here is to determine the current compensation levels of the people being acquired, as well as how these pay levels compare to both internal and industry pay standards, and the presence and cost of any long-term compensation agreements. The core asset of many companies is its employees, acquirer should focus a considerable proportion of its time in the areas of; employee compensation, long-term compensation agreements, current turnover rate, employee benefits, grievance records etc.

➢ **Analysis of Intellectual Property Portfolio:** A target company may possess IPs portfolio of patents, trademarks, copyrights, trade secrets, etc., that can be used to enhance the value of the buyer's products. The primary analysis focuses on the number of years remaining prior to patent expiration and (especially) the expected cash flows to be obtained from them prior to expiration. The analysis intellectual property largely focuses on the existing costs and revenues currently experienced by target's patent and copyright holdings. The buyer should review the estimated additional revenues and costs that will subsequently be incurred by its use of the patent, which may vary from the use to which it has been put by the current patent owner. Acquisition analysis should also encompass patent risks out of technology change in future.

➢ **Brand Name Analysis:** This is sometimes a good reason to acquire a target company, and is most common in the consumer goods industry. The investigation focuses on the incremental profits to be gained by use of the brand name in relation to the cost of acquiring and maintaining the brand. A brand name can be extremely valuable, but its true value can be subject to a broad range of interpretation. The quantitative view of brand value covers, amount of annual trademark fees., clear title to the brand name, amount and trend of any current cash inflows from the brand name and also amount and trend of any legal fees needed to stop infringement.

➢ **Acquisition Analysis - Risk Management:** A target with an excellent risk management program is more valuable to the buyer, because the buyer is less likely to incur unexpected losses following the acquisition transaction. The risk management policies of the target company can be of concern to the buyer, because inadequate risk management likely to give additional expenditures in future. The areas to investigate are claim terms, deductibles, penetrated aggregates, premium adjustments, self-insurance, site security, uninsured risks etc.

➢ **Analysis of Operational Capacity:** This analysis focuses on the age and usefulness of the machinery and facility purchased. When a buyer purchases a manufacturing facility from another company, it is usually doing so to increase its capacity. With this in mind, the key analyses revolve around the condition and cost of the facility, determine the amount of replacement machinery to install, as well as the actual production capacity percentage, the cost per unit/percentage of capacity, and the facility's overhead cost. The analysis covers; determining the facility overhead cost required for minimum, standard, and maximum capacity, ascertaining the amount of capital replacements needed, finding out the periodic maintenance cost of existing equipment, determining the maximum production capacity, investigating any environmental liabilities and determine the cost of modifications needed to increase the capacity of the facility.

➢ **Assets Analysis:** When assets are purchased, the buyer can be quite selective in buying only those assets that are of the most value, such as patents, brands, or personnel (which have been covered in previous sections). Prior to an acquisition buyer should conduct a fixed asset audit, appraise the value of fixed assets, ascertain the existence of liens against assets, determine the possibility of collecting accounts receivable, verify the bank reconciliation for all bank accounts, review existing product line, investigate inventory and determine the value of any tax loss carry-forward.

➢ **Liabilities Analysis:** If the buyer decides to purchase a target as a complete legal entity, rather than buying pieces of it, then it must also review the target's liabilities. The liability analyses covers; reconcile unpaid debt to lender balances, look for unrecorded debt, review debt terms, audit accounts payable and accrued liabilities.

➢ **Equity Analysis:** Buyers should investigate about key shareholders and their super voting rights before going in for acquisition. The areas to investigate are to calculate exercisable options and warrants, investigate registration rights agreements, obtain the shareholder list and investigate special voting rights

➢ **Profitability Analysis:** This requires a detailed review of the target's income statement, broken down by subsidiary, customer, and product. The intent of these analyses is to quickly determine the current state and trend of a target's profits, as well as to pinpoint those customers and costs that are associated with the majority of profits and losses, gross margins, gross profit by product, overhead personnel per major customer and delayed expenses

➢ **Cash Flow Analysis:** If a company has a large cash flows, it is a prime target for purchase by companies that need the cash to fund further acquisitions. The cash flow analyses focus on review trend line of net cash flow before debt and interest payments, review trend line of working capital, segment working capital investment by customer and product and review trend line of capital purchases

➢ **Acquisition Analysis - Customers:** The relationship that a target has with its customers is a key concern to the buyer, but many times not investigated in detail. The buyer should review the length of relationships, profitability by key customer, complaint records, contracts, and related issues, customer complaints, personal relationships, profitability analysis and customer contracts. Here, the best scenario is to have a broadly distributed group of customers with a long history of purchases from the target, who appear to be well taken care of, and are not especially price sensitive.

➢ **Analysis of Product Development Projects:** A target with a long-term commitment to product development is quite valuable. Some key areas to investigate are; product under R&D, development personnel, product launches, product flaws, development plan and costing. Here, the buyer should look for a few key success factors when reviewing a target's product development efforts; an ongoing funding commitment, a development strategy, a strong team to carry out that strategy, and a record of bringing new products to market in a time and within allocated cost.

➢ **Production Process Analysis:** The buyer should examine its work flows, throughput and industrial engineering capabilities. A strong driver of profitability is the target's production process. Buyer should find out; work flow layout, throughput philosophy, industrial engineering practices, engineering change order policies, work safety, shipping delays, cost estimating procedures and pricing procedures. In many cases the presence of significant problems in the production area may cause production delays leading to cost overruns an production wastages and losses.

➢ **IT System Analysis:** The information technology (IT) system of a target company is likely to play a key role in its operations, so it needs to be investigated in details. Many buyers do not have sufficient IT expertise to properly evaluate the systems of a target company. But ignoring IT systems in target company may prove costly when these need replacement or up-gradation.

➢ **Analysis of Legal Issues:** There are many of legal issues that the buyer must review. The analysis issues are related to various kinds of contracts. Key legal issues are; articles of incorporation, certificate of incorporation, employment contracts, environmental exposure, expiring contracts, insurance policies, labor union agreements, leases, licenses, supplier or customer contracts, trade secrets, Intellectual Property Rights etc.

➢ **Other Issues:** The level of complexity and risk is increased when revenue is derived from multiple businesses, since the buyer must devote additional levels of management resources to each of those businesses. Complexity and risk also increase when a significant percentage of revenue is derived from a small number of large transactions that are custom-tailored to individual customers. These transactions tend to be highly volatile in their amount and frequency, making it difficult to estimate future revenue levels and attendant cash flows. The tax rate can also contribute to complexity and risk. Another indicator of complexity is the presence of off-balance sheet assets and liabilities, such as variable-interest entities, research and development partnerships, and operating leases.

SUMMARY

A merger is like a marriage; the two partners must be compatible. Each side should add value so that together the two are much stronger. Unfortunately, many mergers fail to work. Overpaying for the acquisition is a common mistake because of an incomplete valuation model. Therefore, it is essential to develop a complete valuation model, including analysis under different scenarios with recognition of value drivers. A good starting point for determining value is to extend the Discounted Cash Flow Model since it corresponds well to market values. Core value drivers (free cash flows) should be used over traditional type earnings (EBITDA).

The purpose of due diligence is to give the buyer some degree of exposure to the target company's operations, and to thereby gain an understanding of the risks to which it will be exposed. Based on this information, the buyer will also likely adjust the proposed purchase price based on any excessive risks it may find, or at least attempt to shift some risks to the buyer. Further, the buyer may uncover possible synergies that it was not previously aware of, and which may increase his interest for the deal. For these reasons, due diligence is an absolutely mandatory part of the acquisition process. Though there is usually a tight time line within which due diligence is conducted, the buyer should be willing to expand that timeline to ensure that all required review activities are completed to the satisfaction of the due diligence team. Only after the buyer has thoroughly investigated all key areas of concern should it proceed to the next step in the acquisition process, which is the purchase agreement.

Some key points to remember in the valuation process include; discount rate used should match-up with the associated risk of cash flows, forecast should focus on long-term cash flows that captures a normal operating cycle for the company and final forecast should be tested against independent sources.

Review Questions

1. The Valuation Process will often analyze several value drivers in order to understand where value comes from. Which of the following value drivers would be least important to the valuation?
   (a) Return on Invested Capital
   (b) Earnings per Share
   (c) Cash Flow Return on Investment
   (d) Economic Value Added
2. What are the various factors which the buyer takes into consideration in acquisition?
3. Discuss the various method used for target company valuation during acquisition/merger process.

Video Links

1. http://www.youtube.com/watch?v=J-t6zD5G4bk&feature=related, Mergers and Acquisitions
2. http://www.youtube.com/watch?v=yb_JpkWe_08, Business Brokers | Mergers & Acquisitions | Business Valuations

ASSIGNMENTS

Find out two recent merger or acquisition cases that has taken place in different industry . Study their balance sheets and use a returns-based approach, in addition to traditional valuation metrics, to measure the degree to which firms are priced. Also find out the risk-adjusted returns prior to the announcement of an acquisition to measure the degree to which firms are overvalued or undervalued before using above metrics.

BIBLIOGRAPHY

1. Aswath Damodaran, (2009), *Damodaran on Valuation,* Wiley India, ND
2. Brian Coyle, (2000), *Mergers and Acquisitions: Corporate Finance Corporate Finance,* Glenlake Publishing Company, London
3. Chris M. Mellen, Frank C. Evans (2010), *Valuation for M&A: Building Value in Private Companies,* John Wiley, New Jersy,
4. Dash A. P., (2010), *Mergers and Acquisitions,* International Publishing House ND
5. Dennis J. Roberts, (2009), *Mergers & Acquisitions: An Insider's Guide to the Purchase and Sale of Middle Market Business Interest,* John Wiley, NJ
6. Fruhan, W.E., W.C. Kester, S.P. Mason, T.R. Piper and R.S. Ruback, (1992), *Congloeum, Case Problems in Finance,* Irwin.NY
7. Gaughan, P.A., (1999), *Mergers, Acquisitions and Corporate Restructurings,* John Wiley & Sons.NJ
8. Kamal Ghosh Ray(2010), *Mergers and Acquisitions, Strategy, Valuation and Integration* PHI ND
9. Kapil Sheeba, (2011) *Financial Management,* Dorling Kindersley ,ND
10. Lanning Bryer, Melvin Simensky (2002), *Intellectual Property Assets in Mergers and Acquisitions,* John Wiley, NY
11. Ravindhar Vadapalli, (2007) *Mergers, Acquisitions and Business Valuation,* Excell Books, ND

8

CHAPTER

Valuation of Intangible Assets

> *"If this business were split up, I would give you the land and bricks and mortar, and I would take the brands and trademarks, and I would fare better than you."*
>
> **— *John Stuart, Chairman of Quaker (ca. 1900)***

Learning Objectives

To understand:

- Intangible assets
- Intellectual property valuation
- Goodwill valuation
- Brand valuation

Intellectual property and intangible assets have important characteristics that make them different from other business assets. Over the last decade, intellectual properties and intangible assets have become very important to businesses. In many instances, it may comprise the largest component of value for a business. Because of their importance, these assets may require an independent valuation for transaction, licensing, tax, litigation, and strategic purposes. The differences drive the need for more sophisticated valuation expertise. Additionally, there is no single approach that can produce a reliable result in IP valuations and rules-of-thumb and not-so-comparable will not suffice. To value these assets, a valuation expert must have a strong background in financial modeling and economics in order to properly apply the financial approaches and identify truly comparable royalty and transaction rates.

INTRODUCTION

In today's context, intangible assets have become far more important than its tangible counterparts especially in the service industry. Conventional methods of enterprise value such as market capitalization, profit margin, sales growth, etc., have taken backseat since they do not portray the exact financial position of the firm where nearly 75-80 % of the assets are intangible. The valuation exercise complex when human assets and brand image in service sector are to be valuated. In such cases, valuating intangibles assets becomes a challenging task for the valuators. In general valuation of intangible assets, remain highly subjective and complex. It is said thet it's hard to build intangible assets competitively, but it's harder to value them.

Intangible assets don't have the physical value based on plant and machinery. But cannot be ignores as they are not insignificant. They can prove very valuable for a firm and can be critical to its long-term success or failure. Intangibles may include intellectual assets, human capital and intellectual property. These intangible assets have a real value that can be estimated through investigation and systematic calculation. In fact, the actual value of anything, tangible or intangible, is based on what someone else is willing to pay for it. The price paid for an asset has a great deal to do with who can put it to its highest and best use. If one holds a license or copyright on a film or book that is not presently being distributed because he/she cannot afford to do so, that right may still have great value to a larger company with the resources to market.

More and more bankers and financial institutions are agreeing to securiatatize and fund against reputed brands and strong intangibles as collateral security. Hence, the financial role of intangibles has increasingly been recognized and their importance is reflected in the value that the intangibles add to company's bottom line. And it doesn't end there; the value of these intangible assets is required to be monitored on an ongoing basis.

INTANGIBLE ASSETS

In the last twenty years, there is a continuous shift from manufacturing firms to service and technology firms in the global economy. The assets of new generation (pharmaceutical, technology and service) companies are often intangible and invisible - patents, know-how and human capital. Moreover, accounting has dealt with investments in these assets, wherein they are inconsistent with its treatment of investments in tangible assets at manufacturing firms. As a result, many of the basic inputs that are used in valuation (earnings, cash flows and return on capital) are deviated from reality.

Exhibit 8.1: Categories of Intangible Assets

Marketing-related	Trademarks (Brands), trade names, service marks, newspaper, Internet domain names, non-competition agreements
Contract-related	Licensing and royalty agreements, advertising, construction, service or supply agreements, lease agreements, franchise agreements, employment contracts
Technology-related	Patented technology, computer software, know-how, databases, trade secrets such as secret formulas, processes and recipes
Customer-related	Customer lists, order or production backlogs, customer contracts and customer relationships including non contractual relationships
Artistic-related	Plays, operas, ballets, books, magazines, newspapers, pictures, photographs

Intangible assets are defined as identifiable non-monetary assets that cannot be seen, touched or physically measured. These assets are created through time and effort and that are identifiable. These assets can be classified in a separate category of assets. There are two primary forms of intangibles:

- Legal intangibles - Patents, Copyrights, Trademarks, Customer List, etc.
- Competitive intangible - Know-how, Goodwill, Brand name.

The legal intangibles comes under intellectual property rights, which can be defended in a court of law. The competitive intangibles impact effectiveness, productivity, wastage, and opportunity costs within an organization. The competitive intangibles will have impacts on costs, revenues, customer service, satisfaction, market value, and share price. Human capital is the primary source of competitive intangibles for organizations today. Competitive intangibles are the sources from which competitive advantage can be gained.

An intangible asset can also be classified as either indefinite or definite depending on the specifics of that asset. A company brand name is considered to be an indefinite asset, as it stays with the company as long as the company continues operations. However, if a company enters a legal agreement to operate under another company's patent, with no plans of extending the agreement, it would have a limited life and would be classified as a definite asset.

VALUATION EXERCISE

Any valuation exercise can be viewed as a process where each level supports the analysis generated on the level above. IP is never valued for curiosity, it is always valued to resolve a specific business issue. IP valuation analysis has four building blocks[1] such as;

- **Objectives:** The purpose of the valuation defines the legal or regulatory statutes, jurisdictional court of resolution, acceptable methodologies and 'rules-of-thumb' that have developed in that particular field. In general the intangible asset valuations is done for strategic purpose when assets are transferred

1 Paul Flignor and David Orozco, Intangible Asset & Intellectual Property Valuation: A Multidisciplinary Perspective, http://www.wipo.int/sme/en/documents/ip_valuation.htm

in buying-selling process. The second reason is reporting in the annual reports of the company. The third purpose is to compute damage awards in an infringement lawsuit. Valuation is also required to properly dispose off the property in the event of bankruptcy. The other purpose of valuation is financing or securitising the assets. For taxation purpose the valuation is needed by government authorities.

➢ **Description:** Intellectual property refers to patents, trade secrets, copyrights, trademarks/ trade dress. The intellectual property can offer high margins due to low variable costs in licensing. Each resource has distinct differentiating capabilities. In the domain of brands, the trademark offers the ability to leverage existing brand equity within the firm, e.g., through brand extensions, or with partners in the case of franchising, where the mark's goodwill is licensed to franchisees. Patents, if broad enough, can be powerful elements of competitive advantage. This is especially true in new technology markets where early entrants rely on differentiated functionality more than brand recognition. Before the new technology becomes old, patents will be of paramount importance for sustaining competitive advantage. Copyrights covers additional advantage, as a powerful core media asset by virtue of the initial copyright. It generate significant downstream revenues through the exclusivity rights associated with films, apparel, video games and board games.

➢ **Assumptions:** Valuation assumptions refers to how the asset in question will be exploited in the future. A common assumption is the 'best use' concept, which values the asset at the highest value under prevailing circumstances, regardless of current usage. An area where premise is of crucial importance is in bankruptcy, where the distinction between an orderly and a distressed disposition can have a significant impact on valuation.

➢ **Standard:** The most common valuation standard is the 'fair market value' standard, which is commonly defined as the price at which a willing buyer and a willing seller would transact, with each party having access to all relevant information and with neither party under the compulsion to transact. Alternative standards include 'fair value', which is often used in court cases to compensate a party for the involuntary use of an asset, such as eminent domain, where there is no reasonable assumption of a fair market value transaction.

➢ **Profile:** The Profile refers to the legal, business/strategic and financial characteristics of the asset in question. It articulates the business and legal issues that dictate the opportunities and limitations of the asset, and ultimately its ability to generate income and create value. Much of the hard work and creative energy of a valuation analysis takes place at this level. For IP, which has no physical form and for which the marginal cost to replicate is often close to zero, the legal protection provides an important component of value. The value of an intangible asset is ultimately captured through commercial exploitation. Exploitation, in turn, is determined by the strategic and business environment that enables or hinders commercialization. Factors that comprise the business profile include the barriers to exploitation, market life cycle of the offerings, bundled services or other assets, competitor products and services, customer and supplier dynamics, government regulation, and new technologies. An important factor to consider is that most IP is exploited in conjunction with other IP (e.g., technologies are often bundled with trademarks and/or trade secrets), and a careful consideration of the inter-relationships among all IP in the value chain and market life cycle is often important. Economic importance of IP refers to the ability of function or asset to command the residual income of the value chain. Intangible asset has an impact on the value chain of the product or service and the financial profile thereof. This includes typical accounting data, such as revenues, costs and capital investment, other financial result of usage of the subject intangible for directly or indirectly creating value which include after market sales and potential brand extensions. Issues associated with the financial profile include; projected revenues, costs and capital requirements associated with commercializing the intangible, estimated time to commercialize the asset, estimated cost of non-infringing alternatives, time value of money associated with the intangible and impact of the commercialization on working capital.

➢ **Methodology**

Transaction Method is actual price paid for a similar intangible under similar circumstances. This can be used either for direct acquisition or purchase or for the right to use, a license. The transactional method also goes by the name of the 'market approach. 'The transactional approach is appealing because it is a direct measure of the value of the intangible asset. As such, it is often considered to be the most reliable of methods when it can be performed properly. The 'Fair market value,' and 'arm's length standard' two of the most common valuation standards derive from the transaction method. Therefore, as a general rule transaction data can never be ignored in a valuation exercise.

The key to performing a successful transactional approach is to ensure comparability between the outside evidence and the subject asset. Due to the depth of the required information to ensure comparability, often the only good transactional data is considered wherein there is complete access to the legal agreement. Transactional methods are more difficult to apply in contexts where objectivity is critical such as financial reporting, tax, and litigation support and easier to apply in a consulting context where the deliverable is more subjective to the experience of the valuer.

There are two steps to a transactional method valuation - screening and adjustments. Screening refers to the selection process of identifying candidate third party transactions with sufficient information on pricing, scope and terms and conditions to be deemed comparable to the intangible asset in question. The adjustments are also done based on valid assumptions.

VALUATION METHODS

There are two methods most commonly used in IP valuation exercise and these are;

Income Method: It is the most fundamental of the valuation methods. The most basic definition of 'value' is based on the ability of the asset to somehow generate future income. This underlying characteristic is often referred to as the 'intrinsic' value of the asset, and is captured by the ability to directly or indirectly generate a positive cash flow. The cash flow, when appropriately discounted, is the underlying premise of the income method. The income method has three components - projected cash flows, the economic life of the IP, and the discount rate.

Replacement Cost Method: It is the cost to develop similar functionality to the subject IP outside the scope of the legal protection. A common usage of the replacement cost method is the cost to design around a patent or set of patents. This method is based on the principle of substitution - an investor would not pay more for an asset than the cost to obtain similar benefits from another asset. This method is particularly useful when the legal protection is weak or the technology is relatively well-known, and the IP does not produce income currently. The replacement cost method is a forward-looking perspective on how to create an asset with similar functionality to the asset in question

In addition to the above over the past decade there is the growth of a new family of valuation methods based on future contingent events. This family of methods includes real options, binomial models, and Monte Carlo simulations. At the core of each of these methods is a two step process: first, compute the probability of the favorable event occurring that will make the IP valuable and second, compute the pay-off if the favorable event occurs. The real option method is based on the successful Fischer-Black valuation model for pricing options (calls and puts) of financial stocks. The basic premise behind the real option method is that an investment with an asymmetric payoff (potentially large payoff and only limited losses) will have an increased value as the level of uncertainty, known as volatility, increases. Consequently, real option methods have been most useful where large capital investments are required with a highly uncertain and far away pay-off, such as the pharmaceutical and oil exploration industries. In the binomial expansion the required events and decisions are modeled explicitly, each with their own probabilities. However, in building a binomial expansion one has to ensure all potential alternatives and scenarios.

For most IP valuation applications all valuation methods, if applied properly, should converge near a similar valuation estimate. Here, many practitioners suggest employing multiple valuation methods for a given IP asset to demonstrate robustness and completeness of the analysis. In practice this is often difficult as data for multiple methods is unavailable.

WHY IP VALUATION?

The valuation of IP was initially limited to damages calculations in legal cases involving claims against patent infringement. With the introduction of tax planning involving IP, such as transfer pricing and patent donations, the valuation of intangibles became critical in non-litigation circumstances also. Companies were required to include in their tax reporting the fair market value of IP involved in transactions. New accounting GAAP rules in mergers and acquisitions expanded the need for IP valuations. The companies were now required to report the fair value of intangibles in M&A deals. Compliances on the part of the companies to face scrutiny by the regulating authorities, require IP valuation expert's opinion in the form of a valuation report.

The types of activities where IP valuation became important cover spin-offs, demergers, gifts, licensing, patents sales, and other commercialization activities. Since many of these activities are done for planning purposes or do not result in tax or accounting reporting requirements. In these situations, due to the low to medium degree of scrutiny and the lack of reporting requirement, the valuation is often done in-house or between the parties.

The most common complaints with IP valuation usually fall into three categories; first lack of active markets and a good set of comparable, second lack of transparency in valuation methods and third the nature of intangible assets makes their value 'contextual'. This means there is difficulty to assign one value to an asset or to agree on a value between buyer and seller.

In general accounting standards are generally not helpful in representing the worth of IPs in company accounts and IPs are often undervalued, undermanaged or underexploited. Despite the importance and complexity of IPs, there is generally little coordination between the different professionals dealing with an organization's IPs. Exploitation of IPs can take many forms, ranging from outright sale of an asset, a joint venture or a licensing agreement. Inevitably, exploitation increases the risk assessment.

Valuation is, essentially, a bringing together of the economic concept of value and the legal concept of property. The cardinal rule of commercial valuation is; "the value of something can be stated in the value of a thing in a particular place, at a particular time, in particular circumstances". In addition valuation gets impacted by the purpose behind it and for whom it is being done.

The valuations task is not so difficult for IPs such as patents, trademarks copyrights etc when they have been formally protected through law. However for intangibles such as know how, (which can include the talents, skill and knowledge of the workforce), training systems and methods, technical processes, customer lists, distribution networks the valuation is rather difficult identifying them in terms of the earnings and profits they generate.

There are four main value concepts, for IPR:

- **Owner value** - It often determines the price in negotiated deals and is often led by a proprietor's view of value if he were deprived of the property.
- **Market value** - It is the assumption that if comparable property has fetched a certain price, then the subject property will realize a price something near to it.
- **Fair value** - It is based on equitability to both buyer and seller. It recognizes that the transaction is not in the open market and that vendor and purchaser have been brought together in a legally binding manner.
- **Tax value** - It has been the subject of case law and is an confidential practice.

Illustration - Determining the Fair Value of IP in M&A

Rama Photocopying Machines Ltd - Relief from Royalty

Product	**Year 1**	**Year 2**	**Year 3**	**Year 4**	**Year 5**
Sales Proceeds (Rs Crores)					
Light - XLR	68	60	55	50	45
Medium - PLR	120	80	40	20	15
Jumbo LLC	42	30	20	15	
Colour PPC	80	60	50	40	
Totals	310	230	165	125	60
Royalty Rate (1.75%)	1.75	1.75	1.75	1.75	1.75

Royalty savings	5.42	4.02	2.88	2.18	1.05
Less Income Tax (42.024 per cent. This includes a basic tax of 40%, an education cess of 3 per cent and a surcharge of 2.5%)	2.28	1.69	1.21	0.92	0.44
Net Royalty Savings	3.14	2.33	1.67	1.26	0.61
Present Value Factor at 22%	0.81967	0.67186	0.55071	0.45140	0.3700
PV Net Royalty Savings	2.57	1.56	0.92	0.57	0.23
Total for five years	5.85				

$$\text{Fair Value} = \frac{PV \times L}{L - (Fa \times T)}$$

Where,

PV - Present Value - 5.85

L - Remaining tax life -15 (patent's total life is 20 years)

Income Tax - 42.02%

Amortization Factor - (For 12 % interest rate for 15 years) - 1.20

$$\text{Fair Value of Technology} = \frac{5.85 \times 15}{15 - (1.2 \times 0.4202)} = 6.05$$

The above concepts of value has an impact on investment value, liquidation value, and going concern value. Acceptable methods for the valuation of identifiable intangible assets and intellectual property fall into three broad categories. They are:

➢ **Market-based:** The market approach is a valuation method that estimates value based on actual market transactions. The market approach requires the collection of market data from comparable transactions and analysis of the data to estimate the value of the brand or intangible through comparison and correlation.

➢ **Income-based:** This approach considers income and expense data relating to the intangible and estimates value through a capitalization process. Capitalization relates income and value by converting an income amount into a value estimate. This process may consider direct relationships (capitalization rates or multiples), yield or discount rates (reflecting measures of return on investment), or a combination of these. The methods of valuation flowing from an estimate of past and future economic benefits can be broken down in to four as follows;

- Capitalization of historic profits;
- Gross profit differential methods;
- Excess profits methods; and
- The relief from royalty method.

The first one; capitalization of historic profits arrives at the value of IP's by multiplying the historic profitability of the asset by a multiple that has been assessed after scoring the relative strength of the IP. For example, a multiple is arrived at after assessing a brand in the light of factors such as leadership, stability, market share, internationality, trend of profitability, marketing and advertising support and protection. While this capitalization process recognizes some of the factors, which should be considered, it has major shortcomings, mostly associated with historic earning capability. This method does not consider future earning of IP.

The second one; gross profit differential methods are often associated with trade mark and brand valuation. These methods look at the differences in sale prices, adjusted for differences in marketing costs. That is the difference between the margin of the branded and/or patented product and an unbranded or generic product. This formula is used to work out cash flows and calculate value. However, finding generic equivalents for a patent and identifiable price differences is difficult as compared to a retail brand.

The third one; excess profits method takes into consideration the current value of the net tangible assets employed as the benchmark for an estimated rate of return. This is used to calculate the profits that are required in order to induce investors to invest into those net tangible assets. Any return over and above those profits required in order to induce investment is considered to be the excess return attributable to the IPs. While theoretically relying upon future economic benefits from the use of the asset, the method has difficulty in adjusting to alternative uses of the asset.

The fourth one; 'relief from royalty', which considers what the purchaser could afford, or would be willing to pay, for a license of similar IP. The royalty stream is then capitalized reflecting the risk and return relationship of investing in the asset.

Discounted cash flow (DCF) analysis amongst the last three methods and is probably the most comprehensive of appraisal techniques. Potential profits and cash flows need to be assessed carefully and then restated to present value through use of a discount rate(s). The time value of money is calculated by adjusting expected future returns to today's monetary values using a discount rate. The discount rate is used to calculate economic value and includes compensation for risk and for expected rates of inflation.

With the asset under consideration, the valuer will need to consider the operating environment of the asset to determine the potential for market revenue growth. The projection of market revenues will be a critical step in the valuation. The potential will need to be assessed by reference to the enduring nature of the asset, and its marketability, and this must subsume consideration of expenses together with an estimate of residual value or terminal value, if any. This method recognizes market conditions, likely performance and potential, and the time value of money.

The discount rate to be applied to the cash flows can be derived from a number of different models, including common sense, build-up method, dividend growth models and the capital asset pricing model utilising a weighted average cost of capital. The latter will probably be the preferred option.

IPs have a varying ability to generate economic returns dependent upon the main lives. For example, in the discounted cash flow model, it would not be correct to drive out cash flows for the entire legal length of copyright protection, which may be 60 plus years, when a valuation concerns computer software with only a short economic life span of 1 to 2 years. However, the legal life of a patent is 20 years may be very important for valuation purposes, as often illustrated in the pharmaceutical sector with generic competitors entering the marketplace at speed to dilute a monopoly position when protection ceases. When undertaking a valuation using the discounted cash flow modeling, the valuer should never project longer than what is realistic by testing against these major lives.

➢ **Cost approach:** This approach takes into consideration the value intangible assets on the basis of their 'cost-to-create'. For brands, such costs typically include naming, research and product design, packaging, design, advertising and promotional spend. A portion of promotional spend is, by nature, short-term maintenance spend; only part of it creates long-term brand value. Consideration is given to all costs associated with replacing or replicating the asset. The depreciation is deducted from that. Here it may be little or no correlation between the development costs and the impact on financial performance (revenues and profits). The cost to create approach may therefore understate the price at which the asset would change hands between willing parties in an arm's length transaction. The method ignores changes in the time value of money and ignores maintenance.

BRAND VALUATION

The success of many businesses depends on customer awareness and a prominent brand position. A strong brand and a loyal customer base can be the distinct assets owned by a business. Examples of distinct intangible assets include copyrights or trademarks that let a business sell its products for a higher price or in greater quantity than its competition, proprietary mailing lists of customers or prospects, long-term contracts, and franchises with long track records and well-recognized names. Goodwill is defined as the value of the business in excess of its owner's equity.

The term brand name is frequently used when discussing 'Brand', however it is more correctly used when discussing the written or spoken elements of a brand. In this instance a 'brand name' is an example of a trademark, if the brand name identifies (exclusively) the brand owner as the source of certain products or services. By brand finance, one seeks to understand the value of their brand name as part of measuring the value of their intangible assets. A business in any market is normally known by its brands. A brand is an identity or name of a product in a market. It is an intangible asset of the company dealing with or manufacturing it. A brand name makes it easier to differentiate products especially when a single company manufactures a large number of products.

In general, most business owners do not have an adequate understanding of how their brand and customer bases impact the value of their businesses. They go by rule of thumb formulas in some industries. However, a better estimate of value is gained through a more in-depth analysis.

In valuing company's loyal customer base, it's important to remember the 80/20 rule of thumb: that 20 per cent of customers most likely produce 80 per cent of company's profits. Generally, the best method to valuing a customer base is to segment customers into categories based on characteristics that drive profitability. For example, frequency and value (amount) of purchases or longevity of relationship may be important metrics. Using this data, a lifetime customer value may be calculated as the present value result of the average profit per purchase multiplied by the number of purchases per period multiplied by the length of the relationship. This information will prove useful not only in calculating a value for customers, but also in focusing sales efforts on the most profitable customers.

A useful way to combine the analysis of company's brand and its customers is to consider customers' awareness, loyalty and quality perception of the brand. Perceived quality has the strongest linkage to strong profitability, usually because quality brands can demand a price premium.

Customers' loyalty in purchasing is the number-one value-creating factor in brand valuation because it results in an even and predictable revenue stream. Loyalty can also be further categorized into non-customers, price-switchers, passively loyal, fence-sitters and committed customer groups.

In the end, brand recognition and customer loyalty are very important components of the value company's business. The realization of this value is through increased earnings that are received steadily over a period of time. One must understand this value, manage it in the business and convey that understanding to potential buyers.

Every brand has a value depending upon its success in the market. The value is estimated through a process known as brand valuation, which is a very important financial component of mergers and acquisitions. As every brand is unique, it is difficult to lay out a single, standardized mathematical method for all types of valuation. Therefore, the greatest challenge is to eliminate subjectivity as much as possible to arrive at an objective brand value. Brands can be valued using three traditional valuation approaches: cost, market and income;

Cost approach

Relies on 'Creating Cost' or calculating what it would cost another business to duplicate a given asset today. This can be done using an estimation of current costs or by calculating the present value of all past expenses of creating the brand. It involves adding up the cost of different components used in creating the brand. The cost components includes; advertising cost, research cost, manufacturing cost, etc. 'Creation costs' may be estimated by looking back to brand launch and restating actual expenditure in current cost terms. This approach may provide a meaningful number for a new brand, where the time period is short and the costs are readily available. Sometimes costs can be collected consistently but it does not represent the current value of the brand. Even 're-creation costs', which may be also estimated, but there is no such thing as an identical brand to calculate a relevant re-creation value. Brands are valuable because they are unique. By their very nature they are not comparable or replicable. For these reasons cost-based valuations are used for a cross check exercise.

Market approach

Focuses on past sale transactions of brand names. But such past data to use as a comparison may not be available. However, if a brand is identified that is comparable to company's brand name then use it as a proxy, then the market-based valuation analysis is quite reliable. As the name suggests, a brand is compared with other brands under the same product category using various financial ratios like P/E ratios and turnover ratios. This assumes that there are comparable market transactions (specific brand sales), comparable company transactions (the sale of specific branded companies) or stock market quotations (providing valuation ratios against which a comparable branded entity can be valued). A valuation may be based on the disposal of comparable individual brands, specific branded divisions or whole companies where adequate information is made publicly available. In practice, there are few directly comparable transactions. Even where there are sales of specific brands or branded businesses, details are generally not widely available, and it is hard to make comparisons. In addition, the notion of comparability assumes that brands are identical, which is never the case. Market-based valuations also tend to be used only as a cross check.

Income approach

It measures the future benefits (such as sales, profits or cost savings) that the intangible asset will bring to a business, the timing of the receipt of those benefits and the length of time that the business will receive those benefits. Generally, a combination of a discounted cash-flow model and an excess earnings method is used to establish value under the income approach. A variation of this approach is to calculate and capitalize the profits generated by company's business with the strong brand name that are in excess of a similar "unbranded" business. Under this approach, the future economic benefits from the brand are discounted to its present value using various discounting methods. Deciding the discount rate and the tenure is important to derive realistic results. There are two alternative approaches such as; one 'royalty relief' and the second one is 'economic use' method. This considers the economic value of a brand in current use to current owner. In other words, it considers the return that the owner actually achieves by owning the brand - now and in the future. Economic use valuations assume that brands provide their owners with security of demand. In the short run a manufacturer without a brand might enjoy the same sales, the same economies of scale, even the same premium prices as the manufacturer with a brand. However, the non-branded manufacturer could not rely on the same security of knowing that the brand's customers this year are likely to be customers of the brand next year, and for many years after that.

This approach also depends on the accuracy of future sales and earnings projections. It uses the future earnings to a brand after making a fair charge for the tangible assets employed. A charge is also made for tax at a notional rate. The resulting brand earnings are discounted back to a Net Present Value (NPV) representing the current value of the brand. Such brand valuations are based on 3-5 year earnings forecasts. In addition, an annuity is calculated on the final year's earnings on the assumption that the brand continues beyond the forecast period, effectively into perpetuity. As brand rights can be owned in perpetuity and many brands have been around for over 50 years, this is not an unreasonable assumption.

Exhibit 8.2: Value of Global Brands in 2011

Rank 2011	Brand	Value USD bn.	Sector
1	Apple	70.61	Computer Services
2	Google	47.46	Internet Services
3	Microsoft	45.81	Computer Software
4	IBM	39.13	Computer Services
5	Wal-Mart	38.30	Retail
6	Samsung	38.19	Electronic
7	General Electric	33.21	Project Engg
8	Coca Cola	31.08	Beverages
9	Vodafone	30.04	Mobile Handsets
10	Amazon	28.66	Retail

(***Source:*** Brand Finance Global 500, March, 2012, www.brandfinance.com)

GOODWILL VALUATION

Goodwill is an accounting concept meaning the value of an entity over and above the value of its assets. The term was originally used in accounting to express the intangible but quantifiable of an ongoing business beyond its assets. The additional quantifiable value of business is due to the reputation the firm enjoyed with its clients. While goodwill is technically an intangible asset, it is usually listed as a separate item on a company's balance sheet. Goodwill comes into picture in company acquisition transaction . It represents the amount of money a company has paid or would pay over the fair value of the net assets to acquire another company.

Goodwill in financial statements arises when a company is purchased for more than the fair value of the identifiable net assets of the company. The difference between the purchase price and the sum of the fair value of the net assets is by definition the value of the 'goodwill' of the target company. The acquiring company must recognize goodwill as an asset in its financial statements and present it as a separate line item on the balance sheet, according to the current purchase accounting method. In this sense, goodwill serves as the balancing sum that allows one firm to provide accounting information regarding its purchase of another firm for a price substantially different from its book value.

Goodwill can be negative, arising where the net assets at the date of acquisition, fairly valued, exceed the cost of acquisition. Negative goodwill is recognized as a gain to the extent that it exceeds allocations to certain assets. Under current accounting standards, it is no longer recognized as an extraordinary item. For example, a software company may have net assets (consisting primarily of miscellaneous equipment, and assuming no debt) valued at ₹ 5 Crores, but the company's overall value (including brand, customers, intellectual capital) is valued at ₹ 35 Crores. Anybody buying that company would book ₹ 35 Crores in total assets acquired, comprising ₹ 5 Crores physical assets, and ₹ 30 Crores in goodwill. In a private company, goodwill has no predetermined value prior to the acquisition; its magnitude depends on the two other variables by definition. A publicly traded company, by contrast, is subject to a constant process of market valuation, so goodwill will always be apparent.

A business can invest to increase its reputation, by advertising or assuring that its products are of high quality. However, expenses cannot be booked as contributing to goodwill. Hence, there is a disconnect;. goodwill from acquisitions can be booked, since it is derived from a market or purchase valuation, but similar internal spending cannot be booked, although it will be recognized by investors who compare a company's market value with its book value.

There is a distinction between two types of goodwill depending upon the type of business enterprise: institutional goodwill and professional practice goodwill. Goodwill in a professional practice entity may be attributed to the practice itself and to the professional practitioner. On a company balance sheet goodwill and intangible assets are usually listed as separate items on a company's balance sheet. There are three method of valuating goodwill

➢ **Average Profits Method:** Under this method goodwill is calculated on the basis of the average of profit agreed number of past years. The average profit is then multiplied by the agreed number of years. This is the simplest and the most commonly used method of the valuation of goodwill.

Goodwill = Average Profits × Number of years (as agreed)

Before calculating the average profits the following adjustments is made in the profits of the firm.

- Any abnormal profits should be deducted from the net profits of that year,
- Any abnormal loss should be added back to the net profits of that year and
- Non operating incomes (from investments) to be deducted from net profits the year

This is most common and accepted method of valuating a goodwill of a company.

- **Super profits method:** Under this method Goodwill is calculated on the basis of Super Profits, i.e., the excess of actual profits over the average profits. For example if the normal rate of return in a particular type of business is 18% and your investment in the business is ₹ 10,00,000 then your normal profits should be ₹ 1,80,000. But if you earned a net profit of ₹ 2,20,000 then ₹ 2,20,000 - ₹ 1,80,000= ₹ 40,000 are your super profits. For calculating Goodwill Super Profits are multiplied by the number of years of purchase. Here, the goodwill for 10 years purchase will be ₹ 4,00,000.

For calculating Goodwill:-

Normal Profits = Capital Invested × Normal rate of return/100

Super Profits = Actual Profits - Normal Profits

Goodwill = Super Profits x No. of years purchased

- **Capitalization Method:** There are two ways of calculating Goodwill under this method:

The first one is 'Capitalization of Average Profits Method'. Under this method the average profits are calculated and then the capital needed for earning such average profits on the basis of normal rate of return is assessed. Such capital is called capitalized value of average profits. The formula is:-

Capitalized Value of Avg Profits = Avg Profits × (100 / Normal Rate of Return)

Capital Employed = Assets – Liabilities

Goodwill = Capitalized Value of Avg Profits – Capital Employed

The second one is 'Capitalization of Super Profits'. Under this method first calculate the super profits and then calculate the capital needed for earning such super profits on the basis of normal rate of return. This capital is the value of company's Goodwill. The formula is:-

Goodwill = Super Profits × (100/ Normal Rate of Return)

SUMMARY

Intangible Assets are widely accepted to be the key drivers and contributors to the value and growth of businesses. They are critical to the future prospects of any business, they are traditionally considered to be complicated to measure in terms of 'value', and its ongoing management and communication. Intangible asset valuation is done for financial and tax reporting and also in case of M&As. Importance of intangible assets may differ between industries and also amongst companies within a particular industry. For example, consumer products or retail businesses have higher level of marketing related intangible assets like brand as against industrial products where technology may play a more important role. While, telecommunication deal prices would get impacted by availability of license and spectrum, which is a key intangible asset for this industry, while content library could be key intangible for transactions involving media companies. There are three most common approaches in valuing intangible assets such as comparison approach, income approach and cost approach. In the comparison approach, one determines the value of an intangible asset by reference to market activity like transaction prices, bids or offers involving identical or similar assets. Valuation methods under the income approach determine the value of an intangible asset, by reference to the present value of income, cash flows or cost savings that could actually or hypothetically be achieved by a market participant owning the asset. The methods generally used under the 'Income Approach' are royalty relief, premium profit and excess earnings. The royalty relief method considers a hypothetical royalty payment saved through ownership as compared to licensing the asset from third party. The premium profit method involves comparison of future profit streams/cash flows that would be earned by a business using the intangible asset with those that would be earned by a business that does not use the asset. The excess earnings method determines cash flows attributable to the subject intangible asset after excluding the proportion of the cash flows that are attributable to other assets (working capital, fixed assets) and is generally used in practice for those intangibles which have the biggest impact on the cash flows.

Valuations of intangible assets are required for; purchase price allocations, impairment reviews, tax planning and transactions/dispute resolution. It is done for balance sheet purposes, mergers and acquisitions, reporting under Indian GAAP, Joint-venture negotiations, investor relations, licensing and franchising, obtaining finance, colateral & securitisation and finally for bringing the importance of brands to the attention of the board. Valuations also form the basis for risk and performance management.

Review Questions

1. What are the views of the Institute of Chartered Accountants in India about valuating intangible assets?
2. Explain market approach to valuation as it relates to valuing IPs?
3. Explain the income approach to valuation as it relates to brands?
4. What is the proper methodology for determining the fair value of customer relationship intangibles?
5. How 'knowledge workforce' is valued?
6. Explain what is the 'Fair Value' in valuation and where is it used?

Video Linkages

1. http://www.youtube.com/watch?v=8WxFPPSxlS4, Valuing Intangible Assets, Jackie Maguire from Coller IP addresses the BVR IP Summit on Best Practices in IP Valuation and looks at the reasons for valuing IP and other intangible assets.
2. http://www.youtube.com/watch?v=NOqms0b5qiM&feature=related 08 Valuation methods for IP, How to use Intellectual Property for Competitive Advantage in Tough Economic Times Joe Cote, Intellectual Property Expert.

ASSIGNMENT

1. Study a balance sheet of FMCG and IT company and find out how goodwill (amount) is arrived at.

BIBLIOGRAPHY

1. Gordon V. Smith, Russell L. Parr, (1989), *Valuation of Intellectual Property and Intangible Assets,* John Wiley & Sons.
2. Jeffrey A. Cohen, (2005), *IntangibleAssets: Valuation and Economic Benefit,* John Wiley & Sons, NJ
3. Kelvin King, The Value of Intellectual Property, Intangible Assets and Goodwill, http://www.wipo.int/sme/en/documents/value_ip_intangible_assets.htm (visited on Jan 18, 2012)
4. Madhu Dubhashi and D. Murali,, (2006), "The right brand value" - page no. 13, Catalyst Column, The Business Line 8/6/2006,
5. Nan Hua, (2010), *Valuation of Intangible Assets,* VDM Verlag Dr. Mueller e.K.
6. Pablo Fernandez ,(2001) *"Valuation of Brands and Intellectual Capital"* by, IESE Business School, Spain, December 21, 2001
7. Paul Flignor and David Orozco, Intangible Asset & Intellectual Property Valuation: A Multidisciplinary Perspective, http://www.wipo.int/sme/en/documents/ip_valuation.htm
8. Richad Hall, (1992) The strategic analysis of intangible resources, *Strategic Management Journal,* Volume 13, Issue 2, pages 135-144, February 1992, Tulane University,
9. Richard Razgaitis, *Valuing and Pricing of Technology-based Intellectual Property,* John Wiley & Sons, Inc, 2003.
10. Rober F. Reilly. Robert P. Schweihs. (1998) *Valuing Intangible Assets,* McGraw-Hill, NY
11. Tom Copeland & Valdimir Antikarov, *Real Options,* Texere, 2001
12. Geoffrey A. Moore, (2004) "Darwin and the Demon: Innovating With Established Enterprises" *Harvard Business Review,* July 1, 2004.
13. James G. Conley & David Orozco, (2005) "Intellectual Property - The Ground Rules", Kellogg School of Management Technical Note 7-305-501 (August 2005).

9

CHAPTER

Value Enhancement: DCF, EVA and CFROI

> *"There is nothing so dangerous as the pursuit of a rational investment policy in an irrational world."*
>
> ***— John Maynard Keynes***

Learning Objectives

To understand:

- Why value enhancement?
- Approaches to value enhancement
- Value enhancement options

Generating a valuation is basic arithmetic. The key factor to enhancing a company's value is through the execution of opportunities that enhance the future free cash flow of the business. A company's strategic position within an industry with solid growth prospects is essential plus along with a well structured business and an experienced management team. Valuation is an art and not a science, but the process of calculating a company's value in a systematic way can uncover key growth opportunities for a business. Ideally, both EVA and Discounted Cash Flow Valuation should provide us with the same estimate for the value of a firm. The information that is required for both approaches is exactly the same - expected cash flows over time and costs of capital over time. A policy of maximizing the present value of economic value added over time should be the equivalent of a policy of maximizing firm's value.

INTRODUCTION

Enhancing shareholder value is a key objective for the management of both private and public companies. A company's management should have clear cut strategic plan to increase value through a liquidity event such as a flotation, an M&A transaction, or a joint venture. All these transactions require an appreciation of the valuation of a business and how this can be enhanced. Valuing a business is often more an art than a science. For a public company, the market capitalization or the equity value, of the business provides an important reference point based on publicly available information. To assess the full value of a business, the following factors need to be taken into account:

- liquidity of the shares;
- premium required to take control of the business; and
- capital structure.

For private companies and divisions of public companies, straightforward mathematical formulae can be employed. These calculations generate the company's value based on either forecasted cash flow, earnings, or by analyzing the value of comparable listed companies and recent M&A transactions in an industry.

Prior to taking up valuation exercise, it is important to study the industry and of the future prospects of the company in order to place the valuation figures in the current context. An analysis of the competitive environment, barriers to entry, potential for substitute products and the strengths and weaknesses of the company will put the forecasted cash flow and earnings into right perspective.

VALUATION TECHNIQUES

In general the following three valuation techniques are commonly employed;

- **Discounted Cash Flow:** The discounted cash flow (DCF) approach is the most commonly used method to value companies or specific projects. The basis of the calculation is free cash flow. This is cash available for distribution to the debt and equity providers after all planned investments have occurred, including both working capital and taxes. Adjustments are made to the financial statements for non-cash items including depreciation and goodwill. A financial model is developed based on the forecasted profit and loss, balance sheet and cash flow statements for the company. The time horizon is five year period. The assumptions underlying the forecasts are important to the validity of the model. Furthermore, the process of developing the model and checking the consistency with the competitive strategy of the company within the industry is as important a process as the calculation of the final valuation figure.

In general a business will continue to operate well beyond the 5 year forecast period. It is therefore necessary to estimate the "terminal" or "continuation" value of the business. Over time, with competition, a firm's performance tends to average out to the industry average with 5-7% growth rather than say an initial 15-20% growth. Valuation according to comparable multiples will provide accaepable accuracy with normalised cash flow and growth prospects. This is typically an EBITDA multiple; or earnings before interest, tax, depreciation and amortisation. Therefore, the valuation of a company taking into account the time value of money can be separated into its constituent parts.

Value of expected future free cash flows	=	Present value of free cash flows during explicit forecast period	+	Present value of terminal value at the end of the explicit forecast period

The resulting value represents the enterprise value of the business available to all security holders discounted with the Weighted Average Cost of Capital (WACC). The WACC reflects the combined cost of debt and equity with the weights of these capital sources based on their market, rather than book values. The key point to highlight is that a company's WACC declines as it employs additional lower cost debt, thereby reducing the proportion of the more expensive equity. This is due to the tax shield resulting from the tax deductibility of interest payments. Typical WACC rates are set out below. These are not industry specific.

	Large cap	**Mid-small cap**	**Larger private company**	**VC backed private company**
WACC (%)	5	10	15	25

The DCF process provides a valuation of the enterprise. The value of the equity can then be calculated by subtracting the net debt (total debt minus cash) from the enterprise value of the business. To arrive at the correct valuation figure it is necessary to carry out sensitivity analysis around the key assumptions. The focus should be on a valuation range rather than a number.

➢ **Comparable Company Valuations:** A more direct approach often used in practice relies on valuation multiples including:

1. P/E (Price to earnings per share);
2. Price to book (book value of net assets); and the
3. EBITDA multiple (market value plus net debt/EBITDA).

Multiples are estimated from the prices of public companies with growth and risk characteristics comparable to the company being valued. Firms in the same industry are the usual source of comparables. Historical M&A or IPO transactions in the same industry are a good source of information if the targets had similar growth rates and margins. M&A transactions will provide an understanding of the premium paid under recent business scenarios. In the late 1990's the premiums paid approached the 40-50% range. Since then, management teams have become more discerning and have been able to conclude transactions within a more reasonable 15-20% range.

Multiples can be applied to historic financial data and can be used for the termination value in a DCF calculation. A forward multiple can give a better estimate of value because it incorporates expectations about the future. P/E multiples often differ between similar companies due to accounting differences, such as depreciation in earnings calculations. Net debt differences can also affect interest expense and earnings. Hence, EBITDA, or cash flow multiple is often used in calculations. For a business with good growth prospects a forward EBITDA multiple in the 8-12 times range may be used as rule of thumb.

Revenue multiples are calculated by dividing the enterprise value by revenues. They are used to value companies for which no earnings are expected in the short-term. They support valuation where no reliable cost information is available. These multiples are often used for technology companies with strong growth prospects. It must always be remembered that the key element in a company's valuation is not the revenue generated, but the free cash. A comparison of the value of similar public companies can provide a reasonable guide to value, particularly in private situations.

➢ **Valuation in M&A:** The intrinsic value of the business is the net present value of expected future cash flows independent of any acquisition. This is the stand-alone value and the basis for negotiations. Any price paid above the intrinsic value represents the control premium to be shared between the target company and the shareholders of buyer firm. This premium includes a market premium and the potential synergy value. These synergies comprise revenue enhancements, cost savings including financial engineering and tax benefits as well as process improvements.

Hostile bid between Mittal Steel and Arcelor is an interesting example of valuation in M&A discussions. An initial hostile bid in January 2006 valued each Arcelor share at •28.21, a 27% premium to the closing price on the day before the bid. However, the share price increased to •35 and this forced Mittal to increase the price offered to •37. To pre-empt a takeover, Arcelor approached a white knight, the Russian steel company Severstal for a merger. This led at the end of June 2006 to a higher offer from Mittal of •40.4 per share which is 90% above Arcelor's share price in January and is a full price. The transaction is expected to be approved by shareholders. However a minimum of •1.3 billion of synergies is required to generate value for the acquiring shareholders. This transaction highlights that valuation discussions are only one element in the decision to acquire. Strategic interests and in this case the desire to become the largest steel company in the world, are also important factors.

➢ **Valuation at the time of flotation:** With regard to a flotation, or a secondary offering of shares, it is typical for a company to be valued based on the comparable multiples of similar listed companies. In these offerings it is normal for the sale to take place at a slight discount to the existing equity value of companies. This discount is typically in the 2-5% range depending on the situation.

IMPROVING VALUATION PROSPECTS

The strong growth prospects for both an industry and an individual company are important factors in a valuation. However, there are a number of additional factors where a company can improve its prospects prior to a strategic transaction:

- ➢ **Depth of management team:** Developing a core group of managers to lead a business without over-reliance on one person will be value enhancing for new shareholders. It is typical for buyer to enhance a management team with financial expertise whilst retaining an experienced Chief Executive and operating management team. However, in turnaround situations, replacing the top management team is often essential to revitalise the business.
- ➢ **Share Structure:** A simplified share structure with one class of shares and one share one vote will enhance the transparency of the company. Private companies often have several classes of shares, which have been issued during several rounds of financing. Alternatively, certain shareholders often retain voting control irrespective of the amount of financing. A simplified share structure will improve a company's valuation, particularly when a flotation is under consideration.

- **Capital Structure:** An under leveraged balance sheet will provide an opportunity to a private equity firm to restructure a business, increase debt levels and improve the return on equity. Furthermore, existing shareholders should question whether the current or an enhanced management team can restructure the business and increase the value without changing ownership. This has occurred successfully at Marks & Spencer over the last 18 months following the unsuccessful bid from Philip Green who attempted a leveraged public to private transaction.
- **Effective Corporate Governance:** A board with effective independent directors successfully challenging the Chief Executive will lead to improved decision taking compared to an autocratic board. Separating the role of Chairman and Chief Executive has improved the governance at many companies, although in the US there remains a preference for a combined role. A more effective board structure is important for key strategic decisions including acquisitions, divestitures and flotation. All of these transactions have a key impact on valuation.

APPROACHES TO VALUE ENHANCEMENT

To maximize a variable that is correlated with the value of the firm, there are several choices for such a variable. It could be;

- Accounting variable - Earnings or return on investment
- Marketing variable - Market share
- Cash flow variable - Cash flow return on investment (CFROI)
- A risk-adjusted cash flow variable - Economic value added (EVA)

The advantages of using these variables are that they are simpler and easier to use than DCF value.

The disadvantage is that the simplicity comes at a cost; these variables are not perfectly correlated with DCF value.

The value-based metrics (EVA & CFROI) have become popular for two reasons. First, capital markets have forced money managers and corporations to have a renewed focus on the balance sheet. In other words, corporations are not only expected to generate positive earnings and sales growth, they also must provide an adequate return on the money they have invested. Second, accounting information, although necessary, does not explain market valuations nor provide comparability between firms. As per US GAAP, the following are the common accounting distortions that prevent accounting data from reliably capturing a firm's true economic performance:

1. Earnings (economic profitability) does not account for, investment to generate the earnings, cost of capital, inflation and cash flow.
2. Accounting ratios/multiples are not comparable because each company has a different; asset life, asset mix, asset age, capital structure and growth potential.
3. Accounting rules distort economic reality due to; off balance sheet assets/liabilities such as; operating leases, research & development, pooling versus purchase accounting inventory policies.

Value-based metric helps to remove the accounting distortions to provide comparability over time, firms, and industries. In general, the advantages of value-based frameworks, relative to free cash flow and dividend discount models, are that they explicitly do the following;

- company's performance to what it is worth,
- distinguish between the value of a firm's existing assets and future investments, and
- consider competition that impacts returns above/below the cost of capital over time.

Together these advantages form the basis for developing valuation models that provide true insights into what a company is worth.

ECONOMIC VALUE ADDED (EVA)

Investors are currently demanding shareholder value more strongly than ever. It is imperative on the part of the company to have an aim to maximize the wealth of its shareholders. The rational investors expect good long-term yield on their investment. Metrics like 'Return on Investment' and 'Earnings per Share' are used as the most important performance measures. The value-based measures have received a lot of attention in the recent years. Maximizing value means the same as maximizing long-term yield on shareholders' investment. Currently the most popular value-based measure is Economic Value Added,

Shareholder value is being used as a overall term covering various aspects in thinking that promotes the interests of shareholders. Normally the term also means a company's value to its shareholders i.e. market capitalization. Shareholder value approach refers to the focus of organization and management on acting within the interests of shareholders. Hence it means focus on maximizing the wealth of shareholders (creating shareholder value).

Value-based measures are new performance measures that originate from the shareholder value approach. They seek to measure the periodic performance in terms of shareholder value created (or destroyed).

EVA measures whether the operating profit is enough compared to the total costs of capital employed. Stewart defined EVA (1990) as Net operating profit after taxes (NOPAT) subtracted with a capital charge:

$$\text{EVA} = \text{NOPAT} - \text{CAPITAL CHARGE}$$

$$\text{EVA} = \text{NOPAT} - (\text{COST OF CAPITAL} \times \text{CAPITAL EMPLOYED}) \quad (1)$$

Or equivalently, if rate or return is defined as NOPAT/CAPITAL EMPLOYED, this turns into a perhaps more revealing formula:

$$\text{EVA} = (\text{RATE OF RETURN} - \text{COST OF CAPITAL}) \times \text{CAPITAL EMPLOYED} \quad (2)$$

Where:

1. Rate of return = NOPAT/CAPITAL EMPLOYED
2. Capital/Employed = Total balance sheet minus non-interest bearing debt in the beginning of the year

Cost of capital = {[Cost of equity × Proportion of equity from capital] + [Cost of debt × Proportion of debt from capital]} × (1-tax rate).

Cost of capital or Weighted Average Cost of Capital (WACC) is the average cost of both equity capital and interest bearing debt. Cost of equity capital is the opportunity return from an investment with same risk as the company has. Cost of equity is usually defined with Capital Asset Pricing Model (CAPM). The estimation of cost of debt is naturally more straightforward, since its cost is explicit. Cost of debt includes also the tax shield due to tax allowance on interest expenses.

If ROI is defined as above (after taxes) then EVA can be presented with familiar terms to be:

$$EVA = (ROI - WACC) \times CAPITAL\ EMPLOYED\ (3)$$

The idea behind EVA is that shareholders must earn a return that compensates the risk taken. In other words equity capital has to earn at least same return as similarly risky investments at equity markets. If that is not the case, then there is no real profit made and actually the company operates at a loss from the viewpoint of shareholders. On the other hand if EVA is zero, this should be treated as a sufficient achievement because the shareholders have earned a return that compensates the risk. This approach - using average risk-adjusted market return as a minimum requirement - is justified since that average return is easily obtained from diversified long-term investments on stock markets. Average long-term stock market return reflects the average return that the public companies generate from their operations.

EVA is based on the common accounting based items like interest bearing debt, equity capital and net operating profit. It differs from the traditional measures mainly by including the cost of equity. Mathematically EVA gives exactly the same results in valuations as Discounted Cash Flow (DCF) or Net Present Value (NPV), which are the best analysis tools from the Shareholders perspective. These both measures include the opportunity cost of equity, they take into account the time value of money and they do not suffer from any kind of accounting distortions. However, NPV and DCF do not suit in performance evaluation because they are based exclusively on cash flows. EVA in turn suits particularly well in performance measuring. Yet, it should be emphasized that the equivalence with EVA and NPV/DCF holds only in special circumstances (in valuations) and thus this equivalence does not have anything to do with performance measurement.

EVA is an accounting performance measure called residual income and is defined to be operating profit subtracted with capital charge. EVA is aimed to be a measure that tells what have happened to the wealth of shareholders. Thus earning a return greater than the cost of capital increases value (of a company), and earning less decreases value. For listed companies Stewart defined another measure that assesses if the company has created shareholder value. If the total market value of a company is more than the amount of capital invested in it, the company has managed to create shareholder value. If the case is opposite, the market value is less than capital invested, the company has destroyed shareholder value.

Market value added = company's total market value – capital invested and with simplifying assumption that market and book value of debt are equal, this is the same as:

$$\text{Market Value Added} = \text{Market Value of Equity} - \text{Book Value of Equity (4)}$$

Book value of equity refers to all equity equivalent items like reserves, retained earnings and provisions. In other words, in this context, all the items that are not debt (interest bearing or non-interest bearing) are classified as equity.

Market value added is identical by meaning with the market-to-book-ratio. The difference is only that MVA is an absolute measure and market-to-book-ratio is a relative measure. If MVA is positive that means that market-to-book -ratio is more than one. Negative MVA means market-to-book-ratio less than one.

According to Stewart MVA tells us how much value company has added to, or subtracted from, its shareholders' investment. Successful companies add to their MVA and thus increase the value of capital invested in the company. Unsuccessful companies decrease the value of the capital originally invested in the company. Whether a company succeeds in creating MVA (increasing shareholder value) or not, depends on its rate of return. If a company's rate of return exceeds its cost of capital, the company will sell on the stock markets with premium compared to the original capital (has positive MVA). On the other hand, companies that have rate of return smaller than their cost of capital, sell with discount compared to the original capital invested in company. Whether a company has positive or negative MVA depends on the level of rate of return compared to the cost of capital. All this applies also to EVA. Thus positive EVA means also positive MVA and *vice versa.*

Market Value Added = Present value of all future EVA (5)

Market value added is equal to present value of all future EVA. Increasing EVA, a company increases its market value added, or in other words increases the difference between company's value and the amount of capital invested in it. The relationship with EVA and MVA has its implications on valuation.

Market Value of Equity = Book Value of Equity + Present value of all future EVAs (6)

The valuation formula of EVA (formula 2) however is always equivalent to Discounted cash flow and Net present value. Thus the valuation formula (formula 2) gives always the right estimate of value (same as DCF and NPV) no matter what the original book value of equity is. This holds true even though capital is not an unbiased estimate of current value of assets and rate of return is not an unbiased estimate of the true return. That is because an increase in book value decreases the periodic EVA and decrease in book value increases EVA and these changes cancel each other out.

EVA- PERFORMANCE MEASURE AND WEALTH CREATION

EVA is calculated from the accounting-based numbers and some version of accounting return is used in calculating EVA. As a result all the discrepancies in base figures affect EVA. If ROI overstates IRR then EVA also overstates the real shareholder value added. They underestimate the return in the beginning and overestimate it in the end of the period. Some growth phase companies or business units have a lot of new investments. Such growth phase companies are likely to have currently negative EVA although their true rate of return would be good and so their true long-term shareholder wealth added (true long-term EVA) would be positive. Therefore it is said that EVA is a short-term performance measure. Stopping any investments can indeed increase short-term EVA.

EVA does not directly help in finding ways to improve operational efficiency except when improving capital turnover. EVA does not help directly in finding strategic advantages that enable a company to earn abnormal returns and thus create shareholder value. EVA is helpful to understand how the wealth of shareholders can be improved. Increasing EVA falls always into one of the following three categories:

1. Rate of return increases with the existing capital base. It means that more operating profits are generated without tying any more capital in the business.
2. Additional capital is invested in business earning more than the cost of capital. (Making NPV positive investments.
3. Capital is withdrawn or liquidated from businesses that fail to earn return greater than the cost of capital.

The first method includes all the countless ways to improve operating efficiency or increase revenues. Increasing rate of return with current operations and new investments are often linked; in order to improve the efficiency of ongoing operations, companies often do investments which enhance also the return on current capital base.

In the second method fact that the wealth of shareholders increase with investments returning more that the cost of capital if they also use some kind of weighted average cost of capital (WACC) and Net Present Value (NPV) methodology in investment calculations.

The third category, withdrawing capital, is probably not so widely understood and applied as the previous ones. It is however also very important to realize that shareholder value can also be increased if capital is withdrawn from businesses earning less than the cost of capital. This withdrawal will reduce excess inventories and receivables and thus the capital costs caused by them are reduced without corresponding decreases in revenues. This is a simpler way to improve EVA.

Conceptually, EVA is superior to accounting profits as a measure of value creation because it recognizes the cost of capital and, hence, the riskiness of a firm's operations. Return on capital is very common and relatively good performance measure. Different companies calculate this return with different formulas and call it also with different names like Return on investment (ROI), Return on invested capital (ROIC), Return on capital employed (ROCE), Return on net assets (RONA), Return on assets (ROA) etc. The main shortcoming with all these rates of return is in all cases that maximizing rate of return does not necessarily maximize the return to shareholders.

Observing rate of return and making decisions based on it alone is similar to assessing products on the "gross margin on sales" - percentage. The product with the biggest "gross margin on sales" - percentage is not necessary the most profitable product. The product profitability depends also on the product volume. In the same way bare high rate of return should not be used as a measure of a company's performance. Also the magnitude of operations, i.e., the amount of capital that produces that return is important. High return is a lot easier to achieve with tiny amount of capital than with large amount of capital. Almost any highly profitable company can increase its rate of return if it decreases its size or overlooks some good projects, which produce a return under the current rate of return.

The difference between EVA and ROI is actually exactly the same as with NPV (Net present value) and IRR (Internal rate of return). IRR is a good way to assess investment possibilities, but we ought not to prefer one investment project to the other according to their IRR. Assume two good and exclusive investment projects, project 1 and project 2. Project 1 has lower IRR but is much bigger in scope (bigger initial investment and bigger cash flows and bigger NPV). Project 1 (the project offering lower IRR) is better for shareholders even though it has lower IRR. That is because it provides bigger absolute return than project 2. The reason is exactly same as with ROI: maximizing rate of return percentage does not matter. What matters is the absolute amount of shareholders' wealth added.

In the corporate control EVA and NPV go hand in hand as also ROI and IRR. The formers tell us the impacts to shareholders wealth and the latters tell us the rate of return. IRR can always be used along with NPV in investment calculations and ROI can always be used along with EVA in company performance. EVA and NPV should be in the commanding role in corporate control and ROI & IRR should have the role of giving additional information.

RETURN ON EQUITY (ROE)

ROE suffers from the same shortcomings as ROI. Risk component is not included and hence there is no comparison. The level of ROE does not tell the owners if company is creating shareholders wealth or destroying it. With ROE this shortcoming is however much more severe than with ROI, because simply increasing leverage can increase ROE. It is known that decreasing solvency does not always make shareholders' position better because of the increased (financial) risk. As ROI and IRR, return on equity (ROE) is also an informative measure but it should not guide the operations.

EARNINGS PER SHARE (EPS)

EPS is raised simply by investing more capital in business. If the additional capital is equity (cash flow) then the EPS will rise if the rate of return of the invested capital is just positive. If the additional capital is debt then the EPS will rise if the rate of return of the invested capital is just above the cost of debt. In reality the invested capital is a mix of debt and equity and the EPS will rise if the rate of return of that additional capital invested is somewhere between cost of debt and zero. Therefore EPS is inappropriate measure of corporate performance. EPS and earnings can be increased simply by pouring more money into business even though the return on that money would be entirely unacceptable from the viewpoint of owners. EPS, earnings and earnings/EPS growth should therefore not be considered as performance measures.

CASH VALUE ADDED (CVA)

Cash Value Added (CVA) is very similar to EVA except that it includes only cash items. Furthermore it keeps the capital costs constant over certain investment period. CVA is the difference between Operating Cash Flow (OCF) and Operating Cash Flow Demand (OCFD). OCF is the sum of Earnings before Depreciation, Interest and Tax (EBDIT, adjusted for non-cash charges), working capital movement and non-strategic investments. OCFD represents the capital costs. It is the average capital cost per year (in absolute terms) that meets the investors' financial requirements. OCFD is constant over the investment period.

Unlike EVA other shareholder value measures are based more on cash flows than EVA. Therefore they do not normally suffer from the same imperfections as EVA does. Hence the rate of return used with these other metrics is usually a good estimate of the underlying true rate of return without any adjustments. CFROI and CVA defer most of the depreciation into later years in order to achieve smooth return or smooth capital costs. CFROI includes also some salvage value in calculations. These features make the return to divide more evenly between different periods but they also make the performance measures more subjective.

Some Value-based measures have been found to correlate better with share prices than EVA. For example Cash Flow Return on Investment (CFROI) explains share price movements better than EVA. Of course EVA can also be modified in order to avoid some accounting distortions and to correlate better with share prices, but then we have almost as complicated measure as CFROI. All the shareholder value metrics are said to be identical to discounted free cash flow method. CFROI calls for taking into account the effects of inflation to asset values and this in turn takes time and resources. Hence,the other metrics do not pass a prudent cost-benefit analysis; the additional costs with implementing them instead of EVA are often more than the incremental information achieved with them.

The Economic Value Added (EVA) is a measure of surplus value. In this one has to define the return on capital (ROC) to be the "true" cash flow return on capital earned on an investment and also define the cost of capital as the weighted average of the costs of the different financing instruments used to finance the investment. It is:

EVA = (Return on Capital – Cost of Capital) (Capital Invested in Project)

The CFROI is a measure of the cash flow return made on capital, It is:

CFROI = (Adjusted EBIT + Depreciation & Other Non-cash Charges) / Capital Invested

For measuring EVA, the firm has to use the book value of capital invested as their measure of capital invested. The book capital may not reflect the value of intangible assets such as research and development. The operating income has to be cleansed of any expenses which are really capital expenses or financing expenses. The cost of capital for EVA purposes should be computed based on market values. If one estimates return on capital and cost of capital correctly in DCF valuation, then those numbers can be used to calculate EVA.

Economic Value Added is a residual income variable. It is defined as Net operating profit after taxes subtracted with the cost of capital tied in operations. Standard EVA corresponds mathematically the standard DCF formula because it is a modified version of DCF. EVA's equivalence with DCF and NPV holds in valuations although DCF and NPV are based only on cash flows and EVA is based also on historical accounting items. Inflation can distort the values of EVA. Furthermore EVA suffers from wrong periodization. In most cases the impacts of these shortcomings are however fairly small. They can also usually be eliminated for major parts with some corrective adjustments.

In spite of its faults, EVA seems to have importance for companies as a performance measurement and controlling tool. First of all it is fairly simple measure but still measures well the ultimate aim of any given company, the increase or decrease in shareholders' wealth. Maximizing traditional performance measures like ROI is not theoretically in line with maximizing the wealth of shareholders. Therefore EVA is superior to conventional performance measures. The premise behind EVA - that businesses must cover their capital costs - is neither new nor peculiar.

At operational level this new approach leads often to increased shareholder value through increased capital turnover. In many companies everything has been done in cutting costs but the capital efficiency has been ignored. EVA has been helpful because it forces to pay attention to capital employed and especially to excess working capital. Allocating the capital costs to their originators i.e. individual functions of organization can further reinforce this impact.

One of EVA's most powerful features is that it is a good way to increase shareholder value. The good feasibility for this purpose is due to the nature of EVA as excess return to shareholders. EVA is closely related to NPV. It avoids the problems associated with approaches that focus on percentage spreads - between ROE and Cost of Equity and ROC and Cost of Capital. These approaches may lead firms with high ROE to turn away good projects to avoid lowering their percentage spreads.

CASH FLOW RETURN ON INVESTMENT (CFROI)

This product is evolved by Boston Consulting Group (BCG) and HOLT Value Associates. It is the long-term internal rate of return defined almost as common IRR. CFROI is determined by converting profitability data into gross cash flow and using real gross assets as an implied investment. CFROI is calculated in two steps; first inflation-adjusted cash flows available to all capital owners in the firm are measured and they are compared with the inflation-adjusted gross investment made by the capital owners. After that the ratio of gross cash flow to gross investment is translated into an internal rate of return by recognizing the finite economic life of depreciating assets and the residual value of non-depreciating assets such as land and working capital.

CFROI is an internal rate of return (IRR) type metric which measures the return expected to be generated by a firm's existing assets throughout their useful lives. CFROI can be calculated in five steps:

1. Compute the average life of assets by dividing gross assets by depreciation expense;
2. Compute gross cash flow by adjusting net income for non-cash charges, financing expenses, operating lease payments and equity reserve accounts;
3. Compute the gross investment as gross plant and equipment adjusted for reserves, capitalized expenses, restructuring charges, amortization and the present value of operating leases;
4. Compute the value of any assets that will not depreciate (which will represent the future value); and
5. Solve for IRR (or CFROI)

CFROI takes a very different approach relative to EVA. Instead of being a measure of economic profit, CFROI is an internal rate of return. As a rate of return, it provides a consistent basis from which to evaluate companies regardless of their size, which a rupee-based measure of economic profit cannot do. This characteristic of CFROI has made it very popular in the money management area, as investors need to compare many companies against each other to make investment decisions.

It is, important to understand the limitation that ratios have when used to measure wealth creation. First, IRRs by themselves do not provide any indication as to whether a firm is destroying or creating shareholder value. Second, an IRR is a non-linear measure, which creates communication issues among non-financial managers. For instance, how much would a manager need to improve cash flow to obtain a 10% increase in IRR? As a form of an IRR, CFROI faces these issues.

In managing to an internal rate of return, the CFROI also mixes operating and financing decisions exactly like a Return on Equity (ROE) calculation. The primary goal of a this value-based metric is to provide comparability over time, firms, and industries. The mixing operating and financing, CFROIs can change when there has been no change in a firm's underlying operating performance. This is similar to the behavior of a ROE.

Instead of being a measure of economic profit, CFROI is an internal rate of return. As a rate of return, it provides a consistent basis from which to evaluate companies regardless of their size, which other rupee based measures of economic profit cannot do. This characteristic of CFROI has made it very popular in the money management area, as investors need to compare many companies against each another to make investment decisions.

RESTRUCTURING AND OTHER OPTIONS

Continuous growth in shareholder value remains the key business objective for private and public business enterprises. However, growing revenue and profitability year after year in competitive markets is a challenge that few companies achieve on a consistent basis. Expansion through acquisition, whilst tempting for revenue growth, can lead to complex integration issues and periods of under performances.

Companies will therefore have periods where restructuring and business refocusing is required. It is crucial that the board of directors and the management team recognise the requirement to restructure, develop an executable plan and, if necessary, negotiate with creditors and shareholders. In cases where financing difficulties become apparent, the court based solutions of administration and/or insolvency can be avoided if the need for change is accepted.

There are several reasons why companies reach a situation where a refocusing, or a restructuring, is required. These include changes in the competitive environment and an inappropriate cost or capital structure.

➢ **Changing Market Dynamics:** The globalisation of business has lead to a rapidly changing environment. The winners are the companies able to embrace these changes by reducing costs, whilst increasing the quality of their products and services to their customers. In the food retailing sector, both Wal Mart in the US and Tesco in the UK have used the latest technology to manage their supply chain and distribution networks, resulting in consistent lower prices for their customers. This has also allowed both companies to broaden their offering of products and services, thus expanding their served market from initially low cost foods to multi product offerings internationally. Companies that have been unable to adapt to these developments have lost market share and have been forced to restructure or to sell their businesses. In the US, Kmart was recently purchased by a hedge fund intent on an aggressive restructuring. In the UK, food retailers including Sainsbury, Morrison/Safeway and Marks

& Spencer have been forced to change their management teams and their strategies in an attempt to regain market share. The constant threat of a hostile bid retains the management focus.

➢ **Capital Structure:** In a low interest rate environment, there is a tendency for companies to leverage their balance sheets as the cost of debt is significantly lower than the cost of equity. Finance theory also highlights the advantages of holding a certain amount of debt on a company balance sheet to benefit from the tax shield effect of interest payments. Furthermore, the leverage buy-out specialists have found that a significant amount of debt on the balance sheet matched with the necessary incentives, focuses the attention of the management team to cut costs drastically, expand the company's markets and repay debt as rapidly as possible. However, in a competitive environment, with declining revenues and profitability, inappropriate amounts of debt on the balance sheet requires quick action.

➢ **Cost Structure:** Companies that are unable to reduce their costs in comparison with their competitors will rapidly lose profitability. Maintaining a flexible cost base in rapidly changing market conditions is an important goal for companies. The ability to outsource production and services provides a company with the opportunity of converting fixed into variable costs. There are of course limitations to outsourcing, particularly in the areas where companies need to develop and maintain their competitive edge, such as product development. However, the cost advantages versus the potential loss of control of certain aspects of the business have to be considered carefully. Dell has been able to redefine the PC hardware business through direct marketing to consumers. The company has employed the latest technology to manage their distribution systems and suppliers, resulting in very low inventory levels. Dell built itself over 20 years, in a fiercely competitive market, through organic growth and no acquisitions. Compaq, which initially had a dominant position in the PC hardware market, was unable to transform its expensive distribution structure. HP acquired the company in 2002 and restructuring the two unprofitable PC hardware businesses has been, until now, unsuccessful. There are many restructuring options available to the companies, a few are as follows;

Private equity firms, due to their effective monitoring role of management, can often force change in a company's management team and accelerate a restructuring more rapidly than in a public company situation. In some cases, a change of senior management is required in order to refocus the business. In any case, the commitment of the senior management team must be secured as early as possible in the process and an executable short to medium term plan must be put in place with clearly identifiable targets.

➢ **Cost Cutting:** Stage one of the restructuring process is for the company to cut costs and to redeploy resources as rapidly as possible. Once the decision on the direction of the company has been taken, the disposal of surplus assets needs to be executed. Whilst a rapid sale reduces the proceeds, a structured auction with sufficient competitive tension ensures that a market price is obtained for the assets. In the situation where assets are required for the future business, it may be possible to remove them from the balance sheet through sale and leaseback transactions, or through the formation of joint ventures and alliances with partners. Throughout this process, it is essential to reduce the uncertainty for employees through constant communication. A well executed cost reduction plan needs to include careful management of the free cash flow generated by the business.

➢ **Negotiating with Creditors and Shareholders:** With falling profitability, early discussions with creditors and shareholders are essential in order to develop a realistic workout plan. Whilst shareholders may be unwilling to inject further funds into an ailing business, creditors will be keen to avoid, as far as possible, a court based administration and insolvency procedure due to the high costs involved. With a credible plan and management team, convincing creditors to accept significant reductions in their repayments is an achievable objective. Deals can be structured creatively to include short term payment holidays or balloon payments, once the business has been transformed. Equity sweeteners also can be added to provide creditors with upside potential in return for a lengthening of the repayment period, the injection of further debt and/or the reduction of liabilities.

➢ **Merger into another Firm:** During the restructuring and asset sale process it may become apparent that a full sale, or merger of a business, either to a competitor, or to a financial investor is required. The existing business either can be fully absorbed into another company in a similar sector to generate synergy benefits, or can be retained as an independent subsidiary under new direction. In either case, such a strategic transaction is transformational for the business and provides a catalyst for the successful restructuring of the business.

SUMMARY

Financial analysts are increasingly utilizing value-based metrics, such as EVA and CFROI, to help them understand a firm's performance and determine its value. Each measure provides unique advantages over traditional non-economic metrics such as EPS and ROE. Economic Margin is a new metric that links the EVA and CFROI combining their strengths and minimizing their weaknesses. The EVA provides managers a single metric that summarizes wealth creation, and avoids the goal setting problems found with ratio-based and IRR measures. The CFROI framework's core strength is that gives it a strong link to market values. This allows analyst and investors the ability to understand the performance expectations built into a company's market valuation. The Economic Margin Framework is unique in that it combines the advancements in value-based metrics made by economic profit and IRR-based metrics. The Economic Margin is a cash flow-based economic profit measure. Economic Margins use gross assets to avoid the "old plant" accounting distortions inherent in most economic profit measures. Since the metric begins as a money measure of profit, it ensures that managers always pursue opportunities that create wealth. This eliminates the conflicts created by IRR based frameworks that put managers in the awkward position of accepting opportunities that reduce the average IRR of their division. Economic Value Added is a residual income variable. It is defined as net operating profit after taxes subtracted with the cost of capital tied in operations. Standard EVA corresponds mathematically the standard DCF formula because it is a modified version of DCF. In periodical performance measurement EVA can however in some occasions give misleading information because it suffers from the same shortcomings as accounting rate of return (ROI). Inflation can distort the values of EVA. Furthermore EVA suffers from wrong periodization. In spite all this, EVA seems to have importance for companies as a performance measurement and controlling tool. First of all it is fairly simple measure but still measures well the ultimate aim of any given company, the increase or decrease in shareholders' wealth. Maximizing traditional performance measures like ROI is not theoretically in line with maximizing the wealth of shareholders. Therefore EVA is superior to conventional performance measures.

Review Questions

1. How can the valuation prospects of the business be enhanced?
2. What are the different approaches to enhance the business valuation?
3. Explain EVA and CFROI and how are used in business valuation?
4. What are the different options available for business value enhancement?

Video Linkages

1. http://www.youtube.com/watch?v=L9Mzx5pdWwM,Understanding How CFROI is Used in Valuation
2. http://www.youtube.com/watch?v=4KT-hE0RII8, Investment and Business Valuation with Economic Value Added Calculation
3. http://www.youtube.com/watch?v=ZCaeMTSTWYs, [MVA] Market Value Added & [EVA] Economic Value Added

ASSIGNMENT

Take two companies in any one industry sector, study their annual reports and value enhancement prospects in each of the cases. Recommend the measures.

BIBLIOGRAPHY

1. Aswath Damodaran, (2009), *Damodaran on Valuation,* Wiley (2nd Edn).
2. Aswath Damodaran, (2002), *Investment Valuation,* Wiley (2nd edn).
3. Aswath Damodaran, (2002), *The Dark side of Valuation,* Wiley.
4. Andre F. Perold, *Ford Motor Co.'s Value Enhancement Plan (A),* Harvard Business School, Publishing, Jan 22, 2001.
5. Biddle, G., Bwen, R.M., Wallace, J.S., (1996). Abstract of "Evidence on the relative and incremental information content of EVA, residual income, earnings and operating cash flow". University of Washington, Seattle, WA.
6. Bacidore, J.M. Boquist, J.A. Milbourn, T.T. Thakor, A.V. (1997). "The Search for the Best Financial Performance Measure". *Financial Analysts Journal.* May/June 1997.pp.11-20.
7. Birchard, B. (1996). "Do it yourself': How Valmont Industries implemented EVA". *CFO*. Mar 1996. pp. 34-40
8. Blair, Alistair (1997). "Watching the new metrics", *Management Today,* Apr 1997, pp. 48-50.
9. Brealey Richard A. & Mayers Stewart C. (1991). *Principles of Corporate Finance.* 4th Edition. McGraw-Hill Series in Finance. McGraw-Hill, Inc. NewYork.
10. Copeland, T. E. Weston, F.J. (1992). *Financial Theory and Corporate Policy.* 3rd Edition. Addison-Wesley Publishing Company. New York.

11. De Villiers J. (1989), "Inflation, asset structure and the discrepancy between accounting and true return". *Journal of Business Finance and Accounting*. Volume 16, numb 1 Spring 1989, pp.493-506

12. De Villiers J. (1997), "The distortions in Economic Value Added". *Journal of Economics and Business*. Volume 49, numb 3 May/June 1997, pp.285-300

13. Dodd, James L; Chen, Shimin; (1996), "EVA: A new panacea?", *Business and Economic Review*, Vol 42; Jul-Sep 1996, pp.26-28

14. Economist "Valuing companies: A star to sail by". *The Economist*. August 2nd (1997), pp.57-59.

15. Gee, Andrew (1997), "Kingfisher executive compensation", *CPS Alcair Global Review*, Volume III, Number V, Spring 1997, pp.7-8

16. Glasser, J.J. (1996), "How EVA works against GATX" *Chief Executive*. Jan/Feb 1996. pp.42-43.

17. Grant J. L. (1996), "Foundations of EVA for investment managers" *The Journal of Portfolio Management*, Vol 23, Fall 1996, pp.41-48

18. Gressle, M. (1996), Abstract of "How to implement EVA and make share prices rise". *Corporate Cashflow*. Vol 17 Mar 1996. pp.28-30.

19. Lehn, K & Makhija, A. K. (1996), "EVA and MVA: As performance measures and signals for strategic change" *Strategy and Leadership*. Vol 24 May/June 1996. pp.34-38

10 CHAPTER

Business Valuation Standards

"In today's world business appraisers must not only adhere to the business valuation standards, but I believe they must exceed these standards"

— Gary L. Schroeder, ASA MD

Learning Objectives

To understand:

- What is business valuation standards (BVS)?
- Why BVSs are needed?
- Contents of BVS
- Standards of 'value'
- Valuation methods, tools and reporting

When a business is valued, there must be some standard by which it is evaluated. All of the business valuation standards assume a specific point in time as valuation changes quickly, based on external factors like the economy and the industry, and internal factors like the customer base, advertising, and ownership. The valuation procedures serve as the template for business valuation assignments of all types, demonstrating its relevance for the complex business organizations that exist today. To be specific, the valuation of a business is not an exact science and ultimately depends upon a number of factors like the purpose of valuation, stage of business, past financials, expected financial results, industry scenario, market recognition etc. In nutshell business valuation is the process of determining the "Economic Worth" of a company based on its business model and external environment and supported with reasons and empirical evidence.

INTRODUCTION

The intent of valuation standards is to protect users of valuations and the community at large. Standards typically cover the development and reporting of a valuation. A number of organizations have released valuation standards or guidance. There is no mandatory compliance, and very often buyers and sellers of valuations are not even aware of these standards. No single set of valuation standards covers the valuation of private companies. Business valuation standards began to appear in the late 1980s. The various American institution have taken the lead is issiung the business valuation standards. To name the few, Appraisal Foundation in 1987, American Society of Appraisers (ASA) in 1992, Institute of Business Appraisers (IBA) in 1993, National Association of Certified Valuation Analysts (NACVA) and American Institute of Certified Public Accountants (AICPA) in 2007

In general business appraisers should be aware of general issues that may impact a valuation. Often the business appraisers consult the client's legal counsel for their position on specific issues. Again, the business appraiser must use reasoned, informed judgment in developing an indication of value, considering the case-specific facts relevant to the valuation. All assets, tangible, intangible or IP-related, have legal ownership aspects. The majority of non-IP intangible assets such as customer relationships, water or air rights, and workforce intangibles, are given substance by some form of legal contract. For IP, which has no physical form and for which the marginal cost to replicate is often close to zero, the legal protection provides an important component of value. However, because each IP form has unique characteristics each must be examined within the larger business perspective in view.

Business valuation standards provide a general template for the preparing valuation reports. The past decade has witnessed a good deal of activity regarding professional business valuation standards. In US professional business valuation standards are promulgated by the following organizations and most have made many changes to their standards in subsiquent years:

➢ The American Institute of Certified Public Accountants (AICPA). In June 2007, the AICPA released its newly developed standards, the Statement on Standards for Valuation Services-Valuation of a Business, Business Ownership Interest or Intangible Assets (SSVS1), effective for all valuation engagements accepted on or after January 1, 2008.

➢ The American Society of Appraisers (ASA). In July 2008, the ASA updated and revised its Business Valuation Standards. These revisions significantly expanded the ASA's required reporting and assignment disclosures. Section BVS-IX was added, which deals with "Intangible Asset Valuation" and includes an appendix of intellectual property examples. The ASA standards include "Statements on ASA Business Valuation Standards," which have the full weight of the standards; these also were expanded in 2008.

➢ The Institute of Business Appraisers (IBA). Not changed its standards since October 25, 2001.

➢ The National Association of Certified Valuation Analysts (NACVA). In November 2007, NACVA released its revised NACVA Professional Standards.

➢ The Appraisal Foundation (TAF). The Standard is often referred to as USPAP, an acronym for the Uniform Standards of Professional Appraisal Practice. "Uniform" here refers to a structure providing separate standards for several disciplines (real estate, personal property, and business appraisals) within a single uniform framework. USPAP was released in 2007.

➤ Internal Revenue Service, which released its "IRM 4.48, Engineering Program, Business Valuation Guidelines" in July 2006.

Three significant features of all the above standards are as follows:

➤ All of these standards are considered by their authors to be minimum standards or requirements; the authors intend that, in many cases, the appraiser should expand his/her report and/or his/her analysis.

➤ All of the standards address both the development of a valuation analysis and its presentation in a written report.

➤ All of these standards address ethics, either directly in the body of the standards or by reference to ethical standards printed elsewhere.

Many things are common in these standards. All require the consideration of the asset, market and income approaches; marketability or lack thereof; control or lack thereof; and all require understanding the applicable standard and premise of value. Significantly, all standards recognize a "full" or "comprehensive" valuation report as the point of departure for defining other report forms. And the reporting requirements for full reports are remarkably similar across all organizations.

Each of the major business valuation standards (AICPA, ASA and USPAP) describes valuation engagements and reports using different terminology and requirements. The AICPA and the American Society of Appraisers are prominent business valuation standard setters. Following is an overview of the project and report types under each.

AICPA (THE AMERICAN INSTITUTE OF CERTIFIED PUBLIC ACCOUNTANTS)

In Statement on Standards for Valuation Services (SSVS), the engagement described are of two types:

1. In a valuation engagement, the valuation analyst estimates the value and is free to apply the valuation approaches and methods he or she deems appropriate in the circumstances.
2. In a calculation engagement, the valuation analyst and the client agree on the valuation approaches and methods the valuation analyst will use and the extent of procedures the valuation analyst will perform in the process of calculating the value of a subject interest (these procedures will be more limited than those of a valuation engagement).

AICPA provides for three types of reports:

1. The detailed report provide sufficient information to permit intended users to understand the data, reasoning, and analyses underlying the valuation analyst's conclusion of value.
2. A summary report provide an abridged version of the information that would be provided in a detailed report, and therefore, need not contain the same level of detail as a detailed report.
3. A calculation report is used to report the results of a calculation engagement. It should state that (1) a calculation engagement does not include all of the procedures required for a valuation engagement and (2) had a valuation engagement been performed, the results may have been different.

ASA (AMERICAN SOCIETY OF APPRAISERS)

In ASA Business Valuation Standards (BVS) they describe three types of engagements:

1. The objective of an appraisal is to express an unambiguous opinion as to the value of a business, business ownership interest, security or intangible asset. The opinion is supported by all procedures that the appraiser deems to be relevant to the valuation.

2. The objective of a limited appraisal is to express an estimate as to the value of a business, business ownership interest, security or intangible asset. The development of this estimate excludes some additional procedures that are required in an appraisal.

3. The objective of a calculation is to provide an approximate indication of value of a business, business ownership interest, security or intangible asset based on the performance of limited procedures agreed upon by the appraiser and the client.

BVS discusses one specific type of report:

1. The comprehensive written business valuation report must clearly communicate relevant information, valuation methods and conclusions in a logical progression, and must incorporate the other specific requirements of this Standard, including the signature and certification provisions.

The standards allows a business valuation report to be less comprehensive in content provided that the report complies with the minimum content required by Standard 10.2 of USPAP. BVS also provides an exception for preliminary communications of results to a client, reporting on valuation calculations, or reporting on engagements that do not result in conclusions of value.

USPAP (THE UNIFORM STANDARDS OF PROFESSIONAL APPRAISAL PRACTICE)

USPAP Standard 9 addresses one type of engagement:

1. In developing an appraisal of an interest in a business enterprise or intangible asset, an appraiser must identify the problem to be solved, determine the scope of work necessary to solve the problem, and correctly complete the research and analysis necessary to produce a credible appraisal.

USPAP Standard 10-2 provides for two types of reports:

1. When the intended users include parties other than the client, an Appraisal Report must be provided.

2. When the intended users do not include parties other than the client, a Restricted Use Appraisal Report may be provided.

The minimum content required by Standard 10.2 of USPAP is similar to that of a summary report under SSVS No. 1. If the intended users include anyone other than the client, such as auditors, taxing authorities, or a court of law, a restricted use report would be inappropriate. Anything less than an independent, unrestricted appraisal, such as a calculation, is outside the scope of USPAP and should clearly be labeled as such to avoid misleading users of the analysis.

BACKGROUND

During last decade profound changes in environment have taken place and the pace of growth of business has been phenomenal. The participation of the public in the financial market has increased tremendously resulting into the development of new financial products. All these have led to a greater demand for valuation services as investors and shareholders are interested in up to date information on their assets.

Business valuation is a complex process and it involves a multitude of factors ranging from financial matters to historical perspectives. It is a broad and technically challenging discipline. The valuation is performed in a variety of contexts and for a variety of purposes. The meaning of value is different to different people and the result will not be the same, should the context change. A valuation is not an exact science. The value is subjective term and can have a different connotation. Valuation involves use of professional judgement, knowledge of business, analysis of facts, interpretations and use of different methods and procedures, which may result into different value in each given situation. This implies that the business value must be measured and defined by a 'standard of value' that is relevant, meaningful and reliable.

In Indian context there is no uniform standard for business valuation. Hence, ICAI has decided to develop Business Valuation Practice Standards (BVPS) which would establish uniform principles, practices and procedures for valuers performing valuation services.

The business valuation analysis is performed for variety of purposes such as; acquisitions, mergers, leveraged buyouts, initial public offerings, employee stock ownership plans and other share based plans, partner and shareholder buy-ins or buyouts and stock redemptions. The other purposes are dispute resolution and/ or litigation/pending litigation relating to matters such as dissolution, bankruptcy, contractual disputes, owner disputes, dissenting shareholder and minority ownership oppression cases, employment disputes and intellectual property disputes. For regulatory compliances valuations are also done and these covers financial reporting, income tax, property tax, and tax compliance; purchase price allocations; and charitable contributions. The same business may have different values if different standard of value is used and different approaches are adopted. The rising demand for valuation services has given new avenues for the finance professionals. Hence, in India ICFAI deveopled Business Valuation Standard for the following purposes:

- Provide guidance to the valuers in performing valuation services
- Define general valuation concepts, principles, approaches and methods
- Define basis of valuation and premise of valuation
- Set out a code of conduct

CONTENTS OF STANDARDS

All of the standards have the following in common;

- **Independence** - The appraiser must not act in favor of the client or any other party.
- **Fees not based on appraised value** - Fees based upon, for example, a percentage of the valuation are unethical and are not allowed.
- **Limiting conditions be explicitly stated** - All assumptions must be clearly started in the report for the reader. If a lawsuit is pending against a business, the valuation must explicitly state that the impact of the outcome of the lawsuit will have an unknown effect on the value as the impact have not been considered.
- **Participants in the valuation be disclosed** - All professionals participating in a valuation report must sign it, and must have certification of their independence, fee arrangements, and other factors.
- **Information sources be stated** - Sources used in compiling the report must be stated.

The precise minimum requirements about business valuation report vary from countery to contry. However, they include the purpose and scope of the assignment, the standard of value and specific valuation date being employed, an identification of the specific interest being evaluated, the relevant laws of the land that govern the entity being valued, the scope of the procedures employed during valuation, the nature and history of the business, the historical financial information on the business, a thorough financial analysis of the business comparing the business' performance with industry trends, an overview of the industry in which the business operates and the impact of market conditions on the business, and the current investment climate.

OBJECTIVES AND SCOPE

In general the objective for framing the valuation standards is to provide common standards for business valuers, who are involved in business valuation process/exercise. Business valuations methods and procedures followed may vary, but the principle behind the valuation is same irrespective of the methods followed. Hence, the overall objective is to develop a common standard, whereby all types of valuations are covered under one head. Thereafter a consistent and prudent approach is followed keeping the following objectivs in mind.

- Promoting 'best practices' and fairness in valuation services
- Infusing credibility, relevancy and transparency of valuation information.
- Enhancing quality, consistency, comparability and uniformity in valuation process.
- Applicability to valuation of assets, liabilities and cash flows
- Improving corporate governance.
- Improving public confidence in valuation.

In a standard business valuation, the scope of work is as follows:

1. Appropriate valuation methods and procedures;
2. Collection and analysis of relevant data/information of the business;
3. Study the financial and economic conditions affecting the business enterprise;
4. Historical financial results, current operations, and future prospects of the enterprise;
5. Study of capital stock or other ownership interests in the business enterprise
6. Analysis of sales of similar businesses or capital stock of publicly held similar businesses

Appraiser has to prepare a formal report in accordance with requirements. Sometimes oral appraisal reports are permitted in certain types of engagements.

Some Standards (BVS-I) provide for two types of limited scope appraisals; limited appraisals and calculations. A limited appraisal is an appraisal, which is based on limited procedures to collect and analyze information. In a calculations engagement, the appraiser performs only those procedures which are agreed upon with the client. Business Valuation Practice Standard (BVPS) propose to set out concepts, principles, practices and procedures in context of estimation of value of a subject matter which are generally accepted internationally and which the Council of the Institute of Chartered Accounts considers desirable in the light of prevailing legal framework, procedures and practices in India. The valuers should be aware of any Governmental regulations and other professional standards applicable to the engagement, including the ICAI's Code of Ethics and Schedule 1 and 2 to the "Chartered Accountants Act, 1949".

The business valuation standard framed by ICAI has some exceptions and is not applicable when:

1. Valuation is part of an attest engagement like audit, review, compilation engagement etc.
2. Valuer does not apply valuation approaches and methods and does not use professional judgment.
3. Purpose is for determining economic damages.
4. Valuer is unable to apply valuation approaches/methods mentioned in the standard

ETHICAL ORIENTATION

It is esential on the part of valuation professional to have professional competence with a special knowledge and skill in valuation process. He should have adequate knowledge of valuation principles and theory and a level of skill in the application of such principles. He should be able to identify, gather, and analyze data. He should be able to apply appropriate valuation approaches and methods, and use professional judgment in developing the estimate of business value.

A valuer must take due professional care in the performance of services. He should able to do intitial research to get proper information and adequate documentation. The analyst valuing a subject shall act independently, free from all bias. He shall have no financial or other interests in the subject being valued. He should make disclosure of a potential conflict of interest if any.

A valuer shall always exhibit objectivity which is a state of mind. The analyst should have objectivity in the performance of valuation engagements. He must be fair and must not allow prejudice or bias to override his objectivity. He should maintain an impartial attitude and both be and appear to be free of any interest which might be regarded, whatever its actual effect, as being incompatible with integrity and objectivity. The analyst should respect the confidentiality of information acquired in the course of his work. He should not disclose any confidential information to a third party unless there is a legal or professional duty to disclose. The valuer requires a continuing awareness of developments in valuation and related matters, capital market, economic conditions and relevant regulations and statutory requirements.

A valuer will go for a written or oral understanding of the nature, scope and limitations of services to be performed and the responsibilities of the parties, with his client. If situation calls for changes can be incorporated in the understandings and shall be notified to the client. He will inform the client about conflicts of interest, significant reservations concerning the scope or benefits of the engagement, and significant engagement findings or events.

VALUATION SERVICES

In valuation process valuers should comply with the standards promulgated by governing bodies or authorities. The valuer has to go by the procedure stipulated in the standards. This also called as valuation engagement which results in conclusion of value. The other one is calculation process resulting into number in rupee term. Both above engagement are decided on mutual consents of client and the valuer.

The objective of a valuation engagement is to express an unambiguous opinion as to the value of a business, business ownership interest, security or intangible asset which opinion is supported by all procedures that the appraiser deems to be relevant to the valuation. A valuation engagement requires that a valuer apply valuation approaches or methods to be appropriate under the circumstances. In such an engagement, a valuer is free to apply the valuation approaches and methods he or she deems appropriate in the circumstances. A valuation engagement has the following qualities:

An appraiser (valuer) performs a calculation engagement when the valuer and the client agree on the valuation approaches and methods the valuer will use and the extent of procedures the valuer will perform in the process of calculating the value of a subject interest and the valuer calculates the value in compliance with the agreement. The appraiser expresses the results of these procedures as a calculated value. The calculated value is expressed as a range or as a single amount. A calculation engagement does not include all of the procedures required for a valuation engagement.

Assumptions and limiting conditions are common to valuation engagements. The assumptions and limiting conditions should be disclosed in the valuation report. The valuer should examine whether the assumptions considered in valuation engagement are broadly reliable, relevant, logical, achievable and realistic in terms of the overall business conditions and circumstances. If the limiting conditions are so material in nature that the impact on the overall engagement is very significant in the professional judgment of the valuer, the valuer may not issue any report or may withdraw from the engagement. Also if the scope restriction is so material in nature that significantly impact the basic concepts and principles of the valuation the valuer may consider not to issue any valuation report or may withdraw from the engagement.

VALUATION PROCEDURE

In performing a valuation engagement, the valuer should:

- Define the standard and premise of valuation
- Analyze the subject interest and collect the necessary information
- Adjust the 'Financial Statement' appropriately
- Apply appropriate valuation approaches and methods
- Valuation adjustments
- Conclusion of value
- Subsequent Events
- Prepare and maintain appropriate documentation

Even though the above mentioned procedure is presented in a manner that suggests a sequential valuation process, valuations involve an ongoing process of gathering, updating and analyzing information. Accordingly, the sequence of the requirements and guidance in 'valuation standards' may be implemented differently at the option of the valuer.

'STANDARDS' OF VALUE

Business interests are valued in a variety of contexts and for a variety of purposes. Different standards of value may lead to different conclusions of value. Therefore, it is most important for the valuer to identify a standard or definition of value pertinent to the case. There are broadly four standards of value:

- Fair market value
- Fair value
- Book value
- Asset-based value

- **Fair Market Value:** It is by far the most commonly used standard of value. Fair Market Value is the estimated amount that a business will sell for between a willing buyer and a willing seller on the given date on the open market. Fair Market Value also assumes that both parties involved hold a reasonable level of knowledge regarding the relevant facts. The valuer is also required to make a number of assumptions as to the buyers/sellers behaviour and to the terms and conditions associated with the hypothetical transaction. In fact, Fair Market Value does not take into account the individual circumstances of the buyer and the seller.

- **Fair Value:** The primary difference between Fair Market Value, and Fair Value is that Fair Value relies very heavily on individual circumstances. For Fair Value to be established, both the seller and the buyer must have already been identified, and as such, the resultant value represents a figure beneficial and fair to both parties. Essentially it takes into account what the seller gives up in value and what the buyer acquires in value through the transaction. Being that this type of valuation is a closed market value, the various influences introduced by an open market sale (financial, legal, operational, personnel, ownership, cultural etc) are eliminated.

- **Book Value:** Refers to the depreciated market value of the fixed assets. These may include premises, plant and equipment, vehicles etc. This standard of valuation is considerably less common than Fair Market Value, and Fair Value as it doesn't take into account intangible assets.

- **Asset-based Value:** Though disregarding intangible assets in a similar fashion to book value, Asset Based Value ignores the book value and assigns value according to the potential resale of the physical assets in the market.

The 'Asset-based' values are futher divided into following three categories.

- **Liquidation Value:** It is assigned to businesses that are no longer a going-concern. Value is established by the value of the terminated business, with focus on the value of its fixed assets, net of its liabilities and the inevitable costs generated by discontinuing operations. Though assets can be sold off in an orderly fashion, being that the context is liquidation, the haste of which assets can be sold off is generally taken into account.
- **Fairsales Value:** The price at which assets can be sold in the shortest possible time, regardless of how low the obtained price is.
- **Investment Value:** It is comparable to Fair Value in that it is involved in valuations for a closed market sale. It is specific to an instance where the incorporation of the sellers company into the buyers company represents perceived synergies.

Determining the business value depends upon the situation in which the business is valued, i.e, what is likely to happen to the business beyond the valuation date influences what the business is worth today. The timing of valuation describes the type of market conditions the seller of the business interest might reasonably encounter and should always reflect the facts and circumstances underlying each valuation engagement. Two basic premise of valuation are; value in continuation of business and value in liquidation.

The analysis of the subject interest will assist in considering, evaluating, and applying the various valuation approaches and methods to the subject interest. The nature and extent of the information needed to perform the analysis will depend on various factors. In analyzing the subject interest, the appraiser shall gather, analyze and adjust the relevant information necessary to perform a valuation appropriate to the nature or type of the engagement. Such information shall include:

- Non-financial information
- Ownership details
- Financial Information
- General Information

The type, availability and significance of such information vary with the subject interest.

VALUATION APPROACHES AND METHODS

In general in developing the valuation, the three most common valuation approaches are practiced:

- Asset-based Approach
- Market-based Approach
- Income-based Approach
- Rule-of-thumb Approach

The analyst select and apply appropriate valuation approaches, methods and procedures. He develops a conclusion of value considering the relevant valuation approaches, methods and procedures, the information available and appropriate premiums and discounts, if any.

Asset-based approach

The asset-based approach is a general way of determining a value indication of a business, business ownership interest, security, or intangible asset using one or more methods based on the value of the assets net of liabilities. A frequently used method under the asset approach is the adjusted net asset method. When using the adjusted net asset method in valuing a business, business ownership interest, or security, the appraiser consider, as appropriate, the following information:

- Identification of the assets and liabilities
- Value of the assets and liabilities (individually or in the aggregate)
- Liquidation costs (if applicable)

The asset-based approach may not be the sole valuation approach used in assignments relating to operating companies valued as going concerns unless this approach is used by both seller and buyer. In such cases, the selection of this approach shall be supported by the appraiser. When using methods under the cost to value intangible assets, the appraiser should consider the type of cost to be used such as reproduction cost or replacement cost, and, where applicable, the appropriate forms of depreciation and obsolescence. The direct and indirect costs associated with reproduction or replacement, as the case may be, as well as any loss of value due to functional or economic obsolescence, or reduced life expectancy may be considered.

Market approach

The market approach is a general way of determining a value of a business, business ownership interest, security or intangible asset by using one or more methods. In this approach compared are the subject to similar businesses, business ownership interests, securities or intangible assets that have been sold. Three frequently used valuation methods under the market approach for valuing a business, business ownership interest, or security are:

- Guideline public company method
- Guideline company transactions method
- Guideline sales of business ownership or securities

In market approach valuation methods for intangible assets are the three methods in use are as follows. The first one is comparable transactions method based on arm's-length sales or licenses of comparable intangible assets. The second one is comparable profit margin method based on comparison of the profit margin earned by the subject entity that owns or operates the intangible asset to profit margins earned by comparable companies.The third one is relief from royalty method based on the royalty rate, often expressed as a percentage of revenue that the subject entity that owns or operates the intangible asset would be obligated to pay to a hypothetical third-party licensor for the use of that intangible asset.

While applying the Market approach methods, the appraiser should consider; reasonable basis for comparison, selection of valuation ratios and guideline.

Income Approach (Cash Flows)

The income approach is a general way of determining a value indication of a business, business ownership interest, security, or intangible asset by using one or more methods through which anticipated benefits are converted into value. Anticipated benefits (in money terms) may be reasonably represented by such items as dividends or distributions, or various forms of earnings or cash flow. The anticipated benefits are estimated by considering such items as the nature, capital structure and historical performance of the related business entity, the expected future outlook for the business entity and relevant industries, and relevant economic factors. There are two valuation methods under the income approach. These are; capitalization of benefits method and discounted future benefits method.

Rules of thumb

Some standards indicate about rule of thumb method. Technically it is not a valuation method. Here, benchmark indicator is used as a reasonable check against the values determined by the use of other valuation approaches in a valuation engagement. Rule of thumb may provide insight into the value of a business, business ownership interest, security or intangible asset. However, it should not be used as the only method to determine the value of the subject interest. Value indications derived from the use of rules of thumb should not be given substantial weight unless they are supported by other valuation methods and it can be established that knowledgeable buyers and sellers place substantial reliance on them. The source of rule of thumb data should be documented.

VALUATION ADJUSTMENTS

Need for valuation adjustment may be called for in applicable standard of value, or other circumstances of an engagement, due to differences between the base value and the value of the subject interest. If so, appropriate discounts or premiums should be applied. Examples of valuation adjustments for valuation of a business, business ownership interest, or security include a discount for lack of marketability or liquidity and a discount for lack of control.

To determine whether any adjustment is required to pre-adjusted value, following are considered by the valuer if necessary;

- Marketability and Liquidity
- Ability of the interest to control the operations
- Impact of strategic or synergistic contributions to value

Here, the valuer shall adhere to followings while making any adjustment in pre-adjusted value:

- Specify the base value to which the discount or premium is applied
- Define each discount or premium to be applied to the base value
- State reasons why each selected discount or premium applies
- Specify the evidence considered in deriving discount/premium
- Explanation with reasoning for any discount/premium applicable.

CONCLUSION OF VALUE

The conclusion of value reached by the analyst shall be based upon the applicable standard of value, the purpose and intended use of the valuation, and all relevant information available as of the valuation date in carrying out the type of engagement for the assignment and on value indications resulting from one or more valuation methods performed under the valuation process.

In arriving at a conclusion of value, the valuer should; correlate and reconcile the results obtained under the different approaches and methods used, assess the reliability of the results under the different approaches and assign weights to value indications reached on the basis of various methods, indicate value determined under each method, or whether an indication of value from a single method should dominate.

ADDITIONAL FACTORS FOR CONSIDERATION

As appropriate for the valuation assignment as defined, and if not considered in the process of determining and weighting the indications of value provided by various procedures, the analyst should separately consider the following factors in reaching a final conclusion of value:

- Marketability or lack thereof, considering the nature of the business, the business ownership interest, security or intangible asset
- The effect of relevant contractual and/or other legal restrictions
- The condition of the market(s) in which the valued interest might trade
- The ability of an owner of the valued interest to control the operation, sale, or liquidation of the relevant business
- Such other factors that, in the opinion of the analyst, are appropriate for consideration

SUBSEQUENT EVENTS

The valuation date is the specific date at which the valuer estimates the value of the subject interest and concludes on the estimation of value. Generally, the valuer should consider only circumstances existing at the valuation date and events occurring up to the valuation date. An event that occurs subsequent to the valuation date could affect the value; such an occurrence is referred to as a subsequent event.

Subsequent events are indicative of conditions that were not known or knowable at the valuation date, including conditions that arose subsequent to the valuation date. The valuation would not be updated to reflect those events or conditions. Moreover, the valuation report would typically not include a discussion of those events or conditions because a valuation is performed as of a point in time - the valuation date - and the events described. In situations in which a valuation is meaningful to the intended user beyond the valuation date, the events may be of such nature and significance as to warrant disclosure in a separate section of the report to keep users informed.

VALUATION DOCUMENTATION

Documentation is the important record of information obtained and analyzed, procedures performed, valuation approaches and methods considered and used, and the conclusion of value. The quantity, type, and content of documentation are matters of the valuer's professional judgment. Sufficient documentation should be retained for information relied upon in the valuation process. Inclusion of such information in the report satisfies this standard. In general documentation may include:

- Information gathered and analyzed that may affect the value of the subject interest;
- Assumptions and limitations during the valuation engagement;
- Valuation approaches and methods considered and rationale and support for their use;
- Information relating to subsequent events considered by the valuer;
- Source of data for any rule of thumb used in the valuation;
- Any other documentation considered relevant to the engagement by the valuer.

The documentation needs to be retained for a period of time sufficient to meet the needs of applicable legal, regulatory, or other professional requirements for records retention.

REPORTING

The valuation process results into preparation of final report and submission to the client or users of the report. The form of any particular report will depend on the nature of the engagement, its purpose, its findings and the needs of the decision makers who receive and rely upon it. A valuation report is a written or oral communication to the client containing the conclusion of value or the calculated value of the subject interest. The two types of written reports that a valuer may use to communicate the results of an engagement to estimate value are:

➢ **Valuation Engagement - Detailed/Summary Report:** This report may be used to communicate the results of a valuation engagement (conclusion of value) in detail. For a valuation engagement, the determination of whether to prepare a detailed report or a summary report is based on the level of reporting detail agreed to by the valuer and the client.

➢ **Calculation Engagement - Calculation Report:** This type of report should be used only to communicate the results of a calculated value; it should not be used to communicate the results of a valuation engagement.

A valuation performed for a matter before a court, an arbitrator, a mediator or other facilitator, or a matter in a governmental or administrative proceeding is exempt from the reporting provisions of 'Valuation Standards'. The exemption applies only to the reporting provisions of this Standard.

DETAILED VALUATION REPORT

The detailed report shall provide sufficient information to permit intended users to understand the data, reasoning and analyses underlying the valuer's conclusion of value. A detailed report should include, as applicable, the following sections:

- Letter of Transmittal
- Table of contents
- Introduction
- Sources of information
- Analysis related non-financial information
- Financial statement/information analysis
- Valuation approaches and methods considered and used
- Valuation adjustments
- Valuation of non operating assets/liabilities/deficient assets (if any)
- Representation of the valuer
- Reconciliation of estimates and conclusion of value
- Qualifications of the valuer
- Appendices and exhibits

SUMMARY

Valuation Standards (BVS) are basically codes of practice that are used in business valuation. In the United States they have been around since the late 1980s starting with the Uniform Standards of Professional Practice (USPAP) issued by the Appraisal Foundation in 1987. In 1992 the American Society of Appraisers (ASA) issued business valuation standards which was followed by standards published by the Institute of Business Appraisers (IBA) in 1993. ICAI has also framed the BVS which is widely used in India by valuers. The objective of the Business Valuation Standard is to provide guidance and common standards to the business valuers to follow in preparing business valuation reports. The business valuers are required to observe and comply with the Standard which, have been developed to ensure the highest professionalism, integrity, clarity, reliability and impartiality of business valuation practices. More importantly, the promulgation of the Standard is intended to further enhance the professional standards and status of valuation profession. Business valuation standards have been very important in professionalizing the business valuation field over the past several decades and they continue to be important as a barometer as to the minimum requirements of a business valuation. These Standards provide minimum criteria to be followed by business appraisers in developing and reporting the valuation of businesses, business ownership interests, securities and intangible assets. This seems to imply that quality appraisals and reports should exceed the requirements of the standards.

Review Questions

1. Why Business Valuation Standards are so important?
2. What in general is scope of BVSs?
3. What is covered under the Business Valuation Standards?
4. What are the 'Standard' of value used in valuation process?

Video Linkages

1. http://www.youtube.com/watch?v=1XWuHyLQgmA, Valuation Principles and Standards in America.

ASSIGNMENT

Study the various most popular 'Business Valuation Standards' across the globe and compare the same with ICAI 'Business Valuation Standard' framework.

BIBLIOGRAPHY

1. Business Valuation Standartds - ICAI, www.icai.org/resource_file/17798business_valuation.pdf
2. Pathak, (2007) *Legal Aspects of Business,* Tata McGraw-Hill Education, ND
3. Previts G J , Gary Previts, (2007) *Research in Accounting Regulation,* Volume 19, Elsevier
4. Ramachandran N /Kakani R. (2007), *Financial Accounting For Management,* Tata McGraw-Hill Education, ND
5. The Hong Kong Business Valuation Forum, Business Valuation Standards, Hong Kong Business Valuation Forum, 2005
6. Youngman, Joan, (2006) Legal Issues in Property Valuation and Taxation (Book), Cases and Materials, Lincoln Institute of Land Policy
7. *Websites*

   http://analystnotes.com/browse_subjects.php?id=14995

   http://analystnotes.com/browse_subjects.php?id=14995

   http://www.appraisers.org/Files/Professional%20Standards/bvstandards.pdf

   http://www.appraisers.org/Files/Professional%20Standards/bvstandards.pdf

GLOSSARY

Accounting Consistency: Balance sheets balance and income statements are consistent with retained earnings on the balance sheet.

Accrual Accounting: An accounting method that measures the performance and position of a company by recognizing economic events regardless of when cash transactions occur. This method allows the current cash inflows/outflows to be combined with future expected cash inflows/outflows to give a more accurate picture of a company's current financial condition.

Accruals: Amounts owed for salary, taxes and other items but not yet paid.

Additional Funds Needed (AFN): The extra amount of financing that is required in a given year. Usually is positive if the firm is growing.

Adjusted Book Value Method: Method within the asset approach whereby all assets and liabilities (including off-balance sheet, intangible and contingent) are adjusted to their fair market values from respective book amounts.

Amortization: The paying off of debt in regular installments over a period of time. The deduction of capital expenses over a specific period of time (usually over the asset's life). More specifically this method measures the consumption of the value of intangible assets such as a patent or a copyright.

Arbitrage Pricing Theory: Multivariate model for estimating the cost of equity capital, which incorporates several systematic risk factors.

Articulate: Retained earnings on the balance sheet are equal to the previous year's retained earnings plus the current year's net income, less any dividends paid.

Asset-based Approach: A general way of determining a value indication of a business's assets and/or equity interest using one or more methods based directly on the value of the assets or the business less liabilities. General way of determining a value indication of a business, business ownership interest or security using one or more methods based on the value of the assets net of liabilities.

Asset Sale: A form of acquisition whereby the seller of a corporation agrees to sell all or certain assets and liabilities of a company to a purchaser. The corporate entity is not transferred.

Asset Turnover: Assets/Sales. Sometimes based on average assets: $[(Asset_t + asset_{t-1})/2 /Sales_t$. This ratio is often used as an indicator of efficiency of asset utilization.

Asset Valuation: The process of determining the current worth of a portfolio, company, investment, or balance sheet item. The tools used for asset valuation include quantitative methods and statistics, financial statement analysis, ratio analysis, fundamental analysis and valuation economics.

Beta: Measure risk of a stock; i.e., the tendency of a stock's price to correlate with changes in a specific index. Beta measures a stock's market risk, which is the risk relevant to an investor. Market risk is the amount of risk that a stock contributes to a well-diversified portfolio.

Blockage Discount: An amount or percentage deducted from the current market price of a publicly traded stock to reflect the decrease in the per share value of a block of stock, that is, of a size that could not be sold in a reasonable period of time given normal trading volume.

Bond Rating: A measure of the creditworthiness of a bond. For example, Moody's bond ratings range from AAA down to C and D. AAA means very creditworthy and unlikely to default. Bonds rated BB or below are defined as non-investment grade bonds, commonly called junk bonds.

Book Value: The value of an asset, a liability or a company that is based solely upon the values reported in the company's financial statements. With respect to assets, the capitalized cost of an asset less accumulated depreciation, depletion or amortization as it appears on the books of account of the enterprise. With respect to a business enterprise, the difference between total assets (net of depreciation, depletion and amortization) and total liabilities of an enterprise as they appear on the balance sheet. It is synonymous with net book value, net worth and shareholder's equity.

Business Enterprise: Commercial, industrial, service or investment entity (or a combination thereof) pursuing an economic activity.

Business Risk: Degree of uncertainty of realizing expected future returns of the business resulting from factors other than financial leverage. See Financial Risk.

Business Valuation: Act or process of determining the value of a business enterprise or ownership interest therein.

Capital Asset Pricing Model (CAPM): A model of investor required returns. The required return to equity is the risk free rate plus beta multiplied by the market risk premium: $r_s = r_{RF}$ + Beta (Market risk premium). Model in which the cost of capital for any stock or portfolio of stocks equals a risk-free rate plus a risk premium that is proportionate to the systematic risk of the stock or portfolio.

Capital Budgeting: The process in which a business determines whether projects such as building a new plant or investing in a long-term venture are worth pursuing. Oftentimes, a prospective project's lifetime cash inflows and outflows are assessed in order to determine whether the returns generated meet a sufficient target benchmark. Ideally, businesses should pursue all projects and opportunities that enhance shareholder value. However, because the amount of capital available at any given time for new projects is limited, management needs to use capital budgeting techniques to determine which projects will yield the most return over an applicable period of time. Popular methods of capital budgeting include net present value (NPV), internal rate of return (IRR), discounted cash flow (DCF) and payback period.

Capital Structure: Composition of the invested capital of a business enterprise, the mix of debt and equity financing.

Capital Structure: The composition of a business entity's invested capital.

Capitalization: Conversion of a single period of economic benefits into value. It is the capital structure of a business enterprise. The recognition of an expenditure as a capital asset rather than a period expense.

Capitalization Factor: Multiple or divisor used to convert anticipated economic benefits of a single period into value.

Capitalization of Earnings Method: Method within the income approach whereby economic benefits for a representative single period are converted to value through division by a capitalization rate.

Capitalization Rate: Any divisor (usually expressed as a percentage) used to convert anticipated

Capitalizing Net Income: Determining a future value for the company by dividing the *pro forma* net income by the required Return on Investment (ROI).

Cash flow: Cash generated from a business activity.

Cash Flow: Cash that is generated over a period of time by an asset, group of assets, or business enterprise. It may be used in a general sense to encompass various levels of specifically defined cash flows. When the term is used, it should be supplemented by a qualifier (for example, "discretionary" or "operating") and a specific definition in the given valuation context.

Common Stock: Item on the balance sheet that shows how much stockholders have invested in the company by purchasing stock from the company.

Constant Growth Rate Dividend Policy: Dividends are assumed to grow at a constant rate.

Control Premium: Amount or a percentage by which the prorata value of a controlling interest exceeds the *pro rata* value of a non-controlling interest in a business enterprise, to reflect the power of control.

Corporate Finance: Financial or monetary activity that deals with a company and its money.

Corporate Value: The sum of the value of a firm's operations and the value of its non-operating assets. This is the total value of the firm.

Cost Approach: General way of determining a value indication of an individual asset by quantifying the amount of money required to replace the future service capability of that asset.

Cost of Capital: Expected rate of return that the market requires in order to attract funds to a particular investment.

Cost of Equity: The return stockholders require on their investment in the stock.

Cost of Goods Sold (COGS): Expenses associated with production activities.

Current Assets: Assets expected to be converted to cash within a year. Current assets include inventory, accounts receivable, cash, and short-term investments.

Current Liabilities: Liabilities expected to be paid off within a year. Current liabilities include notes payable, the current portion of long-term debt, and accruals.

Deal Structure: The allocation of the consideration paid for a business. The components could include cash, notes, stock, consulting agreements, earnout provisions and covenants not to compete. The sale could take the form of an asset sale or a stock sale.

Debt Holder: A person or financial institution who owns a bond issued by the company, or a bank that is owed money by the company.

Debt Limitation: A bond covenant that limits or restricts any additional debt that may be incurred by the issuer. Debt limitations look to protect the current lenders by maintaining the firm's degree.

Debt Service: Cash that is required for a particular time period to cover the repayment of interest and principal on a debt. Debt service is often calculated on a yearly basis.

Depreciation: The amount of an asset's purchase price that is taken as an expense during each reporting period over the life of the asset.

Discount Rate: A rate of return used to convert a future monetary sum into present value.

Discounted Cash Flow Method: Method within the income approach whereby the present value of future expected net cash flows is calculated using a discount rate.

Earnings per share: Net income/shares outstanding.

Earnout: The portion of the purchase prices that is contingent on future performance. It is payable to the sellers only when certain pre-defined levels of sales or income are achieved in the years after acquisition.

EBIT: Earnings before interest and taxes.

EBITD: Earnings before interest, taxes and depreciation.

EBITDA: Earnings before interest, taxes, depreciation and amortization.

Economic Benefits: Inflows such as revenues, net income, net cash flows, etc., economic benefits of a single period into value.

Economic Life: Period of time over which property may generate economic benefits.

Economic Profit: A generic name for economic value added

Economic Value Added (EVA): The amount of economic value added to a company during the year. Calculated as: EVA = NOPAT – Operating capital (WACC). Sometimes defined as: EVA = NOPAT – (Operating capital at the beginning of the year) (WACC).

Equity: Owner's interest in property after deduction of all liabilities.

Excess Earnings Method: A specific way of determining a value indication of a business, business ownership interest, or security determined as the sum of a) the value of the assets derived by capitalizing excess earnings and b) the value of the selected asset base. Also

External Financing: Debt or equity raised from newly issued securities.

Extraordinary Items: Items on the income statement that are non-recurring, such as reorganization charges.

Fair Market Value: Price, expressed in terms of cash equivalents, at which property would change hands between a hypothetical willing and able buyer and a hypothetical willing and able seller, acting at arms length in an open and unrestricted market, where neither is under compulsion to buy or sell and when both have reasonable knowledge of the relevant facts.

Financial Recasting: Financial recasting of the historical financial statements adds back items such as superfluous, excessive, or discretionary expenses and non-recurring revenues and expenses. Recasting provides an economic view of the company, and allows meaningful comparisons with other investment opportunities.

Financial Risk: Degree of uncertainty of realizing expected future returns of the business resulting from financial leverage.

Fixed Assets: Real assets with lives longer than a year.

Fixed Payout Ratio: A dividend policy in which dividends are a constant proportion of net income.

Forced Liquidation Value: It is liquidation value at which the asset or assets are sold as quickly as possible, similar to one at an auction.

Free Cash Flow: Cash available for distribution after taxes but before the effects of financing. Calculated as debt-free net income plus depreciation less expenditures required for working capital and capital items adjusted to remove effects of financing.

Fundamental Analysis: Fundamental analysis is basically done for long and mid-term investment which is also called as delivery-based investment or trading. The main important aim behind is to study and understand the company in which you are planning to invest your hard earned money and get excellent returns. Basically one should be able to judge at least how the company has done in past years, its debit status, its current valuation, its future growth prospects, its earning capacity, etc., so that based on these terms he can at least decide whether to invest in this company or not. We should look for the following in a company to invest; about company, earnings, current valuation, future earnings growth, and debt status.

Fundamental Value: The value that results from discounting expected future cash flows at an appropriate cost of capital. Analysts are not likely to agree on this value; it is an intrinsic value.

Going Concern: An operating business enterprise.

Goodwill: It is an intangible asset arising as a result of name, reputation, customer loyalty, location, products, and similar factors not separately identified. The amount by which the consideration paid exceeds the fair market value of the company's operating assets.

Gross Margin: Gross profit/sales.

Income-Based Approach: A general way of determining a value indication of a business, business ownership interest, security, or intangible asset using one or more methods that convert anticipated economic benefits into a present single amount industry specific.

Intangible Assets: Non-physical assets such as franchises, trademarks, patents, copyrights, goodwill, equities, mineral rights, securities and contracts (as distinguished from physical assets) that grant rights and privileges, and have value for the owner.

Interest Coverage Ratio: Operating profit/Net interest expense.

Internal Rate of Return: A discount rate at which the present value of the future cash flows of the investment equals the cost of the investment.

Intrinsic Value - The value that an investor considers, on the basis of an evaluation or available facts, to be the "true" or "real" value that will become the market value when other investors reach the same conclusion. When the term applies to options, it is the difference between the exercise price or strike price of an option and the market value of the underlying security.

Inventory Turnover: Inventory/Sales (sometimes defined as the average inventory during the year divided by the year's sales).

Invested Capital: The sum of equity and debt in a business enterprise. Debt is typically (a) all interest-bearing debt or (b) long-term interest-bearing debt. When the term is used, it should be supplemented by a specific definition in the given valuation context.

Levered Beta: The beta reflecting a capital structure that includes debt.

Liquidation Value: It is an amount that would be realized if the business is terminated and the assets are sold piecemeal.

Liquidity: The ability to quickly convert property to cash or pay a liability.

Market-based Approach: A general way of determining a value indication of a business, business ownership interest, security, or intangible asset by using one or more methods that compare the subject to similar businesses, business ownership interests, securities, or intangible assets that have been sold.

Market Multiple: A factor that can be applied to the subject company's financial, operating or physical data to generate an indication of value. The market multiple is derived from observed transactions in the marketplace where the value can be divided by the comparable companies' financial, operating or physical data to generate the market multiple.

Market Risk Premium: The return over and above the risk free rate that investors require for bearing market risk: RP_M = expected return on market – risk free rate.

Market Value: The price at which the asset may be purchased or sold in the financial markets.

Market Value Added (MVA): Total market value of firm (i.e., market values of debt plus equity) minus total capital contributed to the firm. The total contributed capital is the book value of debt plus the book value of common stock and retained earnings, as shown on the financial statements.

Matching Principle: The principle that irrespective of when cash payments for costs of producing goods are actually made, the costs cannot be incorporated into income until goods that were produced are sold.

Merger and Acquisition Method: A method within the market approach whereby pricing multiples are derived from transactions of significant interests in companies engaged in the same or similar lines of business.

Net Assets: Total assets less total liabilities.

Net Book Value: It with respect to a business enterprise, the difference between total assets (net of accumulated depreciation, depletion, and amortization) and total liabilities as they appear on the balance sheet (synonymous with Shareholder's Equity). With respect to a specific asset, the capitalized cost less accumulated amortization or depreciation as it appears on the books of account of the business enterprise.

Net Cash Flow: Cash available for distribution after taxes and after the effects of financing. Calculated as net income plus depreciation less expenditures required for working capital and capital items.

Net Debt: A metric that shows a company's overall debt situation by netting the value of a company's liabilities and debts with its cash and other similar liquid.

Net Income: Revenue less expenses, including taxes.

Net Operating Profit After Taxes (NOPAT): Operating profit less the taxes due on operating profit. In the simplest firm, this is EBIT (1-T) where T is the tax rate.

Net Present Value: Value, as of a specified date, of future cash inflows less all cash outflows (including the cost of investment) calculated using an appropriate discount rate.

Net Profit Margin: Net Income/Sales.

Net Working Capital: Current assets minus current liabilities.

Non-linear Model: A model for projecting a balance sheet or income statement item in such a way that it is not a linear function of sales.

Non-operating Asset: An asset that is not used in operations, such as short-term investments, excess cash, or land purchased for speculative purposes.

Non-operating Assets: Assets shown on the company's balance sheet that are not used in the operation of the business. That is, "extra" assets that are not necessary to generate the revenue and cash flow stream being valued.

Normal Working Capital: The amount of working capital needed by the company to sustain operations throughout the year. Calculated as the average of current assets (which include a normal amount of necessary cash) minus current liabilities on a monthly basis over the most recent twelve months.

Normalized Earnings: Economic benefits adjusted for nonrecurring, noneconomic, or other unusual items to eliminate anomalies and/or facilitate comparisons.

Operating Capital: The amount of money tied up in operating assets, less any operating liabilities.

Operating Current Assets: Short-term assets used in operations. Doesn't include excess cash or short-term investments.

Operating Current Liabilities: Short-term liabilities used in operations. Doesn't include notes payable.

Operating Long-term Capital: Long-term capital used in operations, such as buildings, equipment, and land.

Operating Margin: EBIT/Sales.

Operating Profit: Profit from operations. Usually EBIT.

Operating Profitability: NOPAT/Sales. It is the contribution that operations make to the firm's overall profitability.

Operating Working Capital: Operating current assets less operating current liabilities.

Payout Ratio: Dividends/Net income.

Pre-tax Margin: Profit before Taxes/Sales.

Present Value: The value today of an amount of cash to be received in the future. The value today of a future payment, or stream of payments, discounted at a risk-adjusted rate of return.

Price to Book Ratio: Market value of a company's stock (per share) divided by the book value of equity (per share).

Prime Rate: The rate that banks offer customers with high credit ratings.

Principal: The initial amount borrowed in a loan. Also called the face value.

***Pro Forma* Financial Statements:** Projected financial statements.

Quick Ratio: (Current assets – inventory)/Current liabilities.

Rate of Return: An amount of income (loss) and/or change in value realized or anticipated on an investment, expressed as a percentage of that investment.

Receivables Turnover: Receivables/Sales.

Residual Dividend: Dividends are set so that assets are equal to liabilities plus owners equity.

Residual Value: Value as of the end of the discrete projection period in a discounted future

Retained Earnings: Item on the balance sheet that shows how much stockholders have contributed to the company as the company reinvests (i.e., retains) earnings rather than pays earnings out dividends.

Return on Assets (ROA): Net income/Assets.

Return on Equity (ROE): It is the amount of net income returned as a percentage of shareholders equity.

Return on Invested Capital (ROIC): NOPAT/Beginning Capital. A measure of how well the company is doing financially with the assets it uses. Sometimes calculated as NOPAT/Capital if used for performance measures.

Risk Averse: Investor attitude towards risk. Investors prefer less risk to more risk, if return is held constant.

Risk Free Rate: The rate of return on long-term Treasury securities.

Risk Premium: Rate of return added to a risk-free rate to reflect risk.

Rule of Thumb: A mathematical formula developed or based on the past experience or observation, indicating certain relationship between price and certain industry specific variables.

Selling, General and Administrative expenses (SGA): Expenses associated with corporate overhead, advertising and administration—mostly expenses not directly associated with production.

Sensitivity Analysis: Using a valuation model to see how variation of the assumptions about operating or non-operating performance affects the value of the firm.

Short Run Projection Period: The period during which projections of operating performance are based on specific plans and circumstances of the firm.

Sinking Fund: A means of repaying funds that were borrowed through a bond issue. The issuer makes periodic payments to a trustee who retires part of the issue by purchasing the bonds in the open.

Spread: The difference in yields between two assets. For example, a bond spread is the difference between the yield on a particular bond and the yield on a Treasury security of the same maturity.

Standard of Value: Type of value being used in a specific engagement; e.g., fair market value, fair value, investment value.

Steady-state Period: The period of a firm's existence during which the forces of competition have eroded the ability of the firm to generate extraordinary returns to its investors. When this period is reached, the growth and profitability performance of the firm will merge with that of other firms in its industry, and ultimately with the performance of the economy at large.

Stock Repurchases: A firm buys back its own stock in order to distribute cash to its shareholders.

Stock Sale: A form of acquisition whereby all or a portion of the stock in a corporation is sold to the purchaser.

Tangible Assets: Physical assets (such as cash, accounts receivable, inventory, property, plant and equipment, etc.).

Terminal Value: The value of the company at the end of the five-year *pro forma* period. Terminal value is determined by dividing the fifth year *pro forma* cash flow (normalized for depreciation and capital expenditures) by the required Return on Investment total capital for a given period.

Total Market Value: Market value of debt plus the market value of equity.

Unlevered Beta: Beta reflecting a capital structure without debt.

Valuation: Act or process of determining the value of a business, business ownership interest, security or intangible asset.

Valuation Method: A specific way to determine value.

Valuation Multiple: A factor wherein a value or price serves as the numerator and financial, operating or physical data of the company being valued serve as the denominator.

Valuation Ratio: Fraction in which a value or price serves as the numerator and financial, operating, or physical data serves as the denominator.

Value: The amount at which a business enterprise passes from a willing seller to a willing buyer. It is assumed that both buyer and seller are rational and have a reasonable knowledge of relevant facts.

Value-based Management: Managing a company to maximize its value for the shareholders.

Value Driver: Something that is an important factor in the determination a company's profitability and value. For example, sales growth or gross margin.

Value of Equity: The value of the common stock, sometimes defined as the projected value of the common stock as predicted by the valuation model (intrinsic value) and sometimes, as the market value of the common stock.

Value of Non-operating Assets: The amount non-operating assets are worth in the market.

Value of Operations: The present value of the free cash flows when discounted at the weighted average cost of capital.

Weighted Average Cost of Capital (WACC): The cost of capital (discount rate) determined by the weighted average, at market value, of the cost of all financing sources in the business enterprise's capital structure. It is the after-tax costs of capital of all of the various sources of financing, weighted by their relative market values.

Working Capital: It also called as current assets. It is an excess of current assets over current liabilities.

Yield: The rate of return that an investor would realize on a bond held till maturity.

ANNEXURES

Table A (a): Future Value Interest Factor of ₹ 1 (Compounded at i% Interest for n Periods)

$$FVIF_{k,n} = (1+k)^n$$

Periods	1 %	2 %	3 %	4 %	5 %	6 %	7 %	8 %	9 %	10 %	11 %
1	1.0100	1.0200	1.0300	1.0400	1.0500	1.0600	1.0700	1.0800	1.0900	1.1000	1.1100
2	1.0201	1.0404	1.0609	1.0816	1.1025	1.1236	1.1449	1.1664	1.1881	1.2100	1.2321
3	1.0303	1.0612	1.0927	1.1249	1.1576	1.1910	1.2250	1.2597	1.2950	1.3310	1.3676
4	1.0406	1.0924	1.1255	1.1699	1.2155	1.2625	1.3108	1.3605	1.4116	1.4641	1.5181
5	1.0510	1.1041	1.1593	1.2167	1.2763	1.3382	1.4026	1.4693	1.5386	1.6105	1.6851
6	1.0615	1.1262	1.1941	1.2653	1.3401	1.4185	1.5007	1.5869	1.6771	1.7716	1.8704
7	1.0721	1.1487	1.2299	1.3159	1.4071	1.5036	1.6058	1.7138	1.8280	1.9487	2.0762
8	1.0829	1.1717	1.2668	1.3686	1.4775	1.5938	1.7182	1.8509	1.9926	2.1436	2.3045
9	1.0937	1.1951	1.3048	1.4233	1.5513	1.6895	1.8385	1.9990	2.1719	2.3579	2.5580
10	1.1046	1.2190	1.3439	1.4802	1.6289	1.7908	1.9672	2.1589	2.3674	2.5937	2.8394
11	1.1157	1.2434	1.3842	1.5395	1.7103	1.8983	2.1049	1.8509	1.9926	2.1436	2.3045
12	1.1268	1.2682	1.4258	1.6010	1.7959	2.0122	2.2522	2.5182	2.8127	3.1384	3.4985
13	1.1381	1.2936	1.4685	1.6651	1.8856	2.1329	2.4098	2.7196	3.0658	3.4523	3.8833
14	1.1495	1.3195	1.5126	1.7317	1.9799	2.2609	2.5785	2.9372	3.3417	3.7975	4.3104
15	1.1610	1.3459	1.5580	1.8009	2.0789	2.3966	2.7590	3.1722	3.6425	4.1772	4.7846
16	1.1726	1.3728	1.6047	1.8730	2.1829	2.5404	2.9522	3.4259	3.9703	4.5950	5.3109
17	1.1843	1.4002	1.6528	1.9479	2.2920	2.6928	3.1588	3.7000	4.3276	5.0545	5.8951
18	1.1961	1.4282	1.7024	2.0258	2.4066	2.8543	3.3799	3.9960	4.7171	5.5599	6.5436
19	1.2081	1.4568	1.7535	2.1068	2.5270	3.0256	3.6165	4.3157	5.1417	6.1159	7.2633
20	1.2202	1.4859	1.8061	2.1911	2.6533	3.2071	3.8697	4.6610	5.6044	6.7275	8.0623
21	1.2324	1.5157	1.8603	2.2788	2.7860	3.3996	4.1406	5.0338	6.1088	7.4003	8.9492
22	1.2447	1.5460	1.9161	2.3699	2.9253	3.6035	4.4304	5.4365	6.6586	8.1403	9.9336
23	1.2572	1.5769	1.9736	2.4647	3.0715	3.8197	4.7405	5.8715	7.2579	8.9543	11.0263
24	1.2697	1.6084	2.0328	2.5633	3.2251	4.0489	5.0724	6.3412	7.9111	9.8497	12.2392
25	1.2824	16406	2.0938	2.6658	3.3864	4.2919	5.4274	6.8485	8.6231	10.8347	13.5855

Table A (b): Future Value Interest Factor of ₹ 1 (Compounded at i% Interest for n Periods)

$$FVIF_{k,n} = (1+k)^n$$

Periods	1 %	2 %	3 %	4 %	5 %	6 %	7 %	8 %	9 %	10 %	11 %
26	1.2824	1.6406	2.0938	2.6658	3.3864	4.2919	5.4274	6.8485	8.6231	10.8347	13.5855
27	1.3082	1.7069	2.2213	2.8834	3.7335	4.8223	6.2139	7.9881	10.2451	13.1100	16.7387
28	1.3213	1.7410	2.2879	2.9987	3.9201	5.1117	6.6488	8.6271	11.1671	14.4210	18.5799
29	1.3345	1.7758	2.3566	3.1187	4.1161	5.4184	7.1143	9.3173	12.1722	15.8631	20.6237
30	1.3478	1.8114	2.4273	3.2434	4.3219	5.7435	7.6123	10.0627	13.2677	17.4494	22.8923
31	1.3613	1.8476	2.5001	3.3731	4.5380	6.0881	8.1451	10.8677	14.4618	19.1943	25.4104
32	1.3749	1.8845	2.5751	3.5081	4.7649	6.4534	8.7153	11.7371	15.7633	21.1198	28.2056
33	1.3887	1.9222	2.6523	3.6484	5.0032	6.8406	9.3253	12.6761	17.1820	23.2252	31.3082
34	1.4026	1.9607	2.7319	3.7943	5.2533	7.2510	9.9781	13.6901	18.7284	25.5477	34.5749
35	1.4166	1.9999	2.8139	3.9461	5.5160	7.6861	10.6766	14.7853	20.4140	28.1024	38.5749
36	1.4308	2.0399	2.8983	4.1039	5.7918	8.1473	11.4239	15.9682	22.2512	30.9128	42.8181
37	1.4451	2.0807	2.9852	4.2681	6.0814	8.6361	12.2236	17.2456	24.2538	34.0039	47.8181
38	1.4595	2.1223	3.0748	4.4388	6.3855	9.1543	13.0793	18.6253	26.4367	37.4043	52.7562
39	1.4741	2.16447	3.1670	4.6164	6.7048	9.7035	13.9948	20.1153	28.8160	41.1448	58.5593
40	1.4889	2.2080	3.2620	4.8010	7.0400	10.2857	14.9745	21.7245	31.4094	45.2593	65.0009
41	1.5038	2.2522	3.3599	4.9931	7.3920	10.9020	16.0227	23.4625	34.2363	49.7852	72.1510
42	1.5188	2.2972	3.4607	5.1928	7.7616	11.5570	17.1443	25.3395	37.3175	54.7637	80.0876
43	1.5340	2.3432	3.5645	5.4005	8.1497	12.2505	18.3414	27.3666	40.6761	60.2401	88.8972
44	1.5493	2.3901	3.6715	5.6165	8.5572	12.9855	19.6285	29.5560	44.3370	66.2641	98.6759
45	1.5648	2.4379	3.7816	5.8412	8.9850	13.7646	21.0025	31.9204	48.3273	72.8905	109.5302
46	1.5805	2.4866	3.8950	6.0748	9.4343	14.5905	22.4726	34.4741	52.6767	80.1795	121.5786
47	1.5963	2.5363	4.0199	6.3178	9.9060	15.4659	24.0457	37.2320	57.4176	88.1975	134.9522
48	1.6122	2.5871	4.1323	6.5705	10.4013	16.3939	25.7289	40.2106	62.5852	97.0172	149.7970
49	1.6283	2.6388	4.2562	6.8333	10.9213	17.3775	27.5299	43.4274	68.2179	106.7190	166.2746
50	1.6446	2.6916	4.3839	7.1067	11.4674	18.4302	29.4570	46.9016	74.3575	117.3909	184.5648

Table A(c): Future Value Interest Factor of ₹ 1 (Compounded at i% Interest for n Periods)

$$FVIF_{k,n} = (1+k)^n$$

Pe-riods	12%	13%	14%	15%	16%	17%	18%	19%	20%	25%	30%
1	1.1200	1.1300	1.1400	1.1500	1.1600	1.1700	1.1800	1.1900	1.2000	1.2500	1.3000
2	1.2544	1.2769	1.2996	1.3225	1.3456	1.3689	1.3924	1.4161	1.4400	1.5625	1.6900
3	1.4049	1.4429	1.4815	1.5209	1.5609	1.6016	1.6430	1.6852	1.7280	1.9531	2.1970
4	1.5735	1.6305	1.6890	1.7490	1.8106	1.8739	1.9388	2.0053	2.0736	2.4414	2.8561
5	1.7623	1.8424	1.9254	2.0114	2.1003	2.1924	2.2878	2.3868	2.4883	3.0518	3.7129
6	1.9738	2.0820	2.1950	2.3131	2.4364	2.5652	2.6996	2.8398	2.9860	3.8147	4.8268
7	2.2107	2.3526	2.5023	2.6600	2.8262	3.0012	3.1855	3.3737	3.5832	4.7684	6.2749
8	2.4760	2.6584	2.8526	3.0590	3.2784	3.5115	3.7589	4.0214	4.2998	5.9605	8.1573
9	2.7731	3.0040	3.2519	3.5179	3.8030	4.1084	4.4355	4.7854	5.1598	7.4506	10.604
10	3.1058	3.3946	3.7072	4.0456	4.4114	4.8068	5.2338	5.6947	6.1917	9.3132	13.7858
11	3.4786	3.8359	4.2263	4.6524	5.1173	5.6240	6.1759	6.7767	7.4301	11.6415	17.9216
12	3.8960	4.3345	4.8179	5.3503	5.9360	6.5801	7.2876	8.0642	8.9161	14.5519	23.2981
13	4.3635	4.8981	5.4924	6.1528	6.8858	7.6987	8.5994	9.5264	10.6993	18.1899	30.2875
14	4.8871	5.5348	6.2613	7.0757	7.9875	9.0075	10.1472	11.4198	12.8392	22.7374	39.3738
15	5.4736	6.2543	7.1379	8.1371	9.2655	10.5387	11.9737	13.5895	15.4070	28.4217	51.1859
16	6.1304	7.0673	8.1372	9.3576	10.7480	12.3303	14.1290	16.1715	18.4884	35.5271	66.5417
17	6.8660	7.9861	9.2765	10.7613	12.4677	14.4264	16.6722	19.2441	22.1861	44.4089	86.5042
18	7.6900	9.0243	10.5752	12.3755	14.4625	16.8790	19.6733	22.9005	26.6233	55.5112	112.4554
19	8.6128	10.1974	12.0557	14.2318	16.7765	19.7484	23.2144	27.2144	31.9480	69.3889	146.1920
20	9.6463	11.5231	13.7435	16.3665	19.4608	23.1056	27.3930	32.4294	38.3376	86.7362	190.0496
21	10.8038	13.0211	15.6676	18.8215	22.5745	27.0336	32.3238	38.5910	46.0051	108.4202	247.0645
22	12.1003	14.7138	17.8610	21.6447	26.1864	31.6293	38.1421	45.9233	55.2061	135.5253	321.1839
23	13.5523	16.6266	20.3616	24.8915	30.3762	37.0062	45.0076	54.6487	66.2474	169.4066	417.5391
24	15.1786	18.7881	23.2122	28.6252	35.2364	43.2973	53.1090	65.0320	79.4968	211.7582	542.8008
25	17.0001	21.2305	26.4619	32.9190	40.8742	50.6578	62.6686	77.3881	95.3962	264.6978	705.6410

Table A(d): Future Value Interest Factor of ₹ 1 (Compounded at i% Interest for n Periods)

$FVIF_{k,n} = (1+k)^n$

Periods	12 %	13 %	14 %	15 %	16 %	17 %	18 %	19 %	20 %	25 %	30 %
26	19.0401	23.9905	30.1666	37.8568	47.4141	59.2697	73.9490	92.0918	114.4755	330.8722	917.3333
27	21.3249	27.1093	34.3899	43.5353	55.0004	69.3455	87.2598	109.5893	137.3706	413.5903	1192.5333
28	23.8839	30.6335	39.2045	50.0656	63.8004	81.1342	102.9666	130.4112	164.8447	516.9879	1550.2933
29	26.7499	34.6158	44.6931	57.5755	74.0085	94.9271	121.5005	155.1893	197.8136	646.2349	2015.3813
30	29.9599	39.1159	50.9502	66.2118	85.8499	111.0647	143.3706	184.6753	237.3763	807.7936	2619.9956
31	33.5551	44.2010	58.0832	76.1435	99.5859	129.9456	169.1774	219.7636	284.8516	1009.7420	3405.9943
32	37.5817	49.9471	66.2148	87.5651	115.5196	152.0364	199.6293	261.5187	341.8219	1262.1774	4427.7926
33	42.0915	56.4402	75.4849	100.6998	134.0027	177.8826	235.5625	311.2073	410.1863	1577.7218	5756.1304
34	47.1425	63.7774	86.0528	115.8048	155.4432	208.1226	277.9638	370.3366	492.2235	1972.1523	7482.9696
35	52.7996	72.0685	98.1002	133.1755	180.3141	243.5035	327.9973	440.7006	590.6682	2465.1903	9727.8604
36	59.1356	81.4374	111.8342	153.1519	209.1643	284.8990	387.0368	524.4337	708.8019	3081.4879	12646.2186
37	66.2318	92.0243	127.4910	176.1246	242.6306	333.3319	456.7034	624.0761	850.5622	3851.8599	16440.0841
38	74.1797	103.9874	145.3397	202.5433	281.4515	389.9983	538.9100	742.6506	1020.6747	4814.8249	21372.1094
39	83.0812	117.5058	165.6873	232.9248	326.4338	456.2980	656.9139	883.7542	1224.8096	6018.5311	27783.7422
40	93.0510	132.7816	188.8835	267.8635	378.7212	533.8687	750.3783	1051.6675	1469.7716	7523.1638	36118.8648
41	104.2171	150.0432	215.3272	308.0431	439.3165	624.6264	885.4464	1248.4843	1763.7259	9403.9548	46954.5243
42	116.7231	169.5488	245.4730	354.2495	509.6072	730.8129	1044.8268	1489.2664	2116.4711	11754.9435	61040.8815
43	130.7299	191.5901	279.8392	407.3870	591.1443	855.0511	1232.8956	1772.2270	2539.7653	14693.6794	79353.1460
44	146.4175	216.4968	319.0167	468.4950	685.7274	1000.4098	1454.8168	2108.9501	3047.7183	18367.0992	103159.0898
45	163.9876	244.6414	363.6791	538.7693	795.4438	1170.4794	1716.6639	2509.6506	3657.2620	22958.8740	134106.8167
46	183.6661	276.4448	414.5941	619.5847	922.7148	1369.4609	2025.6870	2986.4842	4388.7144	28698.5925	174338.8617
47	205.7061	312.3826	472.6373	712.5224	1070.3492	1602.2693	2390.3106	3553.9162	5266.4573	35873.2407	226640.5202
48	230.3908	352.9923	538.8085	819.4007	1241.6051	1874.6550	2820.5665	4229.1603	6319.7487	44841.5509	294632.6763
49	258.0377	398.8814	614.2395	942.3108	1440.2619	2193.3464	3328.2685	5032.7008	7583.6985	56051.9386	383022.4792
50	289.0022	450.7359	700.2330	1083.6574	1670.7038	2566.2153	3927.3569	5988.9139	9100.4382	70064.9232	497929.2230

Table B(a): Present Value of ₹ 1 Discounted at i Per Cent for n Periods

$$PVIF_{k,n} = 1 / (1 + k)^n$$

Period	1 %	2 %	3 %	4 %	5 %	6 %	7 %	8 %	9 %	10 %
1	0.9901	0.9804	0.9709	0.9615	0.9524	0.9434	0.9346	0.9259	0.9174	0.9091
2	0.9803	0.9612	0.9426	0.9246	0.9070	0.8900	0.8734	0.8573	0.8417	0.8264
3	0.9706	0.9423	0.9151	0.8890	0.8638	0.8396	0.8163	0.7938	0.7722	0.7513
4	0.9610	0.9238	0.8885	0.8548	0.8227	0.7921	0.7629	0.7350	0.7084	0.6830
5	0.9515	0.9057	0.8626	0.8219	0.7835	0.7473	0.7130	0.6806	0.6499	0.6209
6	0.9420	0.8880	0.8375	0.7903	0.7462	0.7050	0.6663	0.6302	0.5963	0.5645
7	0.9327	0.8706	0.8131	0.7599	0.7107	0.6651	0.6227	0.5835	0.5470	0.5132
8	0.9235	0.8535	0.7894	0.7307	0.6768	0.6274	0.5820	0.5403	0.5019	0.4665
9	0.9143	0.8368	0.7664	0.7026	0.6446	0.5919	0.5439	0.5002	0.4604	0.4241
10	0.9053	0.8203	0.7441	0.6756	0.6139	0.5584	0.5083	0.4632	0.4224	0.3855
11	0.8963	0.8043	0.7224	0.6496	0.5847	0.5268	0.4751	0.4289	0.3875	0.3505
12	0.8874	0.7885	0.7014	0.6246	0.5568	0.4970	0.4440	0.3971	0.3555	0.3186
13	0.8787	0.7730	0.6810	0.6006	0.5303	0.4688	0.4150	0.3677	0.3262	0.2897
14	0.8700	0.7579	0.6611	0.5775	0.5051	0.4423	0.3878	0.3405	0.2992	0.2633
15	0.8613	0.7430	0.6419	0.5553	0.4810	0.4173	0.3624	0.3152	0.2745	0.2394
16	0.8528	0.7284	0.6232	0.5339	0.4581	0.3936	0.3387	0.2919	0.2519	0.2176
17	0.8444	0.7142	0.6050	0.5134	0.4363	0.3714	0.3166	0.2703	0.2311	0.1978
18	0.8360	0.7002	0.5874	0.4936	0.4155	0.3503	0.2959	0.2502	0.2120	0.1799
19	0.8277	0.6864	0.5703	0.4746	0.3957	0.3305	0.2765	0.2317	0.1945	0.1635
20	0.8195	0.6730	0.5537	0.4564	0.3769	0.3118	0.2584	0.2145	0.1784	0.1486
21	0.8114	0.6598	0.5375	0.4388	0.3589	0.2942	0.2415	0.1987	0.1637	0.1351
22	0.8034	0.6468	0.5219	0.4220	0.3418	0.2775	0.2257	0.1839	0.1502	0.1228
23	0.7954	0.6342	0.5067	0.4057	0.3256	0.2618	0.2109	0.1703	0.1378	0.1117
24	0.7876	0.6217	0.4919	0.3901	0.3101	0.2470	0.1971	0.1577	0.1264	0.1015
25	0.7798	0.6095	0.4776	0.3751	0.2953	0.2330	0.1842	0.1460	0.1160	0.0923

Table: B(b): Present Value of ₹ 1 Discounted at i Per Cent for n Periods

$$PVIF_{k,n} = 1 / (1 + k)^n$$

Period	11%	12%	13%	14%	15%	16%	17%	18%	19%	20%	25%	30%
1	0.9009	0.8929	0.8850	0.8772	0.8696	0.8621	0.8547	0.8475	0.8403	0.8333	0.8000	0.7692
2	0.8116	0.7972	0.7831	0.7695	0.7561	0.7432	0.7305	0.7182	0.7062	0.6944	0.6400	0.5917
3	0.7312	0.7118	0.6931	0.6750	0.6575	0.6407	0.6244	0.6086	0.5934	0.5787	0.5120	0.4552
4	0.6587	0.6355	0.6133	0.5921	0.5718	0.5523	0.5337	0.5158	0.4987	0.4823	0.4096	0.3501
5	0.5935	0.5674	0.5428	0.5194	0.4972	0.4761	0.4561	0.4371	0.4190	0.4019	0.3277	0.2693
6	0.5346	0.5066	0.4803	0.4556	0.4323	0.4104	0.3898	0.3704	0.3521	0.3349	0.2621	0.2072
7	0.4817	0.4523	0.4251	0.3996	0.3759	0.3538	0.3332	0.3139	0.2959	0.2791	0.2097	0.1594
8	0.4339	0.4039	0.3762	0.3506	0.3269	0.3050	0.2848	0.2660	0.2487	0.2326	0.1678	0.1226
9	0.3909	0.3606	0.3329	0.3075	0.2843	0.2630	0.2434	0.2255	0.2090	0.1938	0.1342	0.0943
10	0.3522	0.3220	0.2946	0.2697	0.2472	0.2267	0.2080	0.1911	0.1756	0.1615	0.1074	0.0725
11	0.3173	0.2875	0.2607	0.2366	0.2149	0.1954	0.1778	0.1619	0.1476	0.1346	0.0859	0.0558
12	0.2858	0.2567	0.2307	0.2076	0.1869	0.1685	0.1520	0.1372	0.1240	0.1122	0.0687	0.0429
13	0.2575	0.2292	0.2042	0.1821	0.1625	0.1452	0.1299	0.1163	0.1042	0.0935	0.0550	0.0330
14	0.2320	0.2046	0.1807	0.1597	0.1413	0.1252	0.1110	0.0985	0.0876	0.0779	0.0440	0.0254
15	0.2090	0.1827	0.1599	0.1401	0.1229	0.1079	0.0949	0.0835	0.0736	0.0649	0.0352	0.0195
16	0.1883	0.1631	0.1415	0.1229	0.1069	0.0930	0.0811	0.0708	0.0618	0.0541	0.0281	0.0150
17	0.1696	0.1456	0.1252	0.1078	0.0929	0.0802	0.0693	0.0600	0.0520	0.0451	0.0225	0.0116
18	0.1528	0.1300	0.1108	0.0946	0.0808	0.0691	0.0592	0.0508	0.0437	0.0376	0.0180	0.0089
19	0.1377	0.1161	0.0981	0.0829	0.0703	0.0596	0.0506	0.0431	0.0367	0.0313	0.0144	0.0068
20	0.1240	0.1037	0.0868	0.0728	0.0611	0.0514	0.0433	0.0365	0.0308	0.0261	0.0115	0.0053
21	0.1117	0.0926	0.0768	0.0638	0.0531	0.0443	0.0370	0.0309	0.0259	0.0217	0.0092	0.0040
22	0.1007	0.0826	0.0680	0.0560	0.0462	0.0382	0.0316	0.0262	0.0218	0.0181	0.0074	0.0031
23	0.0907	0.0738	0.0601	0.0491	0.0402	0.0329	0.0270	0.0222	0.0183	0.0151	0.0059	0.0024
24	0.0817	0.0659	0.0532	0.0431	0.0349	0.0284	0.0231	0.0188	0.0154	0.0126	0.0047	0.0018
25	0.0736	0.0588	0.0471	0.0378	0.0304	0.0245	0.0197	0.0160	0.0129	0.0105	0.0038	0.0014

Table B(c): Present Value of ₹ 1 Discounted at i Per Cent for n Periods

$$PVIF_{k,n} = 1 / (1 + k)^n$$

Period	1 %	2 %	3 %	4 %	5 %	6 %	7 %	8 %	9 %	10 %
26	0.7720	0.5976	0.4637	0.3607	0.2812	0.2198	0.1722	0.1352	0.1064	0.0839
27	0.7644	0.5859	0.4502	0.3468	0.2678	0.2074	0.1609	0.1252	0.0976	0.0763
28	0.7568	0.5744	0.4371	0.3335	0.2551	0.1956	0.1504	0.1159	0.0895	0.0693
29	0.7493	0.5631	0.4243	0.3207	0.2429	0.1846	0.1406	0.1073	0.0822	0.0630
30	0.7419	0.5521	0.4120	0.3083	0.2314	0.1741	0.1314	0.0994	0.0754	0.0573
31	0.7346	0.5412	0.4000	0.2965	0.2204	0.1643	0.1228	0.0920	0.0691	0.0521
32	0.7273	0.5306	0.3883	0.2851	0.2099	0.1550	0.1147	0.0852	0.0634	0.0474
33	0.7201	0.5202	0.3770	0.2741	0.1999	0.1462	0.1072	0.0789	0.0582	0.0431
34	0.7130	0.5100	0.3660	0.2636	0.1904	0.1379	0.1002	0.0730	0.0534	0.0391
35	0.7059	0.5000	0.3554	0.2534	0.1813	0.1301	0.0937	0.0676	0.0490	0.0356
36	0.6989	0.4902	0.3450	0.2437	0.1727	0.1227	0.0875	0.0626	0.0449	0.0323
37	0.6920	0.4806	0.3350	0.2343	0.1644	0.1158	0.0818	0.0580	0.0412	0.0294
38	0.6852	0.4712	0.3252	0.2253	0.1566	0.1092	0.0765	0.0537	0.0378	0.0267
39	0.6784	0.4619	0.3158	0.2166	0.1491	0.1031	0.0715	0.0497	0.0347	0.0243
40	0.6717	0.4529	0.3066	0.2083	0.1420	0.0972	0.0668	0.0460	0.0318	0.0221
41	0.6650	0.4440	0.2976	0.2003	0.1353	0.0917	0.0624	0.0426	0.0292	0.0201
42	0.6584	0.4353	0.2890	0.1926	0.1288	0.0865	0.0583	0.0395	0.0268	0.0183
43	0.6519	0.4268	0.2805	0.1852	0.1227	0.0816	0.0545	0.0365	0.0246	0.0166
44	0.6454	0.4184	0.2724	0.1780	0.1169	0.0770	0.0509	0.0338	0.0226	0.0151
45	0.6391	0.4102	0.2644	0.1712	0.1113	0.0727	0.0476	0.0313	0.0207	0.0137
46	0.6327	0.4022	0.2567	0.1646	0.1060	0.0685	0.0445	0.0290	0.0190	0.0125
47	0.6265	0.3943	0.2493	0.1583	0.1009	0.0647	0.0416	0.0269	0.0174	0.0113
48	0.6203	0.3865	0.2420	0.1522	0.0961	0.0610	0.0389	0.0249	0.0160	0.0103
49	0.6141	0.3790	0.2350	0.1463	0.0916	0.0575	0.0363	0.0230	0.0147	0.0094
50	0.6080	0.3715	0.2281	0.1407	0.0872	0.0543	0.0339	0.0213	0.0134	0.0085

Table B(d): Present Value of ₹ 1 Discounted at i Per Cent for n Periods

$$PVIF_{k,n} = 1 / (1 + k)^n$$

Period	11 %	12 %	13 %	14 %	15 %	16 %	17 %	18 %	19 %	20 %	25 %	30 %
26	0.0663	0.0525	0.0417	0.0331	0.0264	0.0211	0.0169	0.0135	0.0109	0.0087	0.0030	0.0011
27	0.0597	0.0469	0.0369	0.0291	0.0230	0.0182	0.0144	0.0115	0.0091	0.0073	0.0024	0.0008
28	0.0538	0.0419	0.0326	0.0255	0.0200	0.0157	0.0123	0.0097	0.0077	0.0061	0.0019	0.0006
29	0.0485	0.0374	0.0289	0.0224	0.0174	0.0135	0.0105	0.0082	0.0064	0.0051	0.0015	0.0005
30	0.0437	0.0334	0.0256	0.0196	0.0151	0.0116	0.0090	0.0070	0.0054	0.0042	0.0012	0.0004
31	0.0394	0.0298	0.0226	0.0172	0.0131	0.0100	0.0077	0.0059	0.0046	0.0035	0.0010	0.0003
32	0.0355	0.0266	0.0200	0.0151	0.0114	0.0087	0.0066	0.0050	0.0038	0.0029	0.0008	0.0002
33	0.0319	0.0238	0.0177	0.0132	0.0099	0.0075	0.0056	0.0042	0.0032	0.0024	0.0006	0.0002
34	0.0288	0.0212	0.0157	0.0116	0.0086	0.0064	0.0048	0.0036	0.0027	0.0020	0.0005	0.0001
35	0.0259	0.0189	0.0139	0.0102	0.0075	0.0055	0.0041	0.0030	0.0023	0.0017	0.0004	0.0001
36	0.0234	0.0169	0.0123	0.0089	0.0065	0.0048	0.0035	0.0026	0.0019	0.0014	0.0003	0.0001
37	0.0210	0.0151	0.0109	0.0078	0.0057	0.0041	0.0030	0.0022	0.0016	0.0012	0.0003	0.0001
38	0.0190	0.0135	0.0096	0.0069	0.0049	0.0036	0.0026	0.0019	0.0013	0.0010	0.0002	0.0000
39	0.0171	0.0120	0.0085	0.0060	0.0043	0.0031	0.0022	0.0016	0.0011	0.0008	0.0002	0.0000
40	0.0154	0.0107	0.0075	0.0053	0.0037	0.0026	0.0019	0.0013	0.0010	0.0007	0.0001	0.0000
41	0.0139	0.0096	0.0067	0.0046	0.0032	0.0023	0.0016	0.0011	0.0008	0.0006	0.0001	0.0000
42	0.0125	0.0086	0.0059	0.0041	0.0028	0.0020	0.0014	0.0010	0.0007	0.0005	0.0001	0.0000
43	0.0112	0.0076	0.0052	0.0036	0.0025	0.0017	0.0012	0.0008	0.0006	0.0004	0.0001	0.0000
44	0.0101	0.0068	0.0046	0.0031	0.0021	0.0015	0.0010	0.0007	0.0005	0.0003	0.0001	0.0000
45	0.0091	0.0061	0.0041	0.0027	0.0019	0.0013	0.0009	0.0006	0.0004	0.0003	0.0000	0.0000
46	0.0082	0.0054	0.0036	0.0024	0.0016	0.0011	0.0007	0.0005	0.0003	0.0002	0.0000	0.0000
47	0.0074	0.0049	0.0032	0.0021	0.0014	0.0009	0.0006	0.0004	0.0003	0.0002	0.0000	0.0000
48	0.0067	0.0043	0.0028	0.0019	0.0012	0.0008	0.0005	0.0004	0.0002	0.0002	0.0000	0.0000
49	0.0060	0.0039	0.0025	0.0016	0.0011	0.0007	0.0005	0.0003	0.0002	0.0001	0.0000	0.0000
50	0.0054	0.0035	0.0022	0.0014	0.0009	0.0006	0.0004	0.0003	0.0002	0.0001	0.0000	0.0000

Table C(a): Future Value of Interest Factors for ₹ 1 Ordinary Annuity Compounded at i Per Cent for n Periods

$$FVIFA_{i,n} = \sum_{t=1}^{n} (1+i)^{t-1}$$

Period	1 %	2 %	3 %	4 %	5 %	6 %	7 %	8 %	9 %	10 %
1	1.000	1.000	1.000	1.000	1.000	1.000	1.000	1.000	1.000	1.000
2	2.010	2.020	2.030	2.040	2.050	2.060	2.070	2.080	2.090	2.100
3	3.030	3.060	3.091	3.122	3.152	3.184	3.215	3.246	3.278	3.310
4	4.060	4.122	4.184	4.246	4.310	4.375	4.440	4.506	4.573	4.641
5	5.101	5.204	5.309	5.416	5.526	5.637	5.751	5.867	5.985	6.105
6	6.152	6.308	6.468	6.633	6.803	6.975	7.153	7.336	7.523	7.716
7	7.214	7.434	7.662	7.858	8.142	8.394	8.654	8.923	9.200	9.487
8	8.286	8.583	8.892	9.214	9.549	9.897	10.260	10.637	11.028	11.436
9	9.368	9.755	10.159	10.583	11.027	11.491	11.978	12.488	13.021	13.579
10	10.462	10.950	11.464	12.006	12.578	13.181	13.816	14.487	15.193	15.937
11	11.567	12.169	12.808	13.486	14.207	14.972	15.784	16.645	17.560	18.531
12	12.682	13.412	14.192	15.026	15.917	16.870	17.888	18.977	20.141	21.384
13	13.809	14.630	15.618	16.627	17.713	18.882	20.141	21.495	22.953	24.523
14	14.947	15.974	17.086	18.252	19.598	21.015	22.550	24.215	26.019	27.975
15	16.097	17.293	18.599	20.023	21.578	23.276	25.129	27.152	29.361	31.772
16	17.258	18.639	20.157	21.824	23.657	25.672	27.888	30.324	33.003	35.949
17	18.430	20.012	21.761	23.697	25.840	28.213	30.840	33.750	36.973	40.544
18	19.614	21.412	23.414	25.645	28.132	30.905	33.999	37.450	41.301	45.599
19	20.811	22.840	25.117	27.671	30.539	33.760	37..379	41.446	46.018	51.158
20	22.019	24.297	26.870	29.778	33.066	36.785	40.995	45.762	51.159	57.274
21	23.239	25.733	28.676	31.969	35.719	39.992	44.865	50.422	56.764	64.002
22	24.471	27.299	30.536	34.248	38.505	43.392	49.005	55.456	62.872	71.402
23	25.716	28.845	32.452	36.618	41.430	46.995	53.435	60.893	69.531	79.542
24	26.973	30.421	34.426	39.082	44.501	50.815	58.176	66.764	76.789	88.496
25	28.243	32.030	36.459	41.645	47.726	54.864	63.248	73.105	84.699	98.346
30	34.784	40.557	47.575	56.084	66.438	79.057	94.450	113.282	136.305	164.491
35	41.659	49.994	60.461	73.651	90.318	111.432	138.236	172.314	215.705	271.018
40	48.885	60.401	75.400	95.024	120.797	154.758	199.630	259.052	337.872	442.580
45	56.479	71.891	52.518	121.027	159.695	212.737	285.741	386.497	525.872	718.881
50	64.461	84.577	112.794	152.664	209.341	290.325	406.516	573.756	815.051	1163.365

Table C(b): Future Value of Interest Factors for ₹ 1 Ordinary Annuity Compounded at i Per Cent for n Periods

$$FVIFA_{i,n} = \sum_{t=1}^{n} (1+i)^{t-1}$$

Period	11 %	12 %	13 %	14 %	15 %	16 %	17 %	18 %	19 %	20 %
1	1.000	1.000	1.000	1.000	1.000	1.000	1.000	1.000	1.000	1.000
2	2.110	2.120	2.130	2.140	2.150	2.160	2.170	2.180	2.190	2.200
3	3.342	3.374	3.407	3.440	3.472	3.506	3.539	3.572	3.606	3.640
4	4.710	4.779	4.850	4.921	4.993	5.066	5.141	5.215	5.291	5.368
5	6.228	6.353	6.480	6.610	6.742	6.877	7.014	7.154	7.297	7.442
6	7.913	8.115	8.323	8.535	8.754	8.977	9.207	9.442	9.683	9.930
7	9.783	10.089	10.405	10.730	11.067	11.414	11.772	12.141	12.523	12.916
8	11.859	12.300	12.757	13.233	13.727	14.240	14.773	15.327	15.902	16.499
9	14.164	14.776	15.416	16.085	16.786	17.518	18.285	19.036	19.923	20.799
10	16.722	17.549	18.420	19.357	20.304	21.321	22.393	23.521	24.705	25.959
11	19.561	20.655	21.814	23.044	24.349	25.733	27.200	28.755	30.403	32.150
12	22.713	24.133	25.650	27.271	29.001	30.850	32.824	34.531	37.180	39.580
13	26.211	28.029	29.984	32.088	34.352	36.786	39.404	42.218	45.244	48.496
14	30.095	32.392	34.882	37.581	40.504	43.672	47.102	50.818	54.841	59.196
15	34.405	37.280	40.417	43.842	47.580	51.659	56.109	60.565	66.260	72.035
16	39.190	42.753	46.671	50.980	55.717	60.925	66.648	72.538	79.850	87.442
17	44.500	48.883	53.738	59.117	65.075	71.673	78.978	87.067	96.021	105.930
18	50.396	55.749	61.724	68.353	75.336	84.140	93.404	103.739	115.265	128.116
19	56.939	63.439	70.748	78.968	88.211	98.603	110.283	123.412	138.165	154.739
20	64.202	72.052	80.946	91.024	102.443	115.379	130.031	146.626	165.417	186.687
21	72.264	81.698	92.468	104.767	118.809	134.840	153.136	174.019	197.846	225.024
22	81.213	92.502	105.489	120.414	137.630	157.414	180.169	206.342	236.436	271.028
23	91.147	104.602	120.203	138.295	159.274	183.600	211.798	244.433	282.355	326.234
24	102.173	118.154	136.829	158.656	184.166	213.976	248.803	289.400	337.007	392.480
25	114.412	133.333	155.616	181.867	212.790	249.212	292.099	342.598	402.038	471.976
30	199.018	241.330	293.192	356.778	434.738	530.306	647.423	790.532	966.698	1181.865
35	341.583	431.658	546.663	693.552	881.152	1120.699	1426.448	1816.607	2314.173	2948.294
40	581.812	767.080	1013.667	1341.979	1779.048	2860.724	3134.412	4153.094	5529.711	7343.715
45	986.613	1358.208	1874.086	2500.464	3585.031	4965.191	6875.008	9531.258	13203.105	18280.914
50	1668.723	2399.975	3459.344	4994.301	7217.488	10435.449	15088.805	21812.273	31514.492	45496.094

Table D(a): Present Value Interest Factors for ₹ 1 Ordinary Annuity Discounted at i Per Cent for n Periods

$$FVIFA_{i,n} = \sum_{t=1}^{n} (1+i)t$$

Period	1 %	2 %	3 %	4 %	5 %	6 %	7 %	8 %	9 %	10 %
1	.990	.980	.971	.962	.952	.943	.935	.926	.915	.909
2	1.970	1.962	1.913	1.886	1.859	1.8333	1.808	1.783	1.759	1.736
3	2.943	2.884	2.829	2.775	2.723	2.673	2.624	2.577	2.531	2.487
4	3.902	3.804	3.717	3.630	3.546	3.465	3.387	3.312	3.240	3.170
5	4.853	4.713	4.580	4.452	4.329	4.212	4.100	3.993	3.890	3.791
6	5.795	5.691	5.417	5.242	5.076	4.917	4.767	4.623	4.486	4.355
7	6.723	6.472	6.239	6.002	5.786	5.582	5.389	5.206	5.033	4.868
8	7.653	7.326	7.020	6.733	6.463	6.210	5.971	5.747	5.535	5.335
9	8.568	8.162	7.786	7.435	7.103	6.802	6.515	6.247	5.995	5.759
10	9.471	8.983	8.530	8.111	7.722	7.360	7.024	6.710	6.418	6.145
11	10.363	9.787	9.253	8.760	8.306	7.887	7.499	7.139	6.808	6.495
12	11.255	10.573	9.954	9.385	8.863	8.384	7.943	7.536	7.161	6.814
13	12.134	11.343	10.635	9.986	9.394	8.853	8.358	7.904	7.487	7.013
14	13.004	12.105	11.296	10.563	9.899	9.295	8.745	8.244	7.786	7.367
15	13.863	12.849	11.938	11.118	10.380	9.712	9.108	8.560	8.061	7.606
16	14.718	13.573	12.561	11.652	10.838	10.106	9.447	8.851	8.313	7.824
17	15.562	14.292	13.166	12.166	11.272	10.477	9.763	9.122	8.544	8.022
18	16.398	14.992	13.754	12.659	11.690	10.828	10.059	9.372	8.756	8.201
19	17.226	15.679	14.324	13.134	12.085	11.158	10.336	9.604	8.950	8.365
20	18.046	16.352	14.878	13.590	12.462	11.470	10.594	9.818	9.125	8.514
21	18.857	17.011	15.415	14.029	12.821	11.764	10.836	10.017	9.292	8.649
22	19.661	17.653	15.937	14.451	13.163	12.042	11.061	10.201	9.442	8.772
23	20.454	18.292	16.444	14.857	13.489	12.303	11.272	10.371	9.580	8.883
24	21.244	18.914	16.936	15.247	13.799	12.550	11.469	10.529	9.707	8.585
25	22.023	19.524	17.413	15.622	14.094	12.783	11.654	10.675	9.823	9.077
30	25.808	22.395	19.601	17.292	15.373	13.765	12.409	11.258	10.274	9.427
35	29.409	24.999	21.487	18.665	16.374	14.498	12.948	11.655	10.567	9.644
40	32.835	27.355	23.115	19.793	17.159	15.046	13.332	11.925	10.757	9.779
45	36.093	29.499	24.519	20.720	17.774	15.456	13.606	12.108	10.881	9.863
50	39.196	31.424	25.730	21.482	18.256	15.762	13.801	12.233	10.962	9.915

Table C(b): Present Value Interest Factors for ₹ 1 Annuity Discounted at it Per Cent for n Periods

$$FVIFA_{i,n} = \sum_{t=1}^{n} 1/(1+i)^t$$

Period	11 %	12 %	13 %	14 %	15 %	16 %	17 %	18 %	19 %	20 %
1	.901	.893	.885	.877	.870	.862	.855	.847	.840	.833
2	1.713	1.690	1.668	1.647	1.626	1.605	1.585	1.566	1.547	1.528
3	2.444	2.402	2.361	2.322	2.283	2.246	2.210	2.184	2.140	2.106
4	3.102	3.037	2.974	2.914	2.855	2.978	2.743	2.690	2.639	2.589
5	3.696	3.605	3.517	3.433	3.352	3.274	3.199	3.127	3.058	2.991
6	4.231	4.111	3.098	3.889	3.784	3.685	3.589	3.498	3.410	3.326
7	4.712	4.564	4.423	4.288	4.160	4.039	3.522	3.812	3.706	3.606
8	5.146	4.968	4.799	4.639	4.487	4.344	4.207	4.078	3.954	3.837
9	5.537	5.328	5.132	4.946	4.772	4.607	4.451	4.303	4.163	4.031
10	5.889	5.650	5.426	5.216	5.019	4.833	4.659	4.494	4.339	4.192
11	6.207	5.938	5.687	5.453	5.234	5.029	4.835	4.656	4.486	4.327
12	6.492	6.194	5.918	5.660	5.421	5.197	4.983	4.793	4.611	4.439
13	6.750	6.424	6.122	5.842	5.583	5.342	5.113	4.910	4.715	4.533
14	6.982	6.628	6.302	6.002	5.724	5.468	5.229	5.008	4.802	4.611
15	7.191	6.811	6.462	6.142	5.847	5.575	5.324	5.092	4.876	4.675
16	7.379	6.974	6.604	6.265	5.954	5.668	5.405	5.162	4.938	4.730
17	7.549	7.120	6.729	6.373	6.047	5.749	5.475	5.222	4.990	4.775
18	7.702	7.250	6.340	6.467	6.128	5.818	5.534	5.273	5.033	4.812
19	7.839	7.366	6.938	6.550	6.198	5.877	5.584	5.316	5.070	4.843
20	7.963	7.469	7.025	6.623	6.259	5.929	5.623	5.353	5.101	4.870
21	8.075	7.562	7.102	6.687	6.312	5.973	5.665	5.384	5.127	4.891
22	8.176	7.645	7.170	6.743	6.359	6.011	5.695	5.410	5.149	4.909
23	8.266	7.718	7.230	6.792	6.399	6.044	5.723	5.432	5.167	4.925
24	8.348	7.784	7.283	6.835	6.434	6.073	5.745	5.451	5.182	4.937
25	8.422	7.843	7.330	6.873	6.464	6.097	5.765	5.467	5.195	4.948
30	8.694	8.055	7.496	7.003	6.566	6.177	5.823	5.517	5.235	4.979
35	8.855	8.176	7.586	7.070	6.617	6.215	5.853	5.539	5.251	4.992
40	8.951	8.244	7.634	7.105	6.642	6.233	5.871	5.548	5.258	4.997
45	9.008	8.283	7.661	7.123	6.654	6.242	5.877	5.552	5.261	4.999
50	9.042	8.304	7.675	7.133	6.661	6.246	5.883	5.554	5.262	4.999